MOTORING

Getting the Maximum from Your New MINI

by Gary Anderson
and
Don Racine

Enthusiast Publications LLC

ISBN 0-9765780-0-X   First printing, February 2005

The publishers welcome any comments or questions regarding this book. Correspondence may be addressed to the copyright address above, or via email to EditorGary @aol.com.

Driving is Dangerous

The authors emphasize that driving any automobile, especially in a high-performance manner that approaches the limits of the automobile or driver, is dangerous to the driver, passengers, and pedestrians. No book can teach all aspects of performance driving or racing. Driving should be done in a conservative and responsible manner, whether on public roads or private tracks or courses. Do not race or practice race driving except on a designated and properly supervised race track. When on public roads, obey all laws and regulations, and drive with full respect for the safety of yourself and others, and the limits of your automobile.

Disclaimers

The information presented in this book is, to the best of the knowledge of the authors, accurate and represents the best information available to them at the time of writing. However, the authors emphasize that automobile driving, whether on the road or the track, is inherently dangerous, and therefore neither the authors nor the publishers assume any liabilities and make no warranties, express or implied, regarding the application of any of the information presented in this book, whether it relates to automobile mechanics, modification, or operation. Readers should not rely solely on the information presented in this book for guidance on automobile operation or modification, and should make their own efforts to verify and expand on the information presented here, taking the advice of experts in motorsports and relying on specialists to carry out the modifications described in this book. The authors and publishers also disclaim all liability for direct, indirect, incidental or consequential damage that may result from use of or reliance on any of the examples, instructions, products and brands, or other information presented in this book.

The authors and publishers recognize that some words, model names, and brand names used in this book are the property of other individuals or companies. The authors' and publisher's use of these trade and service marks and brand names is for the purpose of identification only, and is not meant to indicate or imply any endorsement by, or connection, legal or otherwise, with, the authors or publishers of this book.

In particular, there is no connection between the authors and publishers of this book and the BMW Group, BMW USA or MINI USA.

Photographs of components courtesy of MiniMania. All other images in the book, with the exception of those specifically credited, are by Gary Anderson. Layout design was created by Enthusiast Publications, LLC. Printing and print management by Planet Ink USA in Thailand. planetinkusa.com

Contents

Acknowledgments

We would like to thank the following individuals who helped us with various aspects of writing this book, and for their encouragement in its preparation.

Chuck Heleker for his detailed review of the original manuscript and his editorial suggestions. Phil Wicks for allowing us to participate in his driving schools, and for reading and commenting on the driving techniques discussed in the book. MINI of Moutain View for including us in their track day activities. Stuart Langager for his perspectives on MINIs competing in SCCA autocrossing events. Butch Gilbert for information on race tuning and advice on autocrossing techniques. Graham Robson for his encouragement of Gary Anderson's motor journalism, and for loaning the historic images for Chapter One. Ellie Yasek for reading and editing an early version of the manuscript. Brad Davis, who contributed several images of his car in competition, including the picture on the cover. Allan and Jeannie Cary, enthusiastic owners of a MINI Cooper coupe and a MINI Cooper S convertible, for reading and commenting on the manuscript. Jim Bogard for his comments and advice in shaping the original outline. Walt and Louiseann Pietrowicz and Fred Voit for providing racing photos with little advance warning. Last, but not least, all of the staff of MiniMania for their cooperation and assistance, especially Ken Suzuki for technical assistance and Jan Evers for design contributions and graphics and artistic advice.

On the Covers...

The black and white MINI Cooper pictured on the front cover belongs to Stuart Langager who competes in San Francisco Regional SCCA and national SCCA autocross events in the HS stock MINI Cooper class. The picture of MINIs on tour was taken on the September, 2004 British Car Tour in Palo Alto, CA. Drivers are members of NorCal Minis. The racing MINI is the MiniMania MINI Cooper S, raced by author Don Racine and used to test and improve the MINI components sold through MiniMania (*photo by Walt & Louiseann Pietrowicz*).

Introduction

This book grew out of a series of conversations with new MINI owners like you that we had at various events soon after the introduction of this innovative car. We were impressed with the diversity among the new buyers. They were old as well as young, well-off or living on a budget, and bought the car as primary transportation or a supplementary weekend car. Nevertheless, from them we discovered a common theme. Many owners bought their cars for three very simple reasons: MINIS are practical, cute, and inexpensive.

But as these new owners drove their cars, they discovered something new that they hadn't expected to learn. MINIS are fun to drive for the sheer pleasure of driving. These new buyers were becoming motoring enthusiasts.

As motoring enthusiasts, the new owners had begun to look for more things to do with their MINIS and for ways they could make their MINIS even more fun to drive. Unfortunately, they were discovering that the ways of motoring enthusiasm are often confusing to newcomers. Terminology and principles, whether related to motor sports or to mechanical modifications, can be very difficult to understand. Most of this knowledge was passed on from old hand to novice in conversations in parking lots and track paddocks, and the few books on the topic generally assumed a solid base of car knowledge.

Deeply involved in all aspects of the car hobby, and having been impressed ourselves with this new car and the enthusiasm of its new owners, we decided we could do something about this problem by writing a book specifically about MINIS in motorsports, and write it specifically for new owners who hadn't previously been very involved in motoring.

As you read this book, we hope you'll see the benefit of our approach. We start with the basics of buying and driving a new MINI, and gradually delve more and more deeply into the mechanical aspects of the MINI and into how to drive a MINI better. We're not going to assume you know anything about either as we start the book, so we'll try to explain things as we go along.

We just hope that readers who already know something about auto mechanics and competition driving will bear with us as we explain the basics, so everyone will still benefit from the book's later chapters.

As we go along, we'll provide definitions of basic terms and diagrams of basic principles to help you understand the things we're explaining. There is much more to learn, and in one book we can only begin to scratch the surface of questions of car tuning, car handling, and car control. However, we hope that when you've finished, you'll be ready to go more deeply into these topics if you're interested. If you do, there are lots of books, classes, and opportunities to practice that we've listed in the appendices of this book.

Most of all, we hope that as you learn more about your MINI and how it can be improved and used, that you'll continue to find more and more fun behind the wheel and with your new MINI friends. After all, fun is the basic ingredient in true motoring.

Part One

Buying Your New Mini

Inspired by the enormously popular Mini introduced in 1959 under the Austin and Morris nameplates and produced in the millions until 2000, the new MINI by BMW combines the efficient package and sporting heritage of its predecessors with thoroughly modern technology, creating an automobile that is both fun and practical to own.

This book has been written to help you, as a new MINI owner, get all the fun and enjoyment you can out of this great car. In this first part of the book, we will tell you about the traditions that have been built into this marque, and offer some suggestions on buying your new MINI, if you haven't already purchased one. We will also give you some basic driving tips so you can begin right now developing the driving style that will help you enjoy your new MINI to the maximum.

Chapter 1

It's All in the Breeding

*T*o really understand the new MINI Cooper and MINI Cooper S introduced by BMW in 2001, we need to go all the way back to the source of the original inspiration, the British Motor Corporation Minis—actually the Morris Mini Minor and Austin Se7en (yes, 7 not V)— that were introduced to the world in 1959,

Your Basic Compact Front-wheel-drive Economy Car

When Alec (later Sir Alec) Issigonis set out in 1957 to design a car that could cope with the Suez Canal fuel crisis, he wanted to create a car that would be both practical and affordable. To achieve this, he put his car together in a completely new way. The tiny ten-inch wheels were placed at the outside corners so as not to intrude on interior space. Issigonis supported the suspension on rubber cones which took up much less space than traditional springs and shocks.

The new MINI was inspired by the classic Minis first introduced in 1959. By the mid-1960s, the line-up included the basic Mini in several body styles including the Countryman/Traveller station wagon, as well as the Mini Cooper and Mini Cooper S with larger engines and more power.

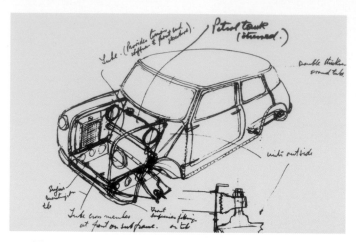

An early Issigonis sketch of the Mini concept illustrated the space for the engine mounted sideways up front with the wheels pushed out to the four corners. *Image courtesy of Graham Robson Archives.*

To save money, British Motor Corporation specified that the new car would use its small four-cylinder A-series engine. To save even more interior space, Issigonis turned the engine sideways, and placed the transmission directly underneath it, effectively in the engine's oil pan. With the transmission connected directly to the front wheels there was no drive shaft, and only a small center hump inside the car for exhaust pipe clearance .

Introduced in 1959 by both Austin and Morris, the two main brands of the British Motor Corporation, the car was first known as the Mini Minor with the Morris badge and grille and the Se7en, using the number seven instead of a V, when carrying the Austin badge and grille. However, with its diminutive size, the car was soon referred to simply as the "Mini."

With its innnovative layout, the car could easily hold four people and their luggage comfortably, but still fit into a space only only ten feet long, five feet wide and four-and-one-half feet high. Making it even more attractive, BMC priced the car at well under $1000 in U.S. dollars, before road tax.

Taking advantage of its small size and economical engine, the Mini Minor could cover over 40 miles on a gallon of gas. As a bonus, the small wheels, tight suspension,

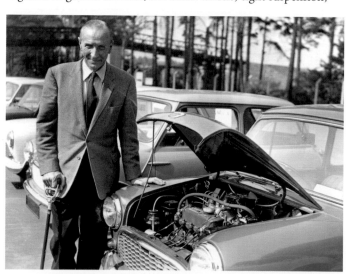

Sir Alec Issigonis, lead designer for the British Motor Corporation, was the source of the inspired Mini design. With its front engine, front drive structure, the Mini created the practical economy car concept.*Image courtesy of Graham Robson Archives.*

Perhaps the most famous Mini was the Mini Cooper S driven to victory in the 1964 Monte Carlo Rally by Paddy Hopkirk and com-memorated with the Monte Carlo 40th An-niversary edi-tion of the new Mini marketed in 2004. *Image courtesy of Graham Rob-son Archives.*

compact size, and direct steering produced a car with surprisingly good handling—a feature that wasn't even on the original wish list.

By the mid-sixties, the Mini had become one of the icons of swinging England, along with the Beatles, Twiggy, and Carnaby Street's mini-skirts. It seemed as if every with-it celebrity owned one, and the cars played starring roles in the first version of *The Italian Job* and *Return of the Pink Panther.*

John Cooper Had Another Idea

At the same time that Issigonis was designing the car, racecar builder John Cooper was adapting the same BMC A-series engine to his Formula Junior racecars and was running the BMC works racing teams. It was only a matter of time before Cooper dropped a race-tuned A-series engine, with modified bore and stroke producing 997cc (below the important one-liter limitation for several racing classifications), into the great-handling Mini to produce a candidate for sedan racing and rallying. In 1961 the Mini Cooper was born.

Never one to be content with just enough, Cooper worked his magic again and, used his Formula Junior engine-tuning experience to develop an 1100cc competition version of the A-series engine. A 1071cc street version of this engine became the basis for the Mini Cooper S, introduced in 1963. A year later, a 1275cc version of the Mini Cooper S was introduced. This little buzzbomb could go from zero to 60 in less than 11 seconds and continue accelerating up to 97 miles per hour, capable of beating most sedans and many sports cars on the road.

With the handling that was already recognized as a strong suit for the Minis, the Cooper S was well-suited for the challenging long-distance European road rallies. A factory team running the Cooper S won the Monte Carlo Rally in 1964 with Paddy Hopkirk at the wheel, and in 1965 with Timo Makinen. In 1966 Mini Cooper Ss took first, second, and third place in the Monte Carlo Rally, only to be disqualified because the bulbs in the fog lamps weren't standard production parts.

However, Rauno Aaltonen took revenge for BMC, conclusively winning the 1967 Monte Rally in his Mini Cooper S.

Looking at the new MINI (this is the 2004 40th Anniversary model commemorating Hopkirk's victory at Monte Carlo), it is easy to see how the inspiration for these new cars was drawn from the classic Minis.

Relying on its superior handling and ability to accelerate out of turns, the Cooper S also became very popular in shorter distance track events. The new European Touring Car Championship was a perfect opportunity to show how easily the car could be tuned for high-speed competition in the under-1000cc Group II classification. Minis did very well at Nurburgring, especially against Fiat-Abarths, which were the main competition. International teams from Spain, Sweden, France and Germany as well as Great Britain, ran Minis quite competitively. Works cars were even built to compete in the Tasmanian series in Australia and New Zealand.

End of the Old; Birth of the New

Even though the Mini could no longer be sold in the U.S. after 1967 because smog and safety regulations had become too stringent for the financially-stressed British Leyland company to meet with the Mini, it had made its mark. To keep the cars alive with the loss of the dealer network, Mini clubs sprang up all over the country and several businesses took root to keep Minis running and on the road.

The rest of the world was more fortunate, and the Mini continued to be manufactured and marketed. Being a small right-hand drive car, it was especially popular in Japan. With Minis continuing to be made in Britain, U.S. owners were able to continue to get parts for their Minis. A trickle of slightly-illegal gray-market cars also found their way across the border from Canada. More recently, when it became legal, buyers began importing Minis with pre-1973 chassis numbers into the United States.

In 1994, BMW absorbed the financially strapped Rover Group, by then the successor to British Motor Corporation. In 1996 product planners for BMW decided that nearly four decades was enough for one design, even if it was so good that it would later be anointed the European Car of the Century. Nevertheless, the designers knew they had to find a way of preserving not only the design concepts, but also the "fun and games" quotient of the original Mini.

Development goals were obvious: the new MINI should be small, cheap, practical, fast, and fun. As you will soon find out, if you haven't already made your pilgrimage to the MINI dealer near you, BMW designers succeeded beyond anyone's expectations. As a result, today you can buy a car that is a direct beneficiary of the heritage that dates back to 1959. The new MINI in the showroom is everything the old Mini was, and more.

The ultimate test of whether the new MINI should be considered a legitimate heir to the classic Mini traditions was passed when many of the established Mini clubs and their diehard enthusiast members adopted the new MINI into their clubs. So, when you choose a MINI for your own fun and games, you'll find a ready-made group of like-minded friends to play with.

But enough of history. If you're interested in learning more, there are some wonderful books about the old Minis. Instead, let's talk about tomorrow and your own trip to the MINI dealer.

Chapter Two

What Kind of Motoring Do You Want to Do?

Y ou've probably already gone to the MINI website, www.MINIUSA.com, to see for yourself what all the hub-bub is about, if you've even considered buying a MINI. The website provides a neat way to look at all the options and do some thinking long before you have to sit across the table from a dealer representative.

A MINI Like No One Else's

If you have checked the MINI website, you've probably been impressed with, maybe even been overwhelmed by, all of the choices that are available. First of all, the car is available in two models in the United States, the MINI Cooper and the MINI Cooper S. (The rest of the world can also buy a third model, the MiniOne.) The major difference between the Mini Cooper and the Mini Cooper S is in the engine tuning, with the supercharged Cooper S producing more horsepower. There are also a few cosmetic differences.

Since the fall of 2004, you can also buy your Cooper or Cooper S in two different body styles, the two-door coupe with a hard-top, or the convertible with its three-position soft-top.

In addition, you can choose to add any or all of three major option packages, or select specific options from within those packages. You can also choose from three different sizes of wheels and tires, and there is a long list of other options to consider.

Club touring on local back roads is one of the delightful activities any MINI owner can enjoy. There are already active MINI clubs in many regions of the country, but if there isn't one in your area, maybe it's time for you to start one.

Weekend autocrossing allows you to compete with your MINI while making only a few modifications.

You have all these choices even before you have confronted the truly significant questions of exterior and interior colors and trim materials. You may see lots of other MINIs on the road (and you'll get to wave at all these new friends as soon as you're behind the wheel of your own MINI) but your MINI doesn't have to look like everyone else's.

This seems like an almost overwhelming richness of choice. But making your decisions may not be as complicated as it seems.

We're going to assume that since you bought this book, you do share a few things in common with us. You understand the messages in the MINI ads. You want your car to perform. Getting from Point A to Point B may be enough for most drivers, but you want to enjoy your time behind the wheel. You do want to motor.

Motoring, however, is a broad term. We'll need to get a little more personal and a little more specific here. This is the time to have a heart-to-heart talk between your intellect, your wallet, and the little voice down deep inside you that tells you how hard to push the fast pedal.

Where Do You Want to Go in Your MINI?

A wise person once said that everything had a price. However the price in the catalog isn't the only cost to think about when you decide what you want and don't want to change on your MINI. When you're designing your car, keep in mind that you might have to give up some capabilities in order to get other capabilities. A car that will go faster, or turn quicker on the track or autocross course may not be as comfortable to drive on long-distance tours. A car that has a variety of appearance accessories and a comfortable interior will weigh more and go slower than a stripped-down version.

First, ask yourself a few questions about how you plan to use your MINI. Are you buying the car as your primary mode of weekday transportation with the idea that you'll still want to use it as a major source of weekend fun? Or are you fortunate enough to already have a functioning transportation unit that can take care of the day-to-day stuff, so your MINI will only be taken out to have fun?

If you do plan on using your MINI for workaday tasks, will you be commuting on the highway to the same office each day, or will you be out in the car all day, making sales visits or trouble-shooting calls to places you've never been before?

Next ask yourself, when you do see yourself having fun in the MINI, where do you see yourself? Will you be on a back country road with your friends, taking a long tour to a secluded picnic spot, or will the curves you take have braking and apex markers, a rumble strip, and a corner worker watching the race track for you?

If your pulse does quicken when the green flashes, will you be racing against the clock on a parking lot marked off with yellow cones; will you be more interested in how fast you can beat the other car to the end of the quarter-mile; or will you only be satisfied if you're going wheel-to-wheel on a real race track?

The nice thing about the MINI, of course, is that it can do any of these things. For example, we know at least one company that maintains a fleet of MINIs for its service reps to use to keep their customers' office networks in operation, but then takes the whole fleet and the reps to the race track a couple of times a year to do hot laps just for fun.

But nevertheless, when you're making your buying decision, and when you're laying out your modification and upgrade strategy, it helps to focus on where you're going to want your MINI to really shine. Take the time to read the rest of the first part of this book and you'll be in a better position to consider your options when you do sit down across the desk from the sales manager at the MINI dealer to place your order for your very own MINI.

How Fast Do You Want to Get There?

Another factor to take into account before you buy the car is how much you're eventually going to spend, and how fast you want to spend it. Fortunately, the MINI isn't a very expensive car to start out with, and it is possible to replace and upgrade its components one step at a time. We'll help you start having fun immediately, and then show you how to upgrade slowly if that's what is necessary to keep from maxing out your credit cards.

It's best to first decide what kind of a car you want to have, so that you don't spend more than you need to at the dealer. Then you should consider the parts that you're

Track racing is an exciting way to enjoy your MINI but requires safety and performance upgrades.

going to want to upgrade or add in order to create the MINI that will suit your own ideas of what motoring fun should be. Finally, you should list the parts in the order that you plan to make the changes, so that you get the maximum benefit from each dollar spent and don't waste money doing things that you'll eventually have to do again.

We've written this book to help you make your budgeting and planning decisions in a logical order, taking into account what you want to do with the car and how much fun you want to have. As you get to know the car, you can consider all the ways there are to enjoy it. Each of the four sections of the book will discuss things you can do to have fun with the car, what kinds of modifications and accessories you will want to consider to make the car perform better in those activities, and offer you tips on how to drive better at that level.

This first part of the book will give you some basic buying and driving tips. Then the second part will tell you how to set up your car for better street and touring performance and give you some tips on driving faster while still staying safe. The third part will help you to make your car and your driving more competitive on the track and autocross course, and fun—but safe—on backroads tours. Finally, the fourth part is intended for those of you who want your times to be the fastest on the track or the autocross course, even if that means that space in your back seat is taken up with a roll cage instead of dry cleaning and groceries.

Chapter Three

Tips on Filling Out Your Mini Order

Now that you've spent some time thinking about your ultimate goals, and how fast you want to get there, we can help you sort through the choices you'll need to make before you sign the order form and start counting the days until your very own Mini is produced, shipped, and prepared for you to pick up at the dealer.

Cooper or Cooper S?

The first buttons you'll have to click are the ones labeled Cooper or Cooper S. This is actually pretty simple. Since the Cooper S costs only $3000 more than the Cooper, and offers many more features and capabilities, we think it offers the best value for money.

For starters, the Cooper S has a six-speed manual transmission. That difference alone, in almost anyone's book, would justify the extra money. You're probably already pretty sure that an automatic transmission is for people who want to use their right hand for inane non-motoring activities like shaving or applying make-up. You already know that a quick hand on the gearshift and a good foot on the clutch separate the motorists from those people who buy a car for transportation. And with the Cooper S you get the bolstered sport seats thrown into the bargain.

But it isn't only the gear-shifting and sports seats that you'll be able to look forward to. It's all the extra horsepower potential that separates the Cooper S from the

The Mini Cooper is a good car in its basic form and even with the automatic transmission will be fun to drive. *(Photo courtesy of BMW USA.)*

The Mini Cooper S offers a supercharged engine, sx-speed transmission, sport seats and 16-inch wheels, a solid platform for upgrading your Mini for whatever activities you have in mind. *(Photo courtesy of BMW USA.)*

perfectly-adequate-for-other-people Cooper. The aftermarket catalogs are full of go-fast components that you can use to boost the power to almost twice the showroom levels.

Yes, the Cooper also can be made to go faster. But by the time you've installed everything possible, you will have spent more than the $3000 you saved. Your Cooper will have reached its maximum horsepower potential at just about where the Cooper S starts, and you'll still have only one tail pipe out the back.

By comparison, with a Cooper S, you start with a car that is already pretty quick. After that, how fast you can go just depends on your own goals and skill. So click the button marked Cooper S and we'll move on.

(For those of you who already bought a Cooper before you bought this book, don't worry. Keep on reading and we'll give you all the tips we have on how to get the most out of your Cooper. If you decide you want a little more performance, we'll discuss modifications that will give your Cooper approximately the same horsepower as the standard showroom Cooper S.)

If you do have to drive under conditions where an automatic transmission makes sense—such as long stop-and-go commutes or managing the hills of San Francisco—the Cooper continuously variable automatic and the six-speed automatic on the Cooper S still allow you to upshift and downshift on your own when you prefer, so you still can learn to upshift and downshift at the most efficient shift points.

We also can guarantee, if you learn to be a better driver as we'll teach you along the way, you'll be able to beat many of those manual shift Cooper S owners who think that they can buy fast lap times with their credit card.

Tintop or Ragtop?

We really can't help you much with your decision on whether to buy the coupe or the convertible, often referred to as tintops and ragtops by motoring enthusiasts. BMW has done an excellent job of engineering body stiffness into the convertible so it won't rattle and shake over rough roads and railroad crossings; therefore the convertible will be just as good as the hardtop on back road tours. Also in the convertible, there is the opportunity to look up at the mountains or redwoods when you're driving that scenic byway, instead of craning your neck to peak at them through the windshield.

However, the convertible does have blindspots when the soft top is up that you wouldn't have with the hardtop. This can make it slightly less safe in heavy traffic, or when backing up. More important, most track day activities and some autocross events won't allow a ragtop on the course because it offers less protection in the unlikely event of a roll-over. If you're thinking seriously about high-speed and timed events in your MINI future, the hardtop will be the better choice.

The real question is where, geographically, you're going to be driving. If your home base is blessed with temperate weather all year around, you'll be able to get a lot of driving time with the top down. On the other hand, if your driveway looks like Ice Station Zebra six months of the year, the hard top may be easier to live with.

Premium, Sport, and Cold Weather Packages

After you've clicked the button marked MINI Cooper S, decided on coupe or convertible, and taken a first shot at picking a color scheme (don't worry, you can come back and play with this again later), you'll have to decide whether you want any of the three combination accessory packages—Premium, Sport, or Cold Weather—that the MINI dealer will offer you. The simple answers, we think, are "no," "maybe," and "it depends."

We would say no to the $1350 Premium package because the primary component in it is the sunroof. A sunroof is certainly very nice if you want to cruise down the highway with the sun fighting the sunblock you just applied. But if you contemplate using the car on the track, where you're going fast and concentrating on your driving, it's just a noisy distraction. Also, it adds weight, something the person seeking performance isn't going to want. Besides, if you envision your perfect car with a checkered flag, Union Jack, or custom graphics on the roof, they won't work over the sunroof.

The other components in the premium package, including cruise control, multifunction steering wheel, automatic air conditioning, and on-board computer are all nice touches and worth having, but at most dealers can each be ordered as separate options which will save you some money. (Note that all options and packages were current at the beginning of 2005, but may have changed subsequently, but the relative comparisons should still apply.)

The convertible MINI is built on a stong chassis and has a unique three-position top to provide topless motoring enjoyment in all weather. But if you expect to drive it on the track, check with your organization to make sure it will be legal without a rollbar. *(Photo courtesy of BMW USA.)*

On the other hand, if you have your heart set on the sun roof—and it certainly is the closest you can come to a convertible without buying the cabriolet—and think you want any one of the other convenience items and can live with the rest, then the premium package would be a bargain.

The Sport package is a definite maybe. It includes one thing you will want, the Dynamic Stability Control (DSC) system, and some things you might want, including (on the Cooper S) the Xenon headlamps with powerwashers, fog lamps, and bonnet stripes. The package also includes 7x17-inch MINI S-Lite alloy wheels and run-flat performance tires.

If bought separately, these options would cost a total of about $1900, but the complete package is available for $1350. This price difference makes the choice seem obvious, but it really depends on whether you want all the individual upgrades in the package.

We definitely advise you to buy the DSC, whether or not you buy the rest of the package. Selected separately, this option costs $500. That's a small price for the peace of mind you will have in slippery conditions. If you hit a patch of wet pavement or black ice on a dark night while cruising down the road, sensors in the DSC system will tell your throttle to ease back and apply the brake on the spinning wheel to keep you from skidding, all in the fraction of a second it will take you to realize you are in danger of spinning into oncoming traffic.

Sure, you'll switch off the DSC before your turn in the next autocross competition, but the rest of the time, you'll want it on. And yes, the standard traction control system will keep your wheels from spinning under most circumstances, but it won't help you much in the turns.

The main issue with the sport package is the wheels and tires that are included. We're going to recommend you buy performance wheels and tires from aftermarket sources, since there are better choices out there. Unless you definitely want the Xenon headlights (separately $550), fog lights ($140), and bonnet stripes ($100), you'll save money by not buying the Sport Package, and you can use that cash to get the high-performance wheels and tires you want.

Alpha-Brake Soup

The MINI Cooper S is equipped with several safety packages that are often referred to by their abbreviations:

ABS—Anti-lock Braking System

Standard: Senses when wheels are about to lock up under heavy braking, then pulses brakes to regain traction.

ASC—All-Season Traction Control

Standard on MCS: Prevents front wheel spin when engine torque is applied, and increases torque to non-spinning front wheel for better traction and control.

CBC—Corner Brake Control

Standard: Senses when brakes are applied heavily during turns or lane changes and feeds more braking force to outside front wheel to counteract oversteer and keep rear end from sliding out.

DSC—Dynamic Stability Control

Option: Senses relative changes in wheel speeds that occur if car starts to skid, and uses throttle control and selective wheel braking to regain car control.

EBD—Electronic Brakeforce Distribution

Standard: balances front and rear brake force to maintain front-to-rear stability under varying vehicle load conditions and avoid front or rear lock-up on hard braking.

If you have decided that you do want to get the lights and stripes, as well as the DSC, then you might as well get the whole Sport combo. There's nothing wrong with the bigger wheels and tires offered in the Sport package, and by the time you've paid for the other parts of the package, the wheels and tires are effectively free with the full package (you can do the math). Then wait until you've worn out your first set of tires before ordering your own set of wheels and tires from your favorite aftermarket supplier.

As for the Cold Weather package, that depends on where you live and drive. If you live where winter lasts four months of every year or more, with colder-than-whatever mornings, accompanied by slush on the road and the sun not even over the horizon yet, then the warmers for the seats, mirrors, and windshield washers will be very good things to have, indeed. Especially since they won't slow you down during the fast season. Those warm seats are also a nice option in other parts of the country if you're buying a convertible and like to drive with the top down, even on chilly mornings.

John Cooper Works Tuning Kit

You said you wanted performance, right? Then why not go for the whole deal and have your local dealer install the BMW-approved John Cooper Works Tuning Kit? The tuning kit includes an improved supercharger with smaller pulley, a two-stage air intake box, a high-performance cylinder head, and reprogramming for the engine control unit.

With these tweaks, the kit takes horsepower from 168 to 207 ponies, and brings torque up to 180 pound-feet from 162 in the stock Cooper S. With that power, you can get from zero to 60 in 6.5 seconds (more than a second faster than the stock Cooper S) and, if you can find enough space on a closed course, get up to 140 miles per hour. And you get a slick cold air box, intercooler cover and and engaving on the exhaust pipes to prove you're faster than the average bear. Now that's motoring.

If you want your Mini to perform right out the door, and don't see yourself taking the car to a tuning specialist after you buy it, the JCW package is an easy way to get a significant bump in engine performance quickly. At the same time, you have the comfort that comes from knowing all the modifications are backed by the factory warranty.

However, the JCW kit is expensive. The parts are $4650 in the box, and then you still have to pay your dealer to install them, which takes ten hours of shop time. The whole thing is going to cost from $5000 to $6000 out the door.

There are alternatives you may wish to consider. For the same amount of money, you can easily get even more horsepower, and at the same time improve the tires, wheels, brakes, and suspension by buying aftermarket components and having a good shop install them. If you still need decals to impress the pedestrians, the aftermarket suppliers will be happy to help you out.

In addition, reputable aftermarket suppliers now offer their own warranties on the parts that they sell, and some, such as MiniMania, even guarantee that if their properly-installed parts cause a problem that voids any part of the factory warranty, they'll pay for the repairs and replacement themselves. You should check the fine print for yourself on both the factory and the supplier warranties, but at least you know that you can make changes to upgrade your MINI without worrying that you'll lose the peace of mind of BMW's solid warranty protection.

Getting the Right Rubber for the Road

We've already said that you may not want the wheels and tires that the MINI dealer has to sell you. To understand why, we need to start talking about performance.

Performance, in gearhead terms, is the general measure of how well your car does the four things it is supposed to do: start, run, turn, and stop. To win on the autocross or race course, you need to get up to speed as quickly as possible, go as fast as possible, get around corners as rapidly as possible, and stop in as short a distance as possible.

While many of the components on the car contribute to one or more of those goals, your wheels and tires contribute to all four. More than any other component on your car, the tires and wheels you choose will make significant differences in performance.

Let's be clear about one thing from the very start: there is no such thing as the best tire and wheel for all those jobs. But there are some features that you should consider when buying any tire and wheel. They include weight, flexibility, and grip.

Weight is the most important aspect to consider. When we measure weight in a performance car, we divide it into two categories: unsprung weight, and sprung weight. Unsprung weight is the weight of all those things that stay connected to the road (tires, wheels, brakes, hubs, axles and springs)—or at least should stay connected to the road—when you hit a bump or pour the car into a turn, while the rest of the car, the sprung weight, goes up and down on the springs. In other words, the wheels and tires are most of the unsprung weight.

In order to improve performance, you want to reduce your unsprung weight to the minimum required to get the job done. The first issue with heavy tires and wheels is that it takes more torque to get them up to speed. Further, since heavier wheels have more momentum than lighter wheels when they are spinning, more braking effort is required to slow them down.

Finally, the more unsprung weight you have, the more difficult it will be to adjust the handling of the car. Changing springs, shock absorbers, and anti-sway bars will change how the weight above the springs moves around, but it won't have any effect on movement of unsprung weight.

> ### *Unsprung Weight*
> The weight of the parts of a car not supported by its springs, including wheels, tires, brakes, hubs, springs and shock absorbers.
>
> ### *Sprung Weight*
> The weight of the parts of the car supported by its springs, including the chassis, body, engine, and drive train.

For these reasons, you really want the lightest wheels and tires you can buy within your budget that are still strong enough to do their job. The problem with the original stock or factory-optional wheels is that they're heavy. There are many choices of wheels on the aftermarket that are much lighter because of their materials and construction, yet will still provide all the safety and functionality needed.

Tires are another issue where the aftermarket offers better performance. Your MINI can be purchased with two different types of tires: performance run-flats, and all-season run-flats. Notice that both types are "run-flat." That's a nice engineering feature, assuring that a flat tire won't leave you parked beside the road. They also allowed the designers to avoid having to figure out where to stick a spare wheel and tire, which saved weight and cost.

A wide variety of aftermarket wheels and tires is available for the new Mini. This wheel and tire combination is mounted on a track race car, but would be fine for the street or autocross course. This 17-inch custom wheel has space for an aftermarket brake set and the wheel and aftermarket tire combination weigh considerably less than the stock wheel and tire.

But there are two problems with run-flat tires. In order to provide the run-flat capabilities, the tires are heavier than standard radial tires and they are stiffer than regular radial tires. As a result of the weight, they require more engine power to turn and have more inertia when stopping. Because of the stiff sidewalls, they don't flex as well, so they don't stick to the pavement as well in turns. They also give a rougher ride than most standard radial tires, which may not affect performance, but certainly detracts from comfortable motoring.

So here is where we stick our neck out for the first time and suggest that if performance is your goal, you can improve the performance of your new MINI by buying from sources other than the dealer. Reputable aftermarket dealers offer an extensive variety of wheel designs to choose from at a wide range of prices and varying weights, as well as tires with different performance and behavior characteristics from several different sources.

Tire Rack (www.tirerack .com), for example, lists 42 different wheels, and several different brands of tires, for you to choose from for a high-performance MINI Cooper S. The MiniMania catalog shows 25 different choices of wheels, which are supplied with Kumho Ecsta Supra 712 Z-rated tires, a tire choice that they've tested and liked on their own cars.

Making the change won't even cost too much. A good set of four aftermarket wheels that are much lighter than the MINI wheels, shod with a set of proven performance tires, can be put on the car for between $1000 and $1,300. Of course, you can get much fancier, and more expensive, tires and wheels but at least that gives you a ballpark idea of your costs.

You'll probably want to carry an inexpensive aftermarket tire patch and inflater kit as insurance against being stranded, but the likelihood of getting a flat tire is pretty small with modern tires.

Bottom line, if you don't need or want the other components in the Sport Package, such as the Xenon lights, save your $800 and put it towards a good set of tires and wheels. It will be the single best investment you make to improve the safety and handling of your MINI.

Other Accessories and Choices

But wait, we're still not through with all the choices in all five boxes on the MINI website. We still have to think about interior trim and a few other miscellaneous goodies.

Let's start with seats and upholstery. Since you've probably already opted for the Cooper S, you're going to get a good set of sport seats, with effective bolstering to keep you from sliding around on those tight corners. And you can choose from a variety of different colors. We don't have any advice on most trim decisions but we do suggest that you order the gray cloth upholstery rather than the leatherette or leather.

In our view, cloth upholstery is best because it provides more grip against the seat of your pants in tight maneuvering, helping those bolsters do their job. It's also cooler in summer and warmer in winter, and won't show wear as much as the leather or vinyl.

Best of all, the cloth doesn't add anything to the cost of your MINI. We talked about trade-offs earlier. How about thinking of your decision as trading off the leather, which won't help you go faster, for a set of tires and wheels that cost about the same and will definitely help you go faster. Seems like a fair trade-off to us.

There are a few other choices to make. If you didn't choose the Sport package, you might want to look at those front fog lamps again, but as far as we're concerned they don't really do much good in fog conditions, and they just irritate other drivers ahead of you. On the other hand, rear fog lamps, which provide brighter visibility to drivers overtaking you, are a good option if you ever drive anywhere when you're likely to be in the fog.

The navigation system is another option that depends on what kind of driving you do. If you are going to be driving back and forth to the same office every day, and rarely venture into unknown territory, you can probably pass on this expensive item. It certainly isn't going to be much help getting through the corkscrew at Laguna Seca.

On the other hand, if you're going to be using your MINI to make sales calls or long-distance trips, the navigation system can be a real time-saver. We've tested them and we can say that the latest generation of these high-tech gizmos is pretty terrific. It will change the interior in one important respect, however. The screen goes where that big pie-plate of a speedometer would normally be mounted, and instead you'll get a smaller speedo mounted next to your tach on the steering column. That's actually kind of a good thing.

The multifunction steering wheel and cruise control are also a matter of personal taste and requirements. If you expect to spend long periods of time on the highway, the ability to set the speed and forget it, and also tune the radio without taking your hands off the wheel, is a good thing. If you don't expect to do much over-the-road driving with your MINI, save the $650 to spend on your new go-fast, sound-good exhaust system that we'll discuss in the next chapter.

A new option, called the Chrono Package, was introduced for 2005. With this package, the center space normally occupied by the speedo is filled instead with a set of performance gauges, including oil temperature (almost unheard of on production cars), oil pressure, water temperature, and gasoline level. As with the nav system, a small speedo is mounted on the steering column in tandem with the tachometer. Chrome bezels (edge rings) add a nice touch to the gauges. We would certainly add this option on any MINI Cooper S that might be used for track days or long-distance touring.

The choices for your MINI are almost endless. Colors, stripes, wheels, interiors, tops, mirrors, lights, and we haven't even opened an aftermarket catalog, yet. Owners of these cars took part in a MINI driver training event near Pleasanton, California.

Auto-dimming mirrors, rain-sensitive wipers, and automatic air-conditioning are nice things, we suppose, but these are probably things you can manage to do for yourself rather than paying little robots to do them for you. As for the "park distance control?" Give us a break; the car is barely 12 feet long, for heaven's sake. If you can't get it into a parking place without a back-up beeper, you're never ever going to master the Charlize Theron parking maneuver from *The Italian Job* or even hope to drive your MINI through the Los Angeles subway tunnels without scratching the paint.

On the other hand, if you're ordering a convertible and live where you're going to be driving with the top up, the park distance control might not be a bad idea, since the convertible top creates some pretty severe blind spots when you're backing up in tight spaces.

Two new high-performance options were announced on the 2005 cars, a John Cooper Works performance brake kit and a limited-slip differential. Later in this book we'll discuss various alternatives to upgrade braking, and the purpose and value of the limited-slip differential.

If you already have a pretty good idea of what these components do, and why you might want them, then we encourage you to consider them and compare their price and performance to similar components available in the aftermarket. If you don't know what we're talking about, you're probably better off gaining some experience with your new MINI and wait until later to consider having these options installed.

Whew! Such a wonderful set of choices. But now that you've used the website and your mouse to make all your choices, you should have an idea of what the car is going to cost. You're ready to talk to a real live MINI representative at your nearest dealer (the address of which, of course, can be found on the www.miniusa.com website, along with a map and driving directions).

Chapter 4

Driving Fast Safely

Before you jump in your current transportation module and head out to your Mini dealer, let's take the time to go over a few basic driving tips that you'll be able to use when you buy your new Mini. You can practice them every time you drive so you'll be ready when your very own Mini arrives. And we can guarantee that these tips will help you avoid any life-threatening, or license-threatening, incidents so you'll be safe and alive when the dealer calls you to come pick up your Mini.

Good Driving Starts Before You Turn the Key

We're going to start with the absolute basics. How do you sit in your car? As you go faster, you'll be surprised at the importance of your basic sitting position. We realize it may seem cool to have the seat reclined to the point where the only thing showing above the doorsill is a reversed baseball cap. But from that position it is impossible to stay in control when the motoring gets interesting.

As soon as you get in, push your butt back into the seat until your lower back is against the backrest. Now slide the seat forward or back until you can rest your left foot comfortably flat on that pedal-looking thing (it's often called a "dead pedal" because it doesn't move) on the left side of the floor. The dead pedal is there to reduce driving

Mirrors should be positioned so that the sideview mirrors show the space to the sides of the car and just overlap with the view from the interior rearview mirror at the rear of the vehicle.

fatigue and give you a place to brace against on hard corners when you start to drive the car hard. That should put your right foot on the accelerator with your knee slightly bent.

Now adjust the seat back and steering wheel until your wrists can touch the rim of the steering wheel with your elbows straight. In that position, your hands will rest comfortably on the sides of the steering wheel rim with your elbows slightly bent, making it easy to turn the steering wheel. More important, there should be at least 12-14 inches between your chest and your steering wheel, so that if the air bag explodes it won't hit you in the chest before it does its job of absorbing your forward momentum.

With you and your seat in the proper position, now adjust the rearview mirrors. The center mirror should show the entire rear window, giving you as much vision directly to the rear as possible.

The sideview mirrors are there for a specific purpose. They allow you to see the blind spots beside you that you can't see out of the corner of your eye or in the center rearview mirror. To adjust the left door mirror, lean over until your head is right against the side window. Now adjust the door mirror so that you can just see the left side of your car on the inside edge of the mirror. Adjust the right door mirror by leaning to the center of the car, then adjusting that mirror the same way, so you can just see the side of your car on the inside edge of the mirror.

Now check your whole field of view. The view in your left-hand outside mirror should just overlap the view in your center mirror, and that view should just overlap the view in your right-hand outside mirror. If this is the case, then you'll have no blind spots in which a car can hide to cause problems when you change lanes or later, on the track when you get ready to make that pass.

You can check this when you get out on the highway. As you pass a car, as soon as you can't see it out of the corner of your eye, it should be squarely in the sideview mirror. As it passes out of the sideview mirror, it should be completely in view in the rearview mirror.

Now, you can turn the key in the ignition and head out, comfortable, confident, and in control of your car.

Position the seat far enough back so there is at least 14 inches of space between your chest and the steering wheel. For normal driving, your hands should be positioned at the "four o'clock" and "eight o'clock" positions so that your hands and arms aren't blocking the airbag. Also, for safety, your thumbs should be resting on the rim of the wheel, not wrapped around it.

When you're on the track or autocross course, move your hands up slightly to the "three o'clock" and "nine o'clock" position for better control of the wheel. Never position your hands higher than this on the wheel.

Wait a second. Where should you put your hands? Of course, you've been told to keep both hands on the wheel – no cruising along with one arm on the window sill and one wrist lazily draped over the rim of the wheel – but at what position? When you took driver training in high school, we'll bet you were told to keep your hands at "ten and two o'clock" thinking of the wheel as a big clock face. That may have been all right years ago, with large steering wheels and no air bags, but in today's cars, that won't work.

For everyday street driving, the best position for your hands is at "four and eight o'clock." This position is comfortable, allows you to keep both hands on the wheel for quick response in an emergency. Just as important, the air bag can deploy without hitting your arms, throwing one through your side window and causing the other to knock your passenger unconscious.

We should note that if you take the car out on the race track, you'll probably move your hands up to a "nine and three" position, like your favorite race driver, but on the track you only need to move your hands a few inches each way for most turns, and you want the maximum possible control to cut that corner apex neatly.

In most turns, whether on the track or on the street, don't move your hands on the rim, but rather keep them in place as you turn the wheel. This gives you more control since your hands are always on the wheel, and allows you to respond rapidly to any changes in conditions.

One more thing about those hands. A light grip on the wheel is all you need. Squeezing the rim hard and flexing those biceps isn't going to make the car hold the road any better around the corners. All you will do is tire yourself out.

Look Ahead, Think Ahead

Whether you're just on your way to the grocery store, or coming through that fast right-hander at the race track, it is critical to think far ahead of where you are and where you want to go. You want to be continuously aware of everything around you. This is our second tip in how to drive fast and safely. The moral of this message not only will help you stay safe on the highway, but it will also help you become a faster driver when you do get out on the track.

Get into the habit of continuously scanning your environment, never letting your eyes pause for more than an instant on any one point before you move on to the next point. Look far down the road, then bring your vision closer. Check your left sideview mirror, then your rearview mirror, then your right sideview mirror. Sweep your eyes across your gauges to check not only that your speed and rpm are where you expect, but also your safety gauges—the gas, temperature, and oil pressure, and "idiot" lights—aren't signaling any impending problems. Then do it all again, maintaining a complete picture of everything around you that might in any way affect you.

The problem with most drivers is that when they're in traffic they fixate on the rear bumper of the car ahead of them. If something happens a little further up the road, they don't notice it until after the car ahead does. Then it's too late and they don't have enough time or space to do anything except become part of the accident report.

When you're scanning all the things in your world—what's happening far down the road, what the car ahead of you is doing, what's on either side of you, how wide the shoulders are on the road, the cars behind you and how fast they are overtaking you— you should also be playing a continuous game of forecasting the future.

For example, is that car that just came onto the freeway from the exit ramp ahead going to try to spurt all the way across the road ahead of you and try to cut into your lane? If a car several hundred feet ahead has just put on their brakes, or changed lanes abruptly, could they be reacting to something in the lane that you can't see yet? Is there a driver tailgating you who might not be able to stop when you do if there is an obstacle in your lane?

The trick is to *look ahead, think ahead,* and *decide ahead* of time what you will do if one of the things that could go wrong does go wrong.

A story is told about Juan Manuel Fangio, the famous Argentinian driver of the late forties and fifties—well before our time, of course—in a race in Italy. The photographer on one of the corners said that every time the great driver passed him, Fangio's front wheel would touch the corner within inches of where it had touched the time before and the time before that, exactly on the fastest line around the corner. Then, on one lap, passing that corner Fangio abruptly swerved wide several car widths to the middle of the track.

An instant later, a crash and smoke from around the corner telegraphed the news of a serious accident. But Fangio's car came around again on the next lap without problems. He had managed to swerve offline to miss a spinning car that he couldn't even have seen.

32

When he talked to Fangio afterward, the photographer asked about the accident. Fangio told him, "Every time I came up to that corner, I could see the crowd looking my way. Then on that one lap, they were all looking the other direction, down the track. So I knew something was wrong and moved off the line so I would have room to handle a problem if there was one there. Sure enough, they had seen the driver ahead lose control of his car and spin sideways, but I was able to get around him."

Fangio was not only watching where his car was going, as well as a thousand other details like the condition of the pavement, the feel of his tires, and the gauges on his dashboard, he was even aware of what direction the crowd was looking. And noticing a small change in one detail of his surroundings may have saved his life and certainly helped him to win the race.

While you may not be able to process information as fast as a famous racing driver from history, you can do the same thing he did. You can be aware of changes in your surroundings, and decide what they might mean to you, so you'll be prepared to avoid an accident instead of winding up in the middle of it.

Practice this every time you drive so you can react not just to things after they happen, but be ready for anything that could happen. Soon it will seem as if you not only have 360 degree vision, but also have the ability to predict the future.

Going Fast Safely is All About Stopping

Any racing driver will tell you that speed in itself is not what wins races. That's why most real racing cars don't even have a speedometer. We would argue that the same thing is true in everyday driving. As long as you're not over the speed limit, you won't get a ticket, but that's really the only instance where it even matters what the speedometer says. What does matter is the distance the car will go in the time that it takes to notice and react appropriately to changes in conditions. Here are three rules of thumb that will tell you whether you're going too fast.

We've already recommended that you look a long distance down the road to anticipate what might happen before it happens, but what really matters is how long it takes for you to stop or change directions before you hit the car ahead of you. We all know that the faster we're going, the more distance we'll cover before we can hit the brake pedal, or turn the wheel. We also know that the faster we're going, the further the car will travel before we can bring it to a stop, and that we shouldn't turn the wheel abruptly at high speeds because that will cause the car to swerve.

But we can't look up our speed and distance in car lengths in some book every time we want to know whether we're driving too close to the car ahead, or whether the car behind us has enough room to stop if we do have to stop ourselves.

To determine how close you should be to the car ahead of you, all you need to do is count to three. At highway speeds, it will take three seconds for you to get your foot from the gas to the brake, and bring the car to a stop.

Notice when the car ahead passes a particular point, such as a tree or lane marker. If you can count to three slowly before you get to that point, then you have room to bring your car to a stop, or turn into the next lane, should the car ahead stop or swerve abruptly.

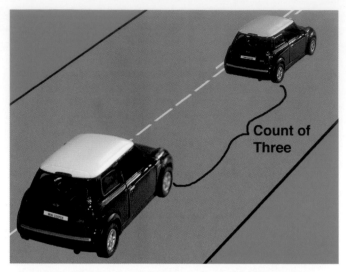

To make sure you're not following the car ahead too closely for the speed you're traveling, pick an object that the car ahead is passing. If you can count to three before you get to that object, you have enough distance to stop without hitting them if you need to.

Count of Three

What about the car behind you? When you're passing, or changing lanes, you want enough room to give the car behind a safe space. As you pass the car ahead, wait until you can see them completely in your inside rearview mirror. If you can see them completely in your rearview mirror, it's safe to move over into their lane. Remember that your side mirrors have been adjusted to cover your blind spots, which are close to you, and that the right mirror says "Objects in the mirror are closer than they appear."

On the road or on the track, it isn't enough just to be ahead of the person you've just passed before you change your line. You need to be far enough ahead of them to cut over into their path and still give them time to react.

But what about when you can't see the car ahead? Curves are another place where we often drive faster than we should. After cleaning auto wreckage off curves for many years, the highway departments of America finally figured this out and started posting warning signs, with a suggested speed for that curve.

Unfortunately, most of us see these signs as challenges since we think they are the fastest speed that the highway department thinks the average driver can get their car around the curve. So we see how much faster we can go than the warning sign. "I took a curve at 40 mph that was posted at 20 mph. I guess I'm twice as good as the average driver," we say.

Too bad that's not what the sign means. What it means is that, if there is something in the road ahead that you can't see, the posted speed is the fastest your car can be going and still have time to stop when you do see the obstacle. You can test the laws of physics if you like, but you won't win.

On an open race track, things will be different. There will be a corner worker looking around the bend for you who will wave a yellow flag if there's a problem while you've still got time enough to stop. That's the place to see just how fast you can get the car around the corner, because if the corner worker isn't waving the flag, you can be sure there isn't anything there. But on the highway, with no corner worker, it's best to slow down to the recommended speed. The stalled driver, bicycle rider, or deer you have time to avoid will thank you for it.

That's enough driving lesson for one day. But if you'll practice a good driving position, get used to thinking 360 degrees and into the future, and not drive faster than you can stop, you'll be a better driver when your new MINI arrives at your dealer, and be ready for our next lesson in motoring.

Part Two

Minis for Streets and Roads

When the original Minis were first introduced, they were intended simply to be used by regular drivers on regular streets and roads. Nevertheless, with a few upgrades, they proved to be great on the long-distance European road rallies such as the Monte Carlo and Alpine rallies where they first made their fame.

In SCCA club racing and later in vintage racing events in North America, the Minis showed their ability to wag their tails at the opposition and then run away and hide until they took first at the checkered flag. They were also very successful in European saloon racing (which isn't racing around liquor bars, as you might expect, but the continental term for sedan racing).

But classic Minis became popular mostly because they were so darned satisfying to drive fast, and because they could go so many places and do so many things better than bigger, more powerful cars.

The new MINIs are stamped from the same mold, fun and practical at the same time. Right out of the showroom, they're able to do the everyday stuff well, and still bring a smile to your face every time you take one around a corner quickly or pass a pokey car on the highway.

But we're here to tell you that you can tweak your MINI just a little bit and make it even better, making your driving around the neighborhood or around the countryside even more fun. With a little professional instruction and some opportunity for practice, you can also learn to drive it better than you've ever driven another car.

Chapter Five

Getting to Know Your New Best Friend

Right off the mark, two things are good about MINIs. First, they're already among the best sports cars on the road in terms of their ability to go fast, corner fast, and stop fast. Second, like other cars that are just plain fun to drive, MINIs have the uncanny ability to gather people together into clubs and organizations that have the sole intent of helping their members enjoy driving their cars.

Combine these two factors, and you have a recipe for easy weekend fun: a good car to drive and a like-minded group of friends to drive with. Our first recommendation is to get to know the car well so you'll know how much fun it can be. Our second recommendation is to join a Mini club so you'll have excuses to have fun with it as soon as possible.

The MINI has been designed by enthusiasts with enthusiasts in mind. What we want to do is show you the difference between simply operating an automobile as a means of transportation, and driving a performance car for the sheer pleasure of it. But where should you start?

We're Serious: Read the Manual

We're going to assume that when you first considered buying a MINI and visited the dealer, the sales rep spent a few minutes showing you the good features before you went out on a test driver, and told you more about how and why things are designed the way they are.

Take the owner's manual out of the glove compartment and read it. Compare what you're reading to what you find on the car so you understand everything thoroughly.

39

We hope that you allowed a little time and curbed your enthusiasm when you first picked your car up to listen again as the rep talked you through the main controls and features. However, we're going to bet you weren't paying much attention. Sitting in your very own brand-new car is just too overwhelming an experience.

So now that you've been driving your new MINI for at least a few days, what should you do? Start with the owner's manual. We'll bet that you've never read the owner's manual from beginning to end for any car you've ever owned. Too bad. There's a lot of information in those manuals so that from the beginning you'll feel confident that you understand your car.

The best way to do that is to take an afternoon in your driveway and sit in the car. As you read each section, look at the diagrams and compare them with the way things actually look in your car. Move, adjust, push, pull, try each of the levers and buttons. Don't just look at the top of the oil dipstick, for example. Take it out and see what real oil looks like. Find the coolant tank, take the cap off and look inside to see where the level should be.

In other words, get to know the car thoroughly. Learn about it as if your life depended on knowing the car thoroughly. Some dark night, it very well might.

If you don't have time to read the owner's manual all the way through right now, then put it in the bathroom. Owner's manuals are great reading material for those few minutes when you really don't have anything else to do. Every time you have a chance, read a section, and then when you go out to your car the next time, try to remember what you just read and check out how it looks in real life.

Another tip: when you're driving your car, try to be as aware as possible about what it does and how it does it. Try to feel how the car moves and sounds when you accelerate, when you take your foot off the gas pedal, and when you put on the brakes. Try to feel what the car is doing when you turn a corner. Turn off your iPod once in awhile and listen for the sounds of the engine as you accelerate and shift gears. Those feelings will be important as you start to plan how you want to improve your MINI and when you work on improving your driving.

Take a Course in MINI Motoring

Once you've read the manual thoroughly, and become an expert on your own car (just try not to bore your MINI-less friends with your new-found knowledge and enthusiasm) and you've been around the block a few times with the car, it's time to get serious about really learning to drive.

First, we want you to go back to school. Yes, we know you've been through that driver training school before you got your license, and some of you might even have already had the experience of taking one of those state-administered driving schools that are offered with the first traffic ticket. Trust us; they didn't even scratch the surface.

When you were driving that little driving school car around your town, did you ever stomp on the brakes hard enough to make the anti-lock braking system kick in? Did you ever take a turn fast enough to make the tires squeal? Did you ever get the car to skid? Intentionally? If you haven't done all of these things, you haven't begun to learn to really drive.

A course teaching street driving skills, especially one tailored to MINI owners, is a great way to get acquainted with the capabilities of your MINI and hone your own skills.

When you've had the chance to learn these things and practice them, the difference will be that when things do go wrong, you'll be able to be a real driver, not just another potential crash dummy or organ donor behind the steering wheel.

What we're talking about is a real driving school, with skilled driving instructors, that combines classroom discussions with practice in a car in a closed area, such as a race track or driving course. We're talking about driving the car close to its limits so you can find out what happens when something unexpected occurs. We're talking about learning what you should do to keep your car from going out of control, and what it feels like when you do lose control. Most important, we're talking about a school that gives you the opportunity to safely practice your skills in steering, braking, and accident avoidance.

Lest you assume that you only need to go to an advanced driving school if you're thinking about racing, let us be very clear. Participating in one of these schools will return every penny it costs and every minute it takes will make you a better, safer driver even if you never put a wheel on a track or autocross course again in your life.

There are lots of different opportunities to learn to drive better. Start by checking with your MINI dealer, since some of them sponsor MINI driving schools, or will be aware of courses in the local area. Check with the websites listed in the back of this book for independent driving schools and those sponsored by, or in conjunction with, the suppliers of aftermarket parts for the MINI.

If there is a automobile race track near you, check with them as well, since many race tracks host driving schools. The best situation is one where you can drive your own car in the course. For example, Car Guys Inc (www.carguysinc.com) offers courses at tracks in Virginia, West Virginia, North Carolina, and New York in which you can use your own car, and advanced street driving instruction in your own car is available at Thunderhill Park near Willows in north-central California (www.thunderhill.com/school.html). A variety of other courses is listed in the driving school directory on the Autoweek website (www.autoweek.com)

At least one driving course has been designed specifically for BMW MINI drivers. The course is presented by the Phil Wicks Driving Academy in several locations around the country. Information is available at www.Minidriving.com.

In this book, we'll be passing on many of the tips that these courses offer their students, but nothing substitutes for the experience of taking a good driving course in your own MINI to put those tips into practice.

Join Your Many MINI Friends

Sure, your MINI will be great for all the normal stuff, getting to work and going out in the evenings, transporting you and your luggage on trips, or moving furniture, plants, or whatever else has to be moved from one place to another on the weekends. But there's no substitute for just taking the car out on a weekend for the sheer pleasure of driving.

If you can combine that with some friendly camaraderie, all the better. And there is where the MINI will excel. When Minis were first introduced in the sixties, their owners immediately recognized that they were a special group of people, able to appreciate the finer things in automobiling, and Mini clubs rapidly grew up all over the world.

Those clubs remained active throughout the dark years when Minis weren't even sold in the United States, and were a ready-made network of friendship and support when the new MINIs were first introduced. Recognizing the common appeal of old and new Minis, many club members were among the first to line up to try and buy the new MINIs, and most Mini clubs have welcomed the new owners with open arms.

Most clubs arrange frequent tours to allow members to get their cars out on the good roads in their areas, as well as organizing social and charitable activities around their cars. You'll be surprised at how many activities are available.

You'll also probably be surprised at the wide range of backgrounds and interests represented by people who have been drawn together by the attraction of this new car. Membership in most of these clubs will span every age, from new drivers to old veterans, and their day jobs will cover every occupation and endeavor.

The nice thing is that, regardless of how much different the members are from one another, you'll all have one common interest in your MINIs, which means there will always be something to talk about as you get to know one another. As one member said recently, "I was surprised at how many friends I had that I had never met before."

In Appendix A to this book, we've listed the contacts for as many of the clubs as we could find at press time. For current information, check with your local MINI dealer, who will know if there is a Mini club in your area, and it won't take you long with an internet browser to find a current list of clubs.

If you can't find a local Mini club, maybe now is the time for you to start one. It won't take much effort. Find a local restaurant or pizza parlor with a back room you can reserve, make up some flyers announcing a meeting in a month or so, then stick them on any MINIs you see. Offer to work with your MINI dealer to start a club. In no time, you can have your own local club.

Chapter Six

Improving Your MINI

You've probably already been impressed by how good the MINI is at what it does. It feels peppy in around-town driving, competent on the highway, and can zip around corners at an enviable clip with almost no body sway or looseness.

Nevertheless, as most car reviews will note, the MINI has some areas where a little improvement wouldn't hurt. Nothing surprising there, all cars are built to please a particular audience as well as meet a particular budget and price target, so compromises were made. But there are some straightforward ways that the MINI can be improved, and we'll describe a logical progression of improvements in the next four chapters.

What's to Improve?

To be more specific about the good points of the MINI, the stock MINI Cooper S can get from zero to 60 in just under seven seconds, which puts it easily in the middle of the pack of what are called "performance cars." Top speed is north of 130 miles an hour, which also makes the car quite respectable in the sports car league. That speed is much faster than most of us should be driving, even on a closed course, though it does mean that at normal highway speeds the engine is right in the middle of its power band with lots of reserve power when needed.

Cornering is where the car really excels. BMW has a well-deserved reputation for suspension engineering, and it is really reflected in this car. Compared to even the best of the performance cars, this car chews up corners without looking back, leaving most of the rest of the pack at its rear.

However, there are still areas where the MINI's performance can be improved. That's not surprising, of course, since the design and development of a modern car is a balancing act. A wide variety of vehicle specifications are affected by laws and regulations. Fuel economy, smog emissions, and crashworthiness requirements all challenge designers by adding weight and putting limits on engine performance. Complicating the problem, different states and countries have differing regulations.

Designers also have the problem of deciding what the market actually wants in a car. Most auto journalists and some potential customers want a car to be fast off the mark, capable of high speeds, and able to corner without body sway. At the same time other buyers simply want a car that is quiet, comfortable, and smooth-riding.

And all of this regulation-following and customer-pleasing has to be put together into a car at a price that will be competitive in the marketplace and still produce a reasonable profit. So automobile designers and engineers have to make compromises.

The great thing about the MINI is that the basic platform is well-designed and very well put together. So once you've decided what kind of a MINI owner you want to be, you can make the changes you want so that your car won't be just some product planner's package of compromises. And with some knowledge and care, you can make your changes without having any bad effects on the overall quality and reliability of the car.

So if you will all take your seats, we'll start the first class in "Maximizing Your MINI 101." In this first class, we're going to focus on the principles of giving the MINI more horsepower and torque and making that power available over a broader range of speeds. We can do that because the steering, handling, and braking are all well above average, so we can save those factors for a later class.

The Basics of Internal Combustion

Let's start at the beginning. Your MINI is powered by an internal combustion engine. Aside from some electric cars, nearly all cars on the road have IC engines. All this means is that the power is produced by rapid burning of an air-fuel mixture— combustion— that happens inside—internal to—the engine.

In contrast, in an electric car the combustion happened somewhere else, at a power plant or in the sun. The resulting energy was sent over the electric power grid to be stored in the car's battery and then used by the car's motor to produce power.

With a hybrid car, the power still comes from internal combustion within the car's engine. However, what makes the car a hybrid is that it also has an electric motor that can be used both to produce power and to generate power. Normally the car is driven by the IC engine, boosted as needed by the electric motor. Any excess power from the gasoline engine is used to make the electric motor generate electricity, which can be stored and used by itself, or in conjunction with the IC engine. But we digress.

In an internal combustion engine, the power is produced by the interaction of three forces: air, fuel, and spark. Air is pulled into the engine, is mixed with gasoline, and then the mixture is compressed by the cylinder and ignited by a spark. As the mixture burns, it expands, which pushes the cylinder down, turning the crank, and producing power. Once the mixture has burned (so rapidly that if we could observe it, it would appear as if it had actually exploded), the only remaining task is to get the combustion byproducts out of the engine as quickly and efficiently as possible, so a fourth factor, the exhaust, enters the equation.

The S Should Stand for Supercharger

In the MINI Cooper S, the engineers added another component, the supercharger, which is only used on high-performance cars. It is used on Jaguars and Bentleys, for example, but on few cars as inexpensive as the MINI. The presence of the supercharger is one of the few major differences between the MINI Cooper and the MINI Cooper S

(Incidentally, the S didn't originally stand for supercharger, since the classic Minis didn't have one. The letter S had come to mean "special" or "sport" on so many other performance cars of the period that it was simply added to the moniker when BMC upgraded the performance of the Cooper. If it ever was defined, that memo has been lost. Even today, with a turbocharged engine on the planning horizon, BMW states unequivocally that S doesn't stand for supercharger.)

But it's still true that the Cooper S has a supercharger, and that component is worth a few words on its own. As we mentioned, in order for the fuel to burn, we need air. If we want more powerful combustion, then we need more air.

This principle first became an issue back in the days when all airplanes used IC engines and the designers wanted their craft to fly higher. However, the higher the airplanes flew, the thinner the air became. With less air, there was less power produced by the engine. So engineers came up with the idea of using a little component with spinning blades, powered off the engine, to compress the air coming into the engine. With more air being forced into the engine—what the engineers call "forced induction"—more power could be produced. They called it "supercharging" the engine.

It wasn't long before automobile designers were using the same invention on the ground to make race engines run faster without having to get bigger. Remember the "Blower Bentleys" that were raced at LeMans in the early 1930s? You probably don't, unless you're an auto history buff. They were probably the earliest well-known application of a supercharger in a racing car. But if you want to impress your car buff friends, just tell them you have a "blown" MINI and refer to your supercharger as the "blower."

It's that same principle we find in the MINI Cooper S today. A small turbine between the air intake and the engine is driven off the main driveshaft by a pulley and belt to compress air coming into the engine. More air means that more fuel can be added, and more power will be produced.

How does the MINI Cooper S engine breathe? Air enters the system through an opening behind the grille (1), flows through the duct (2) and into the air intake box (3)—the air intake box also has a small opening to take in air from the base of the windshield. Passing through an air filter, air flows through another duct (4) into the supercharger and then into the intercooler (5) and finally (6) into the throttle body injection system under the intercooler.

Engines in some other makes of cars address the same problem of compressing the intake air by using turbochargers. The difference between a supercharger and a turbocharger is how the little vanes in the turbine are powered. In a supercharger, the power comes directly off the driveshaft, connected to the supercharger pulley by the main engine belt. In a turbocharger, there are two sets of vanes, connected by a shaft. Exhaust gas coming out of the engine spins one set of vanes, which in turn push the other vanes that push air into the engine.

The advantage of a turbocharger is that it doesn't pull power off the engine to spin the vanes, since it uses exhaust gas pressure. Sitting between the engine and the muffler, it can also reduce exhaust noise.

The problem with a turbocharger is that you've got to wait for the engine to build up some exhaust pressure before the turbo kicks in—what the gearheads call "turbo lag"—which means that the added power isn't immediately available. With a supercharged engine, the supercharger spins faster as the engine gains speed, so the added power is always on tap and ready for use.

Intercooler
A heat exchanger that reduces the temperature of air delivered to an engine by a supercharger or turbocharger, in order to keep the air-fuel mixture denser and, hence, more explosive when burned, which increases engine power.

Running forced induction, whether using a blower or a turbo, engineers have to confront a basic law of physics. When air is compressed, it gets hotter and wants to expand. To keep the air compressed as it is forced into the engine, one other part is almost essential, the "intercooler." On the MINI Cooper S, that part isn't very hard to find; it's the big rectangular box on top of the engine in the middle of the engine compartment.

Basically, the MCS's intercooler is a big air-cooled radiator that surrounds the engine's air intake duct. Air flows in through the hood scoop and across the cooling fins to keep the duct as cool as possible. This type of intercooler is called an "air-to-air" intercooler.

A Shopping List of Basic Improvements

One of the great things about the MINI is the robust nature of the basic engine. It is capable of producing much more power than it does right out of the showroom, even with the supercharger. There are some good reasons why it doesn't.

For one thing, an engine that produces better performance costs more money. Materials used in a high-performance engine are better and the engine is assembled with greater care, both of which add costs.

However, most people really don't care enough about performance to want to pay the extra price. Also, with higher horsepower, the engine doesn't produce as many miles per gallon, and is more difficult to tune to meet emission limitations, so the product designers, even in the MINI, simply had to make some compromises.

But you don't have to compromise. Aftermarket suppliers (companies that make products that are bought by owners after the car is purchased) have developed a number of products to improve the engine performance in the MINI to get better pick-up, higher speed, and simply more driving satisfaction under all speeds and situations.

If we think about that basic air/fuel/spark/exhaust equation, we want to do four things. We want to increase the amount of air entering the supercharger and we want to increase the compression capability of the supercharger, both to get more air into the combustion chambers. Then, we want to have the engine control unit (ECU) take advantage of that added air flow to by altering the fuel mixture and ignition timing for performance efficiency, and we want to make sure that all the smoke from the combustion can get out of the combustion chambers quickly.

We can make those improvements by upgrading the throttle intake and supercharger pulley, reprogramming the ECU, and upgrading the exhaust system. In this chapter, we'll discuss what each of these components does, how it can be upgraded, and the means by which the upgrade improves performance. We'll discuss the upgrades in the order in which they work in the operation of the engine.

Cold Air Intake System

Before we can have combustion, we have to have air. If we can increase the amount of air flowing into the supercharger intake, and keep it as cool as possible, then we'll be helping the supercharger do its job by giving it more air to breath.

We can do this by replacing the standard air intake system with an upgraded "cold air intake system." The standard cold air intake system in the MINI is really not all that complicated. Air flowing into the engine compartment through the grille is channeled into an air intake box on the top of the engine. In the box an air filter removes dust and dirt that would create undesirable wear in the engine. From the air intake box, a duct directs the filtered air into the supercharger. In addition to capturing and filtering the air, the ducts on the standard air intake system have been tuned, like you might tune an organ pipe, so that the air flowing through it produces as little noise as possible.

The standard cold air intake system easily can be swapped for an upgraded one that has been designed with performance in mind. Several aftermarket equipment manufacturers make replacement cold air intake systems for the MINI, but we'll describe two typical designs.

The simplest way to improve the system is to replace the stock air filter with a higher-quality filter that has been designed specifically to increase air flow while still

To improve air flow, as well as improve the efficiency of air intake into the filter, the standard cold air intake box and filter can be replaced by an Ultrik system with circular K&N air filter. The components of the system are shown above, and the installed system at right.

providing the same filtering functions. K&N makes a high-quality flat filter to replace the stock filter without changing the air box. Since the filter can be cleaned and re-used, you won't have to buy a new filter every time the old one gets dirty. (This modification is permitted in SCCA autocross street classes.)

An alternative approach that not only improves filter performance, but also provides additional air flow into the intake is now being manufactured by several companies. The system shown here is an Ultrik system. With this system, the entire air intake box and filter is removed and replaced by a conical filter surrounded by an L-shaped divider. This system helps increase power not only by improving filter efficiency, but also by increasing the flow of air into the system. (This modification is required in BMW CCA MINI Spec Racing.)

This system is designed to do a more efficient job of directing the air from the front grille into the engine's air intake. In addition, by being open at the top and back, it captures air from the grilles below the windshield, which are in an area of the body where air flow creates high pressure. By ducting some of that air into the supercharger in addition to the air coming in through the grille, the system naturally allows more air to enter the supercharger intake.

To make sure there is as little as possible to obstruct the air flow once it gets into the air box, the cold air intake system incorporates a reusable high-flow cone-shaped air filter. K&N's popular re-usable high-performance filters are frequently used in this application. The design of the upgraded cold air intake system offers one other advantage. While providing a direct path for air from outside the car to flow into the supercharger, it blocks off the hot air swirling around the engine. As we learned in science class, hot air is thinner than cold air, so the cooler the air going into the supercharger, the more efficiently the supercharger can do its job.

Though generally similar in design, these systems do vary somewhat from supplier to supplier. Two features should be considered when deciding which one to buy. First, the best dividers are made of shiny stainless steel. As a result they will reflect engine heat back to the outside of the box, so the cool air coming in from outside the car doesn't get heated up before being pulled into the supercharger. Second, the divider should have good space all the way around, so that air can flow into the entire surface of the filter without any restrictions.

A typical cost for the parts for an upgraded cold air intake system is about $200. The design is simple, and can be installed by anyone with the instruction sheet and the proper wrenches in a few hours or less. If it is done in a MINI service shop, it shouldn't take more than half an hour of shop time.

If you own a Cooper model, you can still make improvements in air flow into the engine. A less-restrictive reusable flat filter is available for about $50 to replace the stock filter. Aftermarket developers have also re-engineered the ram air intake duct and air box cover to improve air flow. Installing this improved ducting system in conjunction with a reusable high-performance flat filter will cost about $200 and make a measurable improvement in your Cooper's horsepower.

Making the Supercharger More Super

As we discussed, the supercharger works by forcing more air into the engine. It seems logical to assume, then, that the more air you can get it to push, the more horsepower the engine will produce. In fact, this assumption is true.

The supercharger blower is driven by a shaft connected to a pulley which in turn is rotated by a belt that is driven off the engine drive shaft. (This is the same belt

---

Racing Regulations and MINI Upgrades

There are several motorsports sanctioning bodies in North America that run competitive track and autocross events in which MINIs can compete. However, each of these groups has its own rules that specify the class in which a car may be run, depending on the modifications that have been made to the car.

One of the most popular such groups is the Sports Car Club of America (SCCA), which organizes both track and autocross events throughout the country. A similar body exists in Canada. These organizations have several classes that allow cars to run in street-legal condition. Some modifications and upgrades are permitted depending on the class. However, modifications in these classes are limited in order to keep preparation costs to reasonable amounts and allow drivers to compete against cars with roughly similar levels of modification. What is permitted and not permitted is spelled out in the group's regulations.

Similarly, the BMW Car Club of America (BMWCCA) organizes competitive track racing events for BMW-manufactured cars, including the MINIs. For MINIs that will be run in "Spec" classes, some modifications and upgrades are permitted— some are even mandatory—but other upgrades are not allowed under the rules.

If you are now planning to enter your car in these competitions, or even considering the possibility, you should definitely read the last two parts of this book, and you should obtain a copy of the modification rules that apply to MINIs to make sure that the changes you make to your car will be legal in the group with which you want to run.

Of course, all of the modifications suggested in this chapter can be reversed if they violate the rules of the sanctioning group you want to join, should you make the modifications suggested in this chapter and then decide later that you want to go racing. But if you know now that you intend to race your MINI with a specific sanctioning body, check the rules to save yourself unnecessary time and expense later.

that drives the alternator, and the water pump.) Every time the drive shaft makes a complete rotation, the belt around the supercharger pulley is moved a certain distance.

If you remember your basic geometry from high school, the distance around the edge of a circular object like a pulley—the circumference—is determined by the diameter of the pulley. The smaller the diameter of the pulley, then the smaller the circumference of the pulley. With a smaller circumference, less movement of the belt is required to cause the supercharger shaft of the pulley to make a complete rotation.

Or you can think about it another way. If we put a smaller pulley on the supercharger, then the supercharger will spin more times during the same number of revolutions of the engine. And the faster the supercharger spins, the more air is pushed into the engine.

That's the basis for our next horsepower improvement. By installing a smaller pulley (and the shorter belt that will be required to go with it) we can increase the speed of the supercharger and the amount of air being pushed in. Tuners call this "increasing the boost." Not surprisingly, since the principles are simple, aftermarket suppliers have developed smaller pulleys that you can substitute.

Boost
The amount of pressure above atmospheric pressure at which the supercharger or turbo forces air into the engine. Usually measured in pounds per square inch. With normal atmospheric pressure at 14.7 psi, a blower that provides 10 pounds of boost forces air in at 24.7 psi.

Of course, there are some limits to how much boost an engine can absorb without blowing itself to pieces, so there are limits to how small a pulley can be used effectively. For this reason, BMW may be reluctant to honor its warranty if you replace its very conservatively designed pulley with one that produces more boost.

Most reputable suppliers supply pulleys that are small enough to make a difference in horsepower, but aren't so small that they could blow the engine. As long as the pulley diameter isn't reduced by more than 15 percent, there should be no problems, If the pulley is replaced by one that has a radius of less than 85 percent of the original, it will spin the supercharger in excess of its maxium rated specification, putting the engine itself at risk. Even if the engine isn't pushed hard, if the pulley is too small, the belt angle will be so acute that the belt life will be significantly shortened.

Replacing the original pulley on the engine is not a simple job, since several other components have to be removed to get access to the pulley, and a special tool is needed to remove the pulley. Even with the special tool, an experienced mechanic may take several hours to do the job the first time. With a little practice, the job still takes about an hour.

So if you decide to replace your pulley with the smaller one, you should probably find a shop that has experience in replacing MINI pulleys. The replacement pulley and belt will cost about $200 and the installation requires about two to three hours of shop time. In terms of horsepower improvement per dollar, this is probably the most cost-efficient change you can make to the engine.

Electronic Throttles, ECUs, and Fuel

Until very recently, the amount of fuel that went into an IC engine was controlled by a needle valve in a carburetor, which was connected directly to the gas pedal. You pushed the gas pedal down, the needle valve would open, and gasoline would be mixed with the air being sucked into the engine. The further down you pushed the gas pedal, the more gasoline that would go into the engine, and the faster the engine would go.

With the engine speeding up, there was less time for the fuel/air mixture in the cylinders to burn, so the spark had to occur earlier in the cycle to give the combustion time to really work effectively. This factor is called ignition timing. In cars with a conventional ignition system, a gizmo using weights and springs inside the distributor would compensate for engine speed, changing the timing of the spark.

The process was all very mechanical. And yours was the only brain involved in the system.

> ### *Engine Control Unit (ECU)*
> The computer that is the center of the engine management system. in addition to controlling engine operations, it is connected to the electronic throttle, stability control systems, and auxiliary systems such as air conditioning. This component is also often referred to, for example in the BMW Mini Workshop Manual, as the Engine Control Module, or ECM.

Nowadays, it is a wee bit more complicated. First of all, almost no one uses carburetors any more on street cars. Instead, fuel is added to the air going into the engine with a fuel injection system. A fuel injection system has fewer parts, and therefore is less expensive to make and easier to service, so carburetors have gone the way of crank starters.

There is a second difference. In modern automobiles, to provide the fine-tuning needed to maintain performance while meeting emission regulations, the air/fuel/spark equation is controlled by an engine control unit, generally referred to by its initials, ECU. Also sometimes called an engine control module, or ECM, this component is a small computer that monitors a variety of engine and chassis conditions, as well as reacting to driver inputs to control basic engine operations like fuel mixture and spark timing.

On the MINI, the ECU is linked electronically to the throttle pedal (a set-up that is often referred to as "throttle-by-wire") and to several sensors that measure engine performance and vehicle dynamics. In addition to engine operations, it also controls other systems such as the automatic and dynamic stability control systems.

> ### *Throttle-by-Wire*
> A system which connects the throttle pedal electronically to the engine control unit, which in turn is connected electronically to the throttle body. Rather than being a mechanical connection, as on older cars, the throttle pedal is more like the rheostat you use to dim the lights in your living room.

The ECU tells the fuel injectors how much gasoline to add to the air flowing into the system and tells the spark plugs when to fire during each engine cycle (a factor called "ignition timing"). This little computer bases its calculations not only on how much you push the throttle pedal, but also on the speed of the engine, the amount of unburnt fuel coming through the exhaust system and other factors.

Think of it as a little brain that not only breaks your decision—"I want to go faster"—into many smaller decisions about fuel and timing, but also decides sometimes that you really wouldn't have asked for so much speed so quickly if you knew how much gasoline you were using, and how much exhaust you were pushing into the atmosphere.

In other words, the ECU modifies your decisions in order to help the engine achieve maximum gas mileage and comfortably meet 50-state emission restrictions.

However, within a reasonable range, you would probably want to overrule the computer if you could, or at least modify its decision rules. But for that, you would have to be not only an automotive engineer, but also a computer programmer, wouldn't you?

Not really. The nice thing is that some good automotive engineers and computer programmers have designed a little computer that you can use to tell your MINI's ECU to modify some of its decision rules in order to give you better performance. This process is called "remapping" the ECU.

Remapping the ECU

Changing the programs installed in the engine control unit (ECU), a computer that monitors automotive functions including throttle position, engine heat, emissions characteristics, and accessories, and controls the operation of the throttle body, ignition timing, fuel mixture, and other functions. By reprogramming—remapping—this computer, the engine's operation at various speeds can be modified to improve performance.

These ECU reprogrammer computers modify the software in the your car's ECU to change the ignition timing and fuel relationships at different engine speeds to improve performance. They also change some other factors, such as rev limits, acceleration enrichment, and fuel mixture so that the engine will be more responsive when you push or release the throttle pedal.

One example of these little gadgets is the "Shark Injector ECU Upgrade" designed and programmed for use on the MINI Cooper S. The Shark Injector is designed to change the program in your car's ECU to optimize fuel mixture and ignition timing

The engine control unit can easily be re-mapped to optimize fuel mixture and ignition timing for better torque response using a device like the Shark Injector ECU Upgrade shown here, which plugs directly into the MINI's onboard diagnostics plug.

across the entire engine RPM range, but has been programmed to provide a safe margin in order not to risk any damage to your engine.

The Shark Injector is available in two versions, one to upgrade for use of 93 octane gasoline, and one for 91 octane gasoline. The one you use will depend on the quality of gasoline available in your area.

Reprogramming your ECU is a piece of cake. It's just about as complicated as upgrading a piece of software on your computer. You plug the Shark Injector into the onboard diagnostics data port of your MINI and follow some simple procedures to download the remapped program into the ECU.

If for any reason you want to reverse the process and change your ECU programming back to the way it came from the factory, all you need to do is plug the Shark Injector into the data port again and you can swap the original factory program back into your ECU. You can repeat this process as often as you like, since the job takes less than an hour, and it can be done whenever you want.

Technically, this is probably the easiest performance upgrade you can make to your MINI. ECU remaps typically cost around $400. Since you do the change yourself, there isn't any installation cost.

A similar ECU remapping system designed for your MINI Cooper has been developed by the Evotech company. Used in the same way as the Shark Injector is used on the Cooper S, it is plugged into your Cooper ECM and reprograms it to correct the air-fuel mixture and timing to provide optimum performance at all engine speeds and loads. The price is about $400. The Evotech system has been shown to provide better performance when starting off, improve mid-range throttle response, and increase peak horsepower.

Performance Spark Plugs

To take full advantage of the enhanced performance that can be gained by upgrading the air intake system and remapping the engine control unit computer, you'll also probably want to upgrade your spark plugs. An expanded and more consistent spark flame from good performance plugs will provide more sustained and consistent fuel ignition within the cylinders. This in turn will give you smoother engine operation and more consistent power across the engine revolution range.

One spark plug that we can recommend from our own experience is the NGK Iridium IX, which features a 0.6mm iridium center electrode. The high-tech material improves combustion within the cylinders without sacrificing durability. The tapered ground electrode increases the expansion of the flame center as the spark plug fires, and the superior heat range afforded

Performance spark plugs, such as these NGK Iridium IX plugs, are an inexpensive way to improve engine combustion, and increase horsepower.

by the plug design is well-suited to high-performance driving. These spark plugs retail for about $8, adding less than $32 to the cost of your upgrades. That's a small but sensible investment in engine performance on both the Cooper and Cooper S.

Exhaust Improvements

Of course, the air and fuel going into the engine, and the spark that ignites it, are only the beginning and middle of the process. Horsepower and torque are also affected by how easy it is to get the exhaust gas that is left over after the gas/mixture burns out of the engine. After the piston has been pushed down by the expansion of burning fuel in the cylinder, as it comes back up it pushes the gases from the combustion out the exhaust valve and into the exhaust system. If the gases can't get out as easily as the fuel/air mixture comes in, that puts pressure on the piston, making the engine work harder.

As a result, performance improvements also can be made by improving the exhaust system. In the MINI, the exhaust system consists of "headers"—those pipes into which

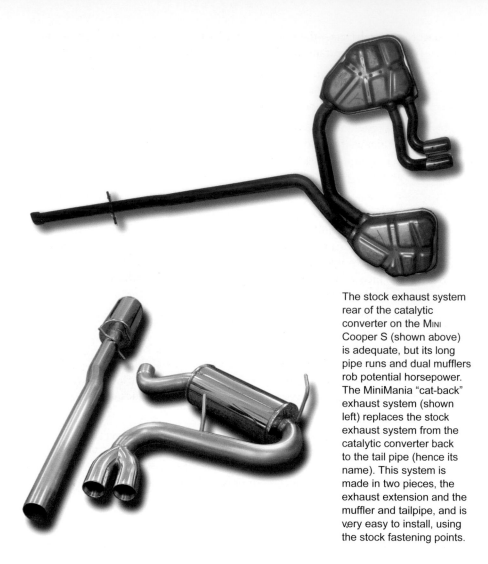

The stock exhaust system rear of the catalytic converter on the MINI Cooper S (shown above) is adequate, but its long pipe runs and dual mufflers rob potential horsepower. The MiniMania "cat-back" exhaust system (shown left) replaces the stock exhaust system from the catalytic converter back to the tail pipe (hence its name). This system is made in two pieces, the exhaust extension and the muffler and tailpipe, and is very easy to install, using the stock fastening points.

the exhaust gas flows after it comes out of the "head"—the top part of the engine. From the header pipes, the exhaust gas flows into a catalytic converter (sometimes called a "cat"), which is the essential element of the modern emission control system that captures contaminants rather than letting them flow out of the tail pipe.

The exhaust gas flowing out of the cat is piped through the muffler to reduce noise, and from there out the tail pipes. The muffler, and the pipes into it and out of it to the tailpipe are often referred to as the "cat-back" part of the exhaust system.

If we can make the exhaust gas flow more easily, we will increase the power that the engine can produce. This can be done by replacing the factory-designed system— which was engineered to a budget and designed to reduce exhaust noise as much as possible—with a more efficient cat-back exhaust system.

A variety of different types of cat-back systems are available for the MINI. The differences among them are cost, installation convenience, performance, and—very important to many drivers—the exhaust tone. Exhaust systems, like the curry in your favorite Indian restaurant, can be ordered in mild, medium, or aggressive form.

Three different systems are good examples of these differences. The least expensive we've found, at about $700, is a two-piece system designed by MiniMania with a single muffler and large-diameter tailpipe outlet.

Though this system uses factory-mounted installation points, it uses a different design than the original, incorporating two sequential mufflers, making it easy to install and weighing approximately 20 pounds less. The system produces increased performance, and has a nice medium-aggressive sound.

Borla, the well-known exhaust company, makes two different cat-back exhaust upgrades for the MINI. Both have a different and slightly more complex design that incorporates two separate mufflers exiting through twin tail-pipe tips at the rear, similar to the original system. The basic system offers good performance improvement, while maintaining a factory-like tone, while the "Sport" catback offers slightly better performance and incorporates different mufflers to produce a much more aggressive tone. Both are priced at about $800.

You MINI Cooper owners can also increase the power on your cars by installing a more efficient cat-back exhaust system. On these kits, a larger primary pipe and low restriction muffler will boost power, and get the bonuses of a little more aggressive exhaust note. At least one attractive system also sports a credibility-building four-inch exhaust tip peeking out under the rear valance. A "silent tip" is included that is easy to install and remove for quiet operation on long trips. These cat-back exhaust kits for the Cooper are available for about $700.

These cat-back exhaust systems aren't difficult to install for anyone with a good set of wrenches and a little garage experience. However, if you don't fancy putting your MINI up on jack stands and crawling under it to make the changes, a good muffler shop can make the substitution in about an hour or two of shop time.

The Total Engine Upgrade Package

Those are the four upgrades—improving air intake, increasing supercharger boost, remapping the ECU-controlled fuel mixture and ignition timing, and installing a more efficient cat-back exhaust— that will take the performance of your MINI engine from very nice to wow, while still being street-legal. If you don't want to go the whole improvement route all at once, you could install these four upgrades in any order you prefer, and with each upgrade you'll notice performance improvements that will make your street driving and touring more fun and exciting.

Street and Touring Engine Upgrades (Approximate costs including installation)	
Cold Air Intake System	$250
Supercharger Pulley and belt	$250
ECM Remap	$400
Iridium Spark Plugs	$ 32
Cat-Back Exhaust	$850-$1000
Total Cost	$1800-$1950

However, since the components all work together, it would be nice to do them all at once. The total cost of the parts and installation should come to around $2000. The total system, based on performance tests, will significantly improve mid-range driving pleasure and should increase peak performance to comfortably over 210 horsepower.

Improving the Handling

Having fun with a car isn't just a matter of how quickly it accelerates or how fast it will go in a straight line. Really enjoying the driving is also a matter of how easily the car can be driven around corners and how stable it is at speed. We've been very impressed with those aspects of the MINI since it was first introduced. We certainly wouldn't argue if you decide to wait until you've gotten some miles on the car and maybe had a chance to really push the car around a race track or autocross course before making any suspension changes.

However, if you're looking at the car now and thinking you'd like to make some changes in its appearance to give it a more custom look, or if you'd like to make a few improvements in its handling right now, we suggest the first thing you consider is replacing those tires and wheels that came with it.

When we were giving suggestions on buying the car, we recommended that you not spend the money on bigger wheels or fancy tires, so if you did take our advice and took delivery of your Cooper S with the standard 16-inch wheels, and didn't opt for the sport package, you've got at least $800 in your piggy bank to buy new tires and wheels.

Changing the wheels and tires also is a fast way to give the Cooper a more sporting appearance while improving its handling. Going to 17-inch wheel from the original 15-inchers will make a major change in the look of the car, immediately giving it that "performance" style.

If you're ready to do it now, look at the wheel and tire suppliers, like Tire Rack or the MINI-specific suppliers and pick some sharp 17-inch wheels. Just remember that you want light wheels, so check those specifications. Look for a wheel that weighs 22 pounds or less, to get the greatest improvements in handling.

The same weight consideration applies to the tires. Those run-flats that came with the car may make you feel a little safer since you won't have to worry about changing a flat tire on the interstate, but they just weigh too much for good performance, and they aren't as responsive as regular radial tires. They also give a rougher ride than regular tires, even the low-profile high-performance tires that you're likely to buy.

Most owners upgrading their wheels are likely to prefer 17-inch wheels, mounted with low-profile tires, because the larger wheels offer more stability, ride more smoothly, and will put more rubber on the road. The larger wheels also are more likely to have the space to fit larger high-performance brakes should you decide to do that later. The low-profile tires also give less squirm in the corners, one of the factors that contributes to that "razor-sharp" handling the car magazines often go on about.

The specific brand of tires is largely a matter of personal preference. Kumho, Yokohama, Bridgestone and other manufacturers all make tires with good performance reputations. Talk to other MINI owners about theirs and we're sure you'll get some good suggestions. MiniMania mounts their wheels with Kumho Ecstas, a good all-around choice for street, autocross, and track use.

As an example of cost, a good set of wheels and tires for your Mini can be purchased for less than $1500. Of course, if you want to get into fancier wheels, the sky's the limit, though much past $1500 you'll be paying for looks more than performance.

As far as the risk of flat tires is concerned, modern tires actually have very few flats under any circumstances, so you don't really have to worry about not having run-flat tires. Nevertheless, several accessory suppliers make a "mobility kit" with an aerosole that will fill the hole in the flat tire and an air compressor that will plug into your car's power outlet to inflate the tire. It certainly is a good idea to have one of those kits in the back. But we'll bet that you'll be much more likely to use the inflator to fill up your beach ball or air mattress, or pump up your tires for autocrossing, than ever fill up a flat tire.

Other Upgrades for Your Mini

There are a number of other upgrades that might be appropriate right now to improve your Mini's performance on the street. Some of these for you to consider include the following.

• Improved brake pads. Better brake pads, such as Greenstuff pads, will reduce brake dust, decrease brake pad heat, and provide more brake bite, while still being completely suitable for street use. Replacing the brake pads is a very simple job and well within the scope of any hobbyist mechanic. If you're going to have an opportunity to take your Mini out on a real track, or expect to do any enthusiastic backroad touring very soon, we strongly recommend doing this upgrade sooner rather than later.

• Short shifter kit. Reduces shift lever movement required to change gears, which improves shifting performance and provides more satisfying shift action.

• Spark enhancement systems. Various products, such as Nology spark plug wires and the Plasma Booster, can improve spark to provide more efficient combustion, increasing horsepower and smoothing out acceleration.

• High-performance street clutch. Provides quicker and more positive clutch take-up, using steel-backed organic clutch disc, high-clamp pressure plate, and modified throw-out bearing. Reduces transition time when shifting gears, increasing acceleration.

We'll review these additional enhancements in more detail in the next chapter when we discuss upgrades that are appropriate for drivers who occasionally use their cars on the autocross course or on the race track at club track days.

Right now, we'll suggest that you wait until you've had the chance to take a driving course and have had the experience of driving on a closed course, before you think about changing brakes, shifter, or clutch. You may be quite happy with the car's performance

Greenstuff brake pads, costing $170 for front and rear sets, are a good upgrade for any Mini owner who plans to go touring on backroads or in the mountains, as well as the owner who expects to participate in an occasional track day or autocross event. They provide better heat performance and produce less dust that has to be cleaned off the wheels. Installation is easy for any driveway mechanic to do with standard tools.

right now, and decide that you don't need all the thrills that high speed and competition can provide.

However, if you find that you enjoy the time you spend on the track, want to hone your skills further, and are already finding that your clutch, brakes, and shifting aren't quite what you want, then you can seriously consider these additional upgrades.

Chapter Seven

Advanced Street Driving Skills

Now that we've spent some time explaining where engine performance comes from, and how to get more out of your MINI Cooper S or Cooper, we need to inject a note of reality. No matter how much potential speed and performance an owner builds into a car, fast is as fast does. At the end of the race, it is going to be the better driver who wins, nine times out of ten.

Any experienced auto racing competitor will tell you that some of the best money you can spend on your car is the money you spend on improving your own driving skills. We can tell you that, without a little training and some practice, no one is capable of driving the MINI anywhere near its limits, even with the equipment it comes with right out of the showroom.

There is a growing number of courses available at tracks around the country where you can receive instruction in advanced street and track driving skills. Some of these courses are taught in cars owned by the school, but in many of them, you can drive your own car so you can apply the lessons you're learning in your own MINI. Courses and references are listed in Appendix A.

But you don't need to wait for the next driving course to start learning how to improve your driving. We'll be happy to pass on some basic information and tips that your instructor also will cover in the first part of these courses. You can begin practicing the tips immediately, so you'll be that much further ahead when you first get behind the wheel in an advanced driving course. We guarantee that you'll be processing so much new information at that point that you'll be glad you did a little homework and practice before you got there.

An advanced driving school, held on a closed course such as a race track, is an ideal place to upgrade and practice your driving skills in a safe environment.

But before we can tell you how to drive, we'll have to introduce some basic terms and principles. Bear with us here; in no time you'll be sounding, and more important, driving, like a pro.

Making the Car Do What You Want

To get your MINI to do what you want it to do on the road, as well as on the track or autocross course, there are two basic principles that you need to keep in mind. Every driving skill is ultimately based on a combination of two things: managing the weight balance of the car and managing to keep the tires stuck to the road.

It's All a Matter of Balance

Good driving is not just a matter of pointing the car where you want it to go and pressing the gas pedal until you get there. If you want to drive well, you must begin by thinking about the weight of the car. This wouldn't be so difficult if your wheels were connected directly to the chassis like they were in your old red wagon. But they're not; instead, the chassis is connected to the wheels with springs and shock absorbers.

This is fortunate, because if you remember that old red wagon, you'll remember what you felt like when it hit a bump. Pretty shook up, as you might recall.

> **Weight Transfer**
> The shifting of the vehicle's weight on its springs, from front to rear with acceleration and braking, and from side to side when turning corners.

Springs and shocks allow you to drive your MINI over pretty bumpy roads with relative comfort and control. The springs absorb the bumps and the shock absorbers keep the chassis from oscillating up and down after the spring takes care of the bump. The combination helps keep the wheels on the pavement, where they can do some good.

However, with springs and shocks, the car will rock when it moves. Accelerate and the car rocks towards the back end. Put on your brakes and the car rocks towards the front end. Turn hard to the right and the car leans to the left, with the right side lifting up. Vice-versa when you turn to the left. The technical term for this is weight transfer.

You might think of the car as suspended on a pin at its very center, able to rock forward and back and side to side. It will even rock from corner to diagonally oppposite corner if your speed is changing at the same time that you are turning a corner or changing lanes.

Really good street driving, and good motorsport driving as well, depend on how well you manage the transfer of weight in your car from back to front and side to side. The reason why weight transfer is important is because when you take the weight off a wheel, it loses traction. Likewise, if you put more weight on a wheel it doesn't move as easily.

In the extreme, take too much weight off a wheel and the car can skid out of control. So, most of what you'll learn in your advanced driving course has to do with managing the factor of weight transfer, so that you can go, stop, and turn corners as fast as possible without losing control of the car.

Where the Rubber Meets the Road

You can spend all your time and budget working on making the engine more powerful and the brakes grippier, but in the end it all comes down to that point at which, as they say, the rubber meets the road.

Tire adhesion, which is affected by balance and weight transfer, is the second factor that will soon come into play as your driving becomes more spirited. When you think about it, it's amazing how much you rely on four tiny patchs of rubber that are in contact with the pavement when you drive. Under most circumstances, fortunately, you don't have to think about it. Most of the time, you'll only be aware of tire adhesion is when you start to push the limits of the tires and you hear the tires squeal.

If you look at your tires on the pavement, you'll see that their contact is only as wide as the tires (maybe seven inches or so) and only as long as the part of the tread that's actually squished down (maybe 3 inches or so). Your car and the pavement are connected over a surface area of about 80 square inches, if you're lucky. That's less square area than can be covered by a handkerchief.

Now think about what those little patches of rubber are being asked to do. When you unleash all those horses and transfer that power to make the wheels turn, they push back against the pavement to make the car go forward. When you hit the brakes, the brakes cause the wheel to slow to a speed slower than the car is going, and those little patches of rubber push forward against the pavement to bring the car to a stop.

Or at least they do unless you put more power to the wheels than the co-efficent of friction between the rubber and pavement can handle, or the wheels lock up before the car is brought to a stop and overwhelm that co-efficient of friction. Either way, the tires spin or skid any time you exceed their adhesion capability.

The same factor applies when you turn. In a turn, to make the car change direction, the rubber of the tire has to push sideways against the pavement in the opposite direction. Turn the steering wheel too much for the speed the car is going and the tire is going to slide sideways, rather than pulling the car around the corner.

Now let's complicate the picture even more. What happens when you try to do two things at once: turning and accelerating, or turning and braking? The problem is that if you've already used up nearly all your adhesion trying to do one thing, such as accelerating, and then you try to do another thing that relies on that adhesion, like braking, it isn't going to do either thing very well. That's the point at which the wheels will lose their grip and the car will begin something called "understeering" or "oversteering."

Start now to think about how the car feels as it accelerates, brakes, and goes around corners. See if you can feel it rocking back as you accelerate, forward when you brake, and from side to side as you turn corners. If your tires start to squeal, try to feel what the car is doing when that happens. It's sort of a Zen thing. You want to try to become one with your car.

When the Car Doesn't Go Where It's Pointed

When we first started driving, it seemed as if the car was always lurching forward or rearing back, and there were those really scary times when the car wouldn't even go where we pointed it. Even though we didn't know it at the time, this was our first experience with the phenomena known as oversteer and understeer.

Push the gas pedal too hard too quickly and the car will rear back, taking weight off the front wheels. Since those are the wheels that provide the car's steering, the front end of the car will become unstable and not respond as readily to movements of the steering wheel. This can be disconcerting, to say the least.

If you throw the car into a turn too quickly, it will rock towards the outside of the curve, taking weight off the opposite side of the car, upsetting your steering. If you're accelerating at the same time, then the car will be leaning back. Put the two motions together, and you have less weight on the steering wheels and less weight on the side towards the turn, meaning that one front wheel will be exerting almost no pressure on the pavement.

As you might guess, it is going to be difficult for the car to make the turn. Instead, it will continue to plow forward. We call that phenomenon "understeer." When a car understeers, instead of turning as you intended for it to do, it continues to go straight down the road. At the extreme, you'll find that you can't get the car to go around the corner. Instead, you wind up plowing off the outside of the road.

Consider the opposite phenomenon. Push the brake pedal too hard too quickly, and the car will rock forward. This takes the weight off the rear wheels and moves it onto the front wheels. If the car is in the middle of a turn, with the back wheels lifting up and losing their grip on the pavement, the car will begin to pivot on the front wheels. This also is not a good thing.

If you're going too quickly when you start to turn and then realize you're in trouble, you might instinctively try to slow down by letting off the throttle and pushing the brake pedal. What happens? The car, which is already leaning out because of the turn, then also starts leaning forward. At that point the weight of the car shifts off the inner rear wheel, which is helping the car stay stable around the corner.

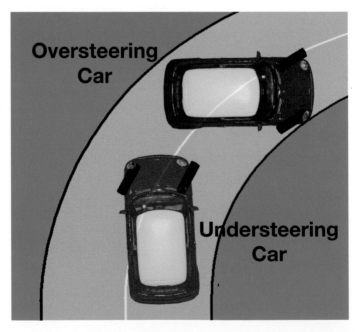

In this figure, the red car is understeering; the driver turned the wheels to go around the corner, but the car didn't turn and instead continued to slide forward across the road.
The blue car is oversteering. As the driver turned the corner, he or she did something abrupt to take traction off the rear wheels, and the rear end slid around towards the opposite side of the road.

Oversteering Car

Understeering Car

With limited traction on one of the rear wheels, the rear end of the car can start to slide out towards the outside of the turn. This phenomenon is called "oversteer." When a car oversteers to an extreme, it will also slide off the road, but this time it will be the rear end that slides off first. Of course, it is possible for an excellent, experienced driver to control the oversteer by turning the front wheels the opposite direction of the skid. This has even been turned into an emerging motorsport, called drifting.

Experienced drivers simpify this oversteer-understeer thing. If the car won't turn as readily as they want it to, they say, that's understeer. On the other hand, if the car turns when they don't want it to, that's oversteer. In racing slang, a car that is understeering is said to "push." A car that consistently oversteers is said to be "loose."

To avoid all of these problems that result in the car doing what you don't want it to, the recipe is to be as smooth as possible when you use the throttle and the brakes. Instead of jamming your foot to the floor to go faster, squeeze the throttle down. Instead of slamming your foot on the brake pedal when you want to stop, roll on to the pedal, feeling it bite as you press it down. Either way, your passengers shouldn't be able to tell when you take your foot off one pedal and push down on the other.

Likewise, when you're turning into a corner, don't change direction any faster than the car can absorb the change. Feel the shift in weight balance as you turn the wheel into the corner, rather than jerking the wheel over and having the car overreact.

Front Wheel Drive

A distinctive feature of the new MINI, as with the classic Minis that inspired it, is that the engine drives the front wheels. For the purpose of making a car that is small and maneuverable while having lots of interior room, that is a good thing. For the purposes of getting the car around the track or autocross course quickly, or being good on the highway, well…let's just say it is different.

So why is front wheel drive so different? With front wheel drive, the car has to be steered and powered by the same wheels. This means that if you're going fast in a straight line, using the traction of the front tires to pull you along, they aren't going to be as effective in making the car change directions, and the car tends to understeer.

Likewise, if you're turning the wheels and using their traction to hold the car in the corner, they are not going to be able to absorb very much forward push. In addition, since a car tends to lean back as it accelerates, it is more difficult in a front-wheel drive car to really put the power to the pavement. As a result, the front wheel drive car needs to be going straight before it can really accelerate out of a corner, and even then will not be able to accelerate as fast as a rear-wheel car with the same torque.

The second part of the difference is that as you accelerate, you're taking weight off the front wheels, making them less effective at steering the car. Likewise, when you put on the brakes the weight shifts to the front of the car, making it understeer even more.

So, what can you do to make the MINI more competitive on autocross courses and race tracks where steering responsiveness matters?

The answer is, first, that you do everything you can to make sure that the car has as much horsepower as available and that it will handle as well as it possibly can. There are modifications to both the engine and suspension that can make that happen.

The second thing you can do is to learn to drive the MINI better, taking into account its quirks, and its advantages.

For example, if you're coming into a corner too fast and the car is understeering—pushing rather than turning—you can briefly ease off on the gas. This allow the weight to transfer to the front end, giving the front wheels more turning traction, and releasing pressure on the rear wheels. The weight change will restore steering control, then all you have to do is accelerate around the corner. Performance drivers call this "steering with the throttle."

Following the same principles of physics, if you find the rear end starting to get loose, especially as you come out of the corner, you don't want to let off on the gas, or worse, hit the brakes. If you do, the car will pitch forward even more, and the rear end will come around with a vengeance. At that point, you may find yourself facing backwards as you slide off the track. Instead, what you want to do is use that power on the front wheels to pull you through the curve. Keep the throttle even, maybe even accelerating a little bit, as you drive your way out of the skid.

This ability to put the power to the front wheels on corners was what made classic Minis so much fun to watch on the track in the sixties. The experienced Mini driver would power deep into the corner, gaining the lead on the rear-drive cars which had to brake sooner.

Then the Mini driver would turn the wheel and briefly release the throttle, or even tap the brakes, to break the rear end loose. As the car rotated and was aimed in the proper direction, the driver would get hard on the power and scoot off down the road, leaving the drivers in rear-drive cars wondering where he had gone.

Rally drivers found the Mini's ability to rotate its rear end and then power out of corners particularly valuable. On a rally route, the surprise of a tight corner might cause a traditionally powered car to slide off the road with the power wheels unable to get traction. Mini drivers, like Paddy Hopkirk for example, would simply let off the throttle and give the handbrake a brief yank to release the rear end and bring it around the corner, then get on the power to drive the car out of the corner. Today, this cornering technique is a standard feature of rally driving; in those days it was revolutionary.

However, right now you'll probably be happiest if your car simply goes around the corner with you in control, without understeering or oversteering. So let's talk about turning corners.

The Best Way Around the Corner

Using the concepts of balance and weight transfer, we can talk about how to take corners in the safest and fastest manner. Sure, you turn corners all the time; you've been doing it since you started driving. But you might be surprised to learn that there is a right way to turn corners, and a variety of wrong ways.

In order to get the car around the corner fast and safely, you want to be as smooth as possible, keeping the car balanced at all times. You don't want to be making abrupt changes in speed, abruptly hitting the gas pedal or brake, while the car is turning. Not only does this upset your passengers, it upsets the car, and that can be much more serious.

Turning corners properly is the most fundamental of driving skills as you start to explore the world of fast track and autocross driving. Everything else in performance driving is built on proper cornering, since most races are won or lost in the turns. How fast a car can go on the straights is pretty much just a function of the car's power; how fast it goes through the turns depends as much on the driver's skill as it does on the capabilities of the car.

To turn the corner smoothly, quickly and safely, you should think about the turn as having three segments: braking, turning, and accelerating.

Before You Get to the Corner

As you prepare to practice the skill of turning corners properly, you should start by running down the driving position check list we discussed earlier. Are you seated comfortably in a reasonably upright position with your back firmly against the back of the seat? Is your seat and steering wheel adjusted so that you can push in the clutch comfortably and hold the steering wheel with your elbows slightly bent?

Are your hands positioned on either side of the wheel just below the sides of the rim, with your right hand somewhere between three and four o'clock and your left hand between eight and nine o'clock? Are the rear-view mirrors set so that you can see directly behind the car and into the blind spot on each side? If so, you're ready to go.

First Segment: Braking to Slow Down

The first segment of the turn is slowing down. First, check your mirrors to make sure there is no one right behind you who could run into you as you slow down and as you turn. On the road, you should also signal for the turn, of course.

While the car is still going straight, you should reduce your speed to the level that your eyes, seat, and brains tell you is slow enough to get around the corner safely without sliding off the outside. You should make sure that you do all of your braking

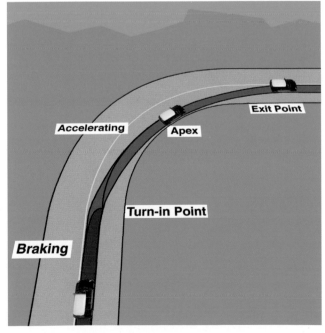

Turning a corner can be divided into three parts: **braking, turn-in, and accelerating**. All braking (indicated in red) is done while the car is going in a straight line. Braking ends and turning and acceleration (indicated in dark green) start at the **"turn-in point."** The steering wheel is turned as far as necessary at the **"apex"** and begins to unwind, and the car is going straight at the **"exit point."**

while the car is pointed in a straight line and before you start to turn. Remember to look as far around the corner as possible. This will feed in the information that your brain needs to tell you when to start braking and when you're going slow enough to complete the turn safely.

Experienced drivers will tell you that the fastest way to get around any corner is "slow in, fast out." Your car should be going at its slowest speed at the point when you begin turning the wheel.

Second Segment: Turn-in and Transition

In the second segment, you will turn the wheel to take the car around the corner to make the turn, move your foot from the brake pedal to the gas pedal and begin to drive the car around the corner. The point at which you begin to turn into the corner is what racers call the "turn-in point." (We realize the terminology is pretty obvious, but it does make sense.)

How can you tell where you should start your turn? Here you'll depend on your eyes, which should have been looking around the corner. Basically, you don't want to make your turn until you have a clear line of sight around the corner. You should be able to see where the path of your car will come closest to the inside of the turn, and where you will finish the turn.

Racers call these two points the "apex" and the "exit" or "track-out" points of the turn. To make the turn as easy as possible, you'll want to start your turn as near to the outside edge of the road as you can, then drive across the lane or road to the inside edge of the turn, and finally back out to the outside edge. Following that line through the corner will make the turn as open and straight as possible, allowing you to turn both more quickly and more safely than if you had to turn more sharply.

Once you are able to see most of the path of your turn you should begin to turn the wheel. (By the way, when we get into how to turn corners quickly on the track or autocross course, you'll discover that this path is the fastest one you can follow.)

You should keep a little pressure on the brake as you begin to turn in, to make sure that the nose of the car stays down, keeping pressure on the steering wheels. But just as soon as you've turned the steering wheel as far as necessary to make the turn and the car is pointed around the corner, it's time to get off the brakes completely and get on the throttle.

The way you make the change from braking to acceleration is important in order to keep the car balanced. On the one hand, you don't want to take your foot off the brake abruptly and immediately slam down the gas pedal. If you had a racing instructor sitting in the passenger seat, they would tell you to "roll off the brake and roll on to the throttle."

On the other hand, there should be no hesitation from the time your foot comes off the brake until you start pushing on the throttle. This is no time to be coasting; as soon as you've finished slowing down and started to make the turn, you should have your foot on the gas to keep the car under control.

Once your foot is on the throttle, you'll want to give the car enough gas to keep the car balanced from front to rear until you finish the turn-in and begin to unwind the steering wheel. How long this period lasts depends on the radius of the corner. In a simple 90-degree turn, this transition period is very short; on a long sweeping corner on the other hand, you may be "balancing the car on the throttle," as racers say, for a long time before you reach the next stage of the turn.

Third Segment: Acceleration and Exit

The third segment of the turn is acceleration. At soon as you have turned as far as you need to and the car is pointed around the corner, you should start to smoothly accelerate. Here you can really take advantage of the front-wheel drive on your MINI. Since your power comes from the front wheels, you can start to accelerate much sooner than is possible in cars with rear wheel drive.

That driver in the rear-wheel drive car has to be very cautious about how much they accelerate at this stage of the turn, since their car's weight isn't back on the rear wheels yet. If they get on the throttle too soon, they can easily break the rear end loose into a skid. In fact, in the middle of the turn they might even still be on the brakes, practicing a technique called "trail braking" which you don't have to even think about.

As you accelerate, you'll pass the apex of the corner when you can begin to allow the steering wheel to unwind as the car moves out to the exit point of the corner. By the time the steering wheel has rotated back and the car is completely straight, you should have the accelerator pedal as far down as circumstances permit. When you get the opportunity to do this on a race track, you'll be able to really put your foot in it, but when practicing this on public streets and highways, you'll of course be limited by the speed limits.

Practicing the Fundamentals

Try to remember this sequence every time you come to a corner, whenever you're driving. Start braking before you get to the corner and before you begin to turn. As soon as you can see your path around the corner, turn the steering wheel and roll off the brakes and on to the throttle.

Keep the car smooth and balanced by lightly using the throttle until the car is aimed towards the exit point. Then get hard on the throttle and let those front wheels pull you through the corner as the steering wheel unwinds.

Practice this sequence every time you turn a corner until it becomes second nature. On the street or highway, your turns will be faster and smoother, but more importantly, you'll be more in control of your car and better able to cope with the unexpected than the person who just blunders around the corners any old way. Mastering these fundamentals in everyday driving also will allow you to begin working on advanced driving skills on the track or autocross course much sooner.

Smoothness and Focus

When you have an opportunity to ride with a very good driver, you're bound to be impressed with how smoothly they drive, especially in the transitions from acceleration to braking, and into and out of turns. We didn't say these transitions were done slowly; we said they should be done smoothly. You never want to do anything abruptly if you can help it but you won't want to be coasting either.

To develop that smoothness yourself, as you drive, pretend that there is a cup sitting on the dashboard, filled to the brim with water. Try to make your transitions and the consequent weight transfers as smooth as possible so that not a drop splashes out of your imaginary cup as you accelerate, brake, and turn.

At the very least, your passengers will enjoy the ride much more if they're not being thrown around, and we guarantee your smoothness will make you a better driver, staying safer on the streets and becoming faster on the track.

One more tip: The position of your head also matters in how well you drive your MINI around the corners. That may seem silly, but in fact most driving instructors can tell a lot about how well a student is driving just by looking at the direction of their head. This all comes back to the point made in the last chapter. To drive well, you must look and think way ahead of where you are.

When you're driving into, through, and out of a corner, you should be looking as far ahead as you can see. It's a proven principle that the car will go where you are looking. If you're looking straight down the racing stripes on your hood, you are unconsciously going to be steering in that direction as well.

So as you come up to the corner, look around the corner as far as you can see. When you start to exit the corner, instead of looking straight ahead at the curbing ahead of you, you should be looking as far past the exit and down the road as you can see. This focus ahead gives your arms and hands the information they need to steer your car around the corner efficiently.

Focusing ahead also insures that should an obstacle appear by surprise as you round the corner, you'll have as much time as possible to react to it. Keep your head up and your vision focused far ahead and your speed into and out of the corner will be improved, not to mention your safety.

What about Crisis Situations?

All of this smoothness we emphasized earlier is a good thing when you're in control of your car and there are no surprises. But what happens when something goes wrong on the road up ahead and you have no choice but to respond in a hurry? Good question. Our discussion of weight transfer will help explain what to do in different types of crisis situations.

Crisis Braking and ABS

Let's talk first about the modern braking system that is standard equipment on your MINI and nearly every other new car on the road. Your MINI is equipped with an anti-lock braking system (ABS). This system is designed to allow you to hit the brakes hard in a situation where you absolutely, positively, must stop as quickly as possible, but without the problems of the old days where the brakes locked up and the car started to skid.

The system is pretty easy to explain, though the mechanics behind it would be impossible without modern electronics. Say you come around a corner and a child chasing a ball suddenly darts out into the street. You jump on the brakes as hard as you can. As you would expect, one or more of the wheels reaches the point where the contact between the brake pads and the brakes is stronger than the contact between the tire and the road and the wheel stops spinning and starts to skid.

In the old days, your instructor would have told you that you should immediately release and re-apply the brakes, (a method called "threshold braking") so that the skidding tire could start to turn and go back to its job of helping the car slow down. However, with the new ABS system, the car can do the job better than you do.

As the wheel starts to skid, sensors in the wheels notice that one wheel has stopped while the other wheels are still turning. The sensor passes this information to the brake system computer, which causes it to go into anti-lock mode. At that point, the computer causes the brake cylinders to start to pulse, alternately pushing and releasing the brakes. This pulsing allows the skidding tire to start to spin, doing exactly what you would do, but much more quickly. With the pulsing brakes, the car can come to a straightline stop very effectively, much better than you could manage.

Why are we telling you this right now? We're going to bet that, unless you've already had this situation happen to you, you've never actually experienced the operation of an ABS system. If you haven't, we'll also bet that the first time that brake pedal starts pulsing on its own, you're going to panic and let of the brake pedal, so that the system stops working.

We recommend that you try out your ABS system as soon as possible. Find a large parking lot that is empty at some point during the week, or a backcountry road with no traffic. When you're sure no one is around, hit the brakes hard. You don't need to be going very fast to get the full effect. Take the car up to about 25 mph and stomp on the brake pedal, then hold your foot down.

Don't panic when the brake pedal starts kicking back against your foot. What you're feeling is the pulsing of the brake system, pushing and releasing the brakes for you. While you keep your foot on the brakes, the car will come to a stop. It won't feel pretty, but it will work better than you could manage on your own; we'll guarantee that.

The key thing is that, in a crisis stop (we won't call it a panic stop, because as a very good driver you won't panic, now that you know what to do) you get your foot on the brakes hard and keep it there until the car comes to a stop.

Crisis Braking and Turning

But what happens if the obstacle is right in front of you, or you're coming around a corner when you have to make the stop? A very good feature of the ABS system is that it will bring you to a smooth stop, while allowing you to continue to turn.

When we mentioned the problem of turning and braking above, we noted that the weight transfer off the steering wheels could cause the car to plow, or skid. However, when the ABS system activates, by pulsing the brakes it helps restore the ability of the wheels to steer the car out of trouble.

That is, the system will do that as long as you can manage to remember to keep your foot firmly on the brake and at the same time keep looking at where you want the car to go, not where it's going. If you look at where you want to go, your hands will automatically turn the wheel to steer the car in that direction.

The first time or two you try this trick, you'll probably have trouble with it. It is tough to remember to keep your eyes up and looking at where you want the car to go, turning the wheel to follow your eyes, while at the same time the ABS system is pounding back on your foot through the brake pedal. Try to find an opportunity to practice this a few times in that vacant parking lot or deserted road to see what it's like.

As you practice it, and if you have to actually do it in a crisis situation, just keep telling yourself: "*Stomp, stay, steer.*" Stomp on the brake pedal, stay on the brake pedal, and steer around the problem. Easier said than done, but with a little practice you should be prepared for problems down the road.

Steering Around Problems

Slamming on your brakes may not always be the best solution to a crisis situation. In particular, a variety of different events can occur on the highway that require a different response. Many times you don't want to brake, with or without turning; instead you're better off steering around the problem.

The most typical situation is one where the car in front of you suddenly changes lanes to avoid that old tire casing or deep pothole that you didn't see until the car ahead moved out of the way. Or as you're driving along, something gets loose from the truck ahead and falls into your lane. Either way, at highway speed you aren't going to have enough distance to stop before running into the junk.

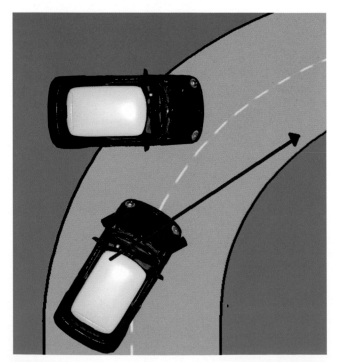

To make your car go where you want in a crisis turn, you have to look at where you want the car to go. The car will follow your eyes. With the ABS system, you will be able to steer around the problem—in this illustration a car ahead that has skidded partially off the road in your lane—provided you stay on the brakes and look where you want to go in order to make the car go in that direction.

Instead, your best response is to rapidly change lanes. You may not even have time to slow down. Nevertheless, even at highway speeds, a MINI (and most other modern cars, as a matter of fact) are stable enough to make a quick lane change without seriously losing equilibrium.

All you need to do is check quickly on both sides of you to pick the lane into which you're going to turn, then give the wheel a definite and strong turn in that direction and then back again to straighten yourself out in the new lane. Incidentally, always being sure that you have space on one side of you or the other so you can execute this maneuver, is an important defensive driving technique.

Keeping some escape space on at least one side of you is also the reason why you want to avoid getting stuck in the middle of a clump of cars when highway driving. By simply backing off a little, you can usually disengage yourself from these pods of accidents waiting to happen and get yourself a nice safe little empty bubble in which to drive.

This technique of accident-avoidance will require a little practice before you will be confident of your ability to pull it off, which is why nearly all advanced driving skills courses teach it, using multiple lanes and stop lights to allow you the chance to improve your reaction time, practice your high speed lane-change skills, and gain confidence in yourself and your MINI.

Chapter 8

Taking It to the Track

Many of the street-driving schools conducted at regular race tracks often include in their curriculum the opportunity to drive some "hot laps" on the track. Also, in most regions of the country, clubs and organizations sponsor track days where you can get out on the track in your MINI. These track events are great opportunities to safely practice and improve your driving skills, even if you never ever plan to race your MINI.

At these track sessions, you'll be put in the novice group, so you don't need to worry about having your doors blown off by some hot-shoe in a track racer. But you will have the opportunity not only to work on your basic car control skills, but also to drive a little faster—maybe even over highway speed limits here and there—and work on some advanced driving skills. Here are some tips on the skills you can work on.

Torque, Power and Gearing

As you watch the races on *Speed Channel*, or in person at a road-racing track, you'll notice the wonderful change in the engines' song as the drivers slow down for corners and then accelerate out. What you're hearing, of course, is the driver downshifting the car before the corner, and then upshifting as the car gathers speed out of the corner. What's this all about?

What the driver is doing is always keeping the car's engine at the point where it can deliver the most acceleration. In an automobile, that relationship is measured not by horsepower, but rather by "torque."

In technical terms, torque is the twisting power exerted by the engine crankshaft as it rotates. In simple terms, torque is the power to get the car to go faster. It's that push you feel in the small of your back as you get on the throttle and start to accelerate.

Car designers point out that while owners argue about which car has the most horsepower (which measures the car's ability to maintain a given speed), the measure that matters more in

> **Torque**
> Turning or twisting effort, measured (in the U.S.) in pound-feet (lb-ft) or in Newton-meters (in Europe). In relation to automobile performance, it is the measure of the ability of the engine to increase the car's forward speed and so is an important measure of track performance.

competition is the torque of the engine, since it is the torque that gets the car to start off from a stop and go faster when needed, such as when passing.

If you've ever looked at the plots of engine torque shown in the car tests in the automobile magazines, you've noticed that as the engine speed ("rpm" in gearspeak short-hand, which stands for revolutions per minute) rises, the torque increases, but only up to a point. At some point, as the engine speed continues to increase, the torque levels off, and then begins to decline.

For example, in stock condition, the MINI Cooper S produces about 135 pound-feet of torque at 2500 rpm. Torque rises rapidly with engine speed, reaching about 150 pound-feet at 3500 rpm, then more slowly until it peaks at 155 pound-feet at 4500 rpm. At that point, as rpm continues to increase, torque declines gradually to 120 pound feet at 7000 rpm.

What this means in practical terms, is that when driving your MINI, you want to have the engine running between 3500 and 4500 rpm at those times when you need greatest responsiveness and pick-up, such as when passing another car on the highway or pulling away after executing a pass on the track.

If you don't upshift as you accelerate down the straight, or fail to downshift when entering a tight corner, you'll find yourself on one side or the other of peak torque just when you need the additional pick-up. That's why shifting gears is important. For best acceleration, you want to keep the engine revs in the range where the engine is generating the greatest torque.

As the car accelerates, good drivers don't want to push the engine past its physical limits, so as they accelerate they shift up to a higher gear. That way the engine is producing as much power as necessary, but at the lowest possible engine speed.

Shifting Gears

Like so many other things we've been doing since we started driving, there is a right way and a wrong way to shift gears to keep your engine at peak power. Assuming you have a manual transmission, let's start with your gear shift and the correct way to change gears. While you're sitting in the car, push in the clutch and then move the gear shift through the gears.

The first thing you'll notice is that the gearshift seems to be pushing against your hand as you move the lever through the gears. This is because the gearshift is spring-loaded—it has two springs pushing it towards the center "gate" of the gearbox. This is done to make it easier for you to make a clean shift and know where you are, provided you do it properly.

Properly means that you shouldn't grip the lever as if it were a baseball or bat. Instead, all you need to do is cup your hand around the lever and nudge it in the proper direction. You use the heel and outside of your palm to push it up into first, and use the palm and base of the fingers to pull it down into second while pulling it towards you against the spring.

To move it up into third take advantage of the spring by simply nudging the shift straight up; the spring will push it out of the one-two channel and into the three-four channel. You can use the inside of your fingers to pull it straight down into fourth without exerting any sideways motion.

When you're ready to shift from fourth into fifth, you use the heel of your hand and base of your thumb to nudge the lever up while pushing over against the spring. From fifth to sixth, you use the inside of your first finger to push the lever away from you against the spring, and the crook of your fingers to pull it down.

Incidentally, most of the shifting can be done with a simple finger and wrist motion. If your arm is moving from the elbow or shoulder, you're using way too much force. And remember, you're just nudging the lever into place; you shouldn't be slamming it in. All that's necessary is that the movement from gear to gear be crisp and definite.

Slamming won't get the job done any quicker. Your shift needn't be slow, but excessive speed is just going to cause you to miss shifts. Under nearly all circumstances, you never want to slam the shifter into the next gear. All this does is cause unnecessary wear on the springs and gears without appreciably speeding up the gear change.

Here's another tip about that gear shift. Casually resting your hand on the gearshift while driving or sitting at the stop light is a definite no-no. It may look cool, but that constant pressure will wear against the springs and gears and eventually cause gearbox problems. Unless you are actually making a shift, your hand belongs on the steering wheel, anyhow.

Heel and Toe Downshifting

In normal driving, very few people downshift, since the MINI engine can pull pretty strongly from very low rpm and there are few times when the additional torque is really necessary. But if you want to practice for the day you start doing hot laps at the race track, you can start working on how to downshift, since you want to have as much power available as possible as you accelerate out of the corner. To do your downshifting as smoothly as possible, you'll be using using the technique called "heel-and-toe" shifting.

Of course, if you remember the original cornering sequence we just discussed, we didn't discuss shifting gears. Downshifting does add one additional step to the sequence. However, the downshifting should be completed during the early part of the braking process, while the car is still going in a straight line. By the time you start to make the turn, you want all your shifting done, so you can have both hands on the wheel through the corner.

In heel-and-toe downshifting, what you are going to do is make it easier for the engine to cope with the changes in gears by giving the throttle a little blip while you're downshifting. That way, before the shift is completed, the engine is already spinning close to the higher rpm required in the lower gear. Done properly, this little blip of the throttle will make your driving much smoother, and eventually much faster.

If you're one of those drivers who believe in the myth of downshifting in order to slow down—using the compression in the engine to slow the wheels—you should change that belief right now. Brakes are much cheaper to replace than engines, so use your brakes to slow down, rather than using your engine. You should be downshifting as you brake, and only for the purpose of matching engine rpm to car speed when you're ready to ac-celerate again.

Heel-and-toe downshifting is done by pushing in the brake pedal with the toe of the right foot, then pushing in the clutch with the left foot while rotating the right foot and using the right heel to blip the throttle pedal just before releasing the clutch.

The one exception is in highway driving on long descents down steep hills. There it can be a good idea to downshift to a lower gear and use the engine compression to slow you down. That way you keep the brakes from overheating in case you need them before you get to the bottom of the hill. However, that is a different matter than spirited backroad or track driving where using the engine compression to slow the car down entering corners is simply a bad idea.

What makes the process of downshifting on the track a little complicated is that you are going to start downshifting at the same time that you are braking to get ready for the corner. At the same time that you're putting on the brake with your right foot, you're going to want to tap the gas pedal with your right foot. "But wait a minute," you say. "I only have one right foot."

Right you are. So what you will do is to push the brake in with the toe of your right foot, and by twisting your foot slightly, give the throttle a nudge with your right heel. If it's more comfortable for you, you can push the brake with your heel and the throttle with your toe. That's why the technique is called heel-and-toe. (Though to be honest, some people use one side of the foot on the brake and the other side of the foot on the gas. Whatever works for you.)

So here's the sequence: As you get ready to turn a slow-speed corner that is going to require a lower gear for a fast exit on the power, you will start to brake with your right foot and at the same time push in the clutch with your left. With the clutch in, you'll slide the gear shift into the next lower gear and about the same time blip the throttle. With the engine still revving up from the throttle blip, you'll let out the clutch. Brake, push clutch, shift/blip, release clutch.

Right now this may seem a little like patting your head while rubbing your stomach, but a little practice will make it all work. Incidentally, if anyone asks, you are not "double-clutching." Double-clutching is actually a more complicated process that requires releasing the clutch slightly at the point that the throttle is blipped in order to get the gears spinning faster, then pushing it back in to shift the gear, before releasing the clutch. Thankfully, with modern engines and gear boxes, the technique is no longer required, except on some really, really old vintage cars.

The Cornering Line

In preparation for your first driving class, and as something else to begin practicing, let's talk about the safest and most efficient way to get around the corner. The choice of turn-in, apex, and exit points, and the pathway between them is what racers refer to as the "line" around the corner.

The optimal line around an individual corner is the one that allows you to wait as long as possible before braking, while still having enough time to bring the car down to a speed that will allow you to take the car around the corner without spinning out or sliding off the track. More important, the optimal line is the one that allows you to be going as rapidly as possible at the point when you exit the corner.

It's an old saying around race tracks that all racing is simply a succession of drag races from corner to corner. Picking the correct line around the corner is not necessarily a matter of just getting around each corner as fast as possible. Instead, it is a matter of setting the car up so that you can be the first to start the drag race to the next corner.

Where you exit, and how fast you exit, depends entirely on where you start to make the turn. Selecting the turn-in point is critical to getting the corner right. After that, everything else is just follow-through.

The first step in taking a corner is to move as wide as possible to the "outside" of the corner (the side opposite to the direction you're turning). On the street or highway, this will usually be the center line or curb. (Of course, on deserted roads with no obstructions, where you can see all the way around the corner and up the road a good distance you might be able to go wider.) Once you're on the track, you'll be moving clear to the edge of the track before beginning your turn.

You'll drive at the edge, while completing your heavy braking (and your downshifting, if the corner requires it), until you can see around the corner. At that point, you'll begin to turn in—which, as we noted earlier, is called the turn-in point— and start to release your brakes.

The path from this point around the corner isn't necessarily the shortest path, but generally it will be the most efficient line around the corner in terms of exit speed. It is also the safest, since you will be able to see any obstructions in your path.

You will want to aim for the inside edge of the corner—remember, earlier we called that the "apex" of the corner—while looking for the point where you will be completing your turn and will once again be at the outside edge of your lane, or the road, at the "exit point" or "track-out point." Remember that you're looking at where you want the car to go, not just where it is aimed at the moment.

You've probably noticed that at most tracks the edge of the track at the apex and exit points will have a little extra curbing, painted in contrasting, usually red and white paint. These strips are often called "rumble strips" because they're generally raised and rough. They are there so that if a driver gets too enthusiastic about cutting the apex tight, or "tracks out" too far, and goes over the edge of the track, there won't be a problem. The car and driver will just get a little shaken up. You'll often see professional

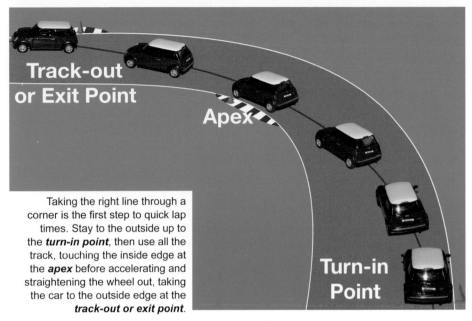

Track-out or Exit Point

Apex

Turn-in Point

Taking the right line through a corner is the first step to quick lap times. Stay to the outside up to the *turn-in point*, then use all the track, touching the inside edge at the *apex* before accelerating and straightening the wheel out, taking the car to the outside edge at the *track-out or exit point*.

drivers hit these strips on every corner, using up all the track, and then some. For now, just skim the edge; it isn't be considered good form for a novice driver to deliberately hit them and you could lose control of the car if you did.

As you reach the apex of the corner you should be off the brakes completely and already starting to ease onto the throttle. As soon as you begin straightening the wheel, you'll roll onto the throttle and start to accelerate.

You can see from the diagram that the arc of your curve is tightest just past the turn-in point, and widest as you come out of the turn. This will allow you to get on the throttle as hard as conditions permit as early as possible and start that drag race to the next turn-in point.

The optimal line through a single corner is going to start and end at the far outside limits of the available track or lane. As you progress in racing, you'll often be reminded to "use all the track." What the instructor means is that if you didn't start and end the curve at the far outside, while nearly touching the inside limit—curb, berm, or edge of the pavement—at the apex point, you will have made too tight a turn and sacrificed some of that precious speed you need.

Also notice that on this line, the apex—the point at which you touch the inside limit—is just a little way around the corner, rather than being at the actual geometric point of the corner. That "late apex" is usually the best line, since you have a good sight-line down the road when you start your turn, and that same long straight line along which to accelerate as you complete the turn.

You might think about what happens if you get a little tense and try to "hurry" the corner. You'll start to turn in sooner than the person who's following the line we've just described, but at best you won't be able to get on the throttle until later in the turn than the other driver. At worst, you will find yourself, as racers say, "running out of road" before you've completed your turn, and risk running off the track.

Now all of that is a lot to practice all at once, which is why we recommend that you start now, rather than waiting until you get into the driving course. Incidentally, during the driving course, the instructor will most likely mark off the course with pylons or markers to show you the turn-in point, the apex, and the exit, which will make it a little easier. But daily driving is like rally driving; no one has put pylons out to show you the correct line, so get used to finding it on every corner on your own.

The entrance and exit ramps on limited-access highways make especially good practice areas, since you aren't likely to encounter anyone going the other way, and the range of speed within legal speed limits is as wide as you'll encounter on most corners of most race tracks.

The best place to practice is on a corner you take every day. That way you can start at a fairly slow speed, and gradually speed up to the legal limit on that road as you get used to the corner, changing the point where you start and end your braking, turn in for the corner, apex it, and come out at the exit point.

If you find that you are having difficulty getting around the corner, having to put on your brakes or pull the wheel over hard to make the turn, it means either that you're going in too fast, or you're turning too early. If that's the case, trying slowing down a little, which will allow you to turn more tightly at the beginning, and turn in later, which will give you more room to finish the corner at the end.

As racing drivers learn new tracks, this is exactly what they are doing; they are finding the optimal points and speeds to start and end each phase of each corner, then memorizing those points so they can repeat them lap after lap during an actual race.

When taking the corners, keep thinking about weight transfer as you brake, turn, and accelerate, feeling the car's weight shift from back to front and corner to corner through the process. Downhill skiers and horseback riders often find that this process is very familiar, it's just that there is a lot more of you to think about as the car increases and extends your mass.

As you round every corner on your way to work or wherever, make your braking, turning, and accelerating as smooth as possible and try to pick a good line around each one of those corners. If you do your practice diligently every chance you get, pretty soon you'll start to feel at one with the car, anticipating the weight transfers and feeling yourself going with them, with no abrupt transitions and with as much speed as the situation allows. In short, you'll really be motoring.

Motoring On

Whether or not you decide to make changes to your MINI right away, or decide to wait, don't wait to start working on your driving. Use a good driving position, practice smoothness in your starts, stops and turns, and try to find a good line around every corner. And take the next possible opportunity to take an advanced driving course so you can learn and practice the skills that will allow you to drive your MINI in the way it was intended.

After your driving school experience and with a few miles under your tires, you may find that you want to get even more out of your MINI. In the next part of this book we'll discuss improvements that will prove their worth on the road track or autocross course, and we'll present some advanced driving skills that will help you take advantage of those improvements.

Part Three

Serious MINIs for Track, Autocross and Touring

By now, we hope you have gotten a few weeks or months experience with your MINI. We also hope you have taken the opportunity to participate in a basic one-day driving school where you got more comfortable with the car's handling and performance, and learned some safe-driving techniques. If not, we hope you've at least used that anti-lock braking system, tried a few quick lane changes, and squealed the tires a little on a back road or empty parking lot.

Perhaps you've also upgraded the basic engine performance and bought those aftermarket wheels and tires that give the car a distinctive appearance and improve its handling. But there is still more to be done and more to experience.

In this third part of the book we'll discuss several ways that you can get a little more excitement out of your motoring experience. We'll offer some ideas for further performance upgrades to suit the driving you're starting to do. Finally, we'll give you some tips on high-performance driving to take advantage of the capabilities of your MINI.

Chapter Nine

What Can We Do Next?

By now perhaps you've discovered in your everyday driving just how much fun your MINI can provide, especially when you can let it out a little bit, and experienced its stimulating performance and handling capabilities. But if you really want to have some fun with that great MINI, we encourage you to try some of the various kinds of organized events that are available to you. You can head out on the highway for club tours, participate in organized track days, or try your mettle against the clock in autocross events.

Backroads Touring

In every part of the country, there are interesting roads that allow you to get off the interstate and enjoy the sights and sounds of nature and geography. When you do that, you begin to experience the automobile not just as a way to get from one place to another, but also as a source of enjoyment in itself. And you discover how much fun driving can be, even within the prescribed speed limits of public roads.

Club tours are one of the fun and relaxing things you can do with your friends and your MINIs. Tours can be simple low-key affairs with a picnic ground for a destination, or challenging rallies with route instructions, timing and scoring. Whether the event is intense or low-key, just getting out with a group of other MINIs will be fun.

You can explore other eras by visiting historical sights; you can expand your senses by getting closer to scenic wonders; or you might just pack a picnic lunch and find a place off the beaten path where you can relax for a few hours away from the noise and confusion of the city. Or if you'd rather, you can spend a day or two becoming one with the spirited handling and performance of your car on some curving backroads through hills and valleys, with no other purpose in mind but to enjoy the drive.

While you can do any of these on your own, simply by getting out your map and guidebook and doing some internet exploring to find places to visit and stay, the trips will be much more fun if there is a Mini in front of you, and another in your rearview mirror. In other words, take a tour with a local Mini club or some Mini friends.

In some parts of the country, competitive time-speed-distance rallies are still sponsored by local sports car clubs. These TSD rallies have a competitive element that often appeals to car enthusiasts, but under controlled legal circumstances. Essentially, a TSD rally measures your ability to drive a route that has been laid out by the "rallymaster" with your results determined by how close you can match the exact speeds driven by the rallymaster over the route.

Directions are spelled out in a shorthand that is defined in the rally's general instructions—"R at 1st op," for example means turn right at the first opportunity after executing the previous instruction—and exact speeds are specified for each leg of the rally, always at levels that can be achieved without exceeding speed limits. By driving each leg at the specified speed—say, 36 mph—and carefully following the instructions, you try to arrive at each checkpoint at an exact time. Points are deducted for each second you arrive early or late to the checkpoint.

These TSD rallies challenge the ability of the driver and navigator to carefully follow the instructions and maintain the specified speeds, which requires a significant amount of driving discipline. The rewards are the opportunities to drive through interesting countryside, and share experiences with other individuals who are trying to meet the same challenges.

The best way to get involved in activities like these is through a local Mini club, if one already exists in your area. If one doesn't exist, your local dealer may be willing to help you organize one, or at least introduce you to some other new Mini owners with whom you can do some driving events.

If there aren't yet enough Minis in your area to have your own single-marque club, you might instead see if there is a local British car club or more general sports car club in your region. Regardless, it shouldn't take long to find a group of like-minded enthusiasts who enjoy driving their cars and organize events for just that purpose.

All that is required to enjoy one of these events is a willing interest to participate and a safe, reliable car that is fun to drive. You supply the first and your Mini will happily fill the bill for the second. Nevertheless, the better your car's performance and handling, the more pleasure you're likely to get out of the experience.

Club Track Days

Perhaps leafy byways aren't your cup of tea, or you just want to really feel what it's like to run your car to its rev limits in fourth gear without watching in the rear view mirror for flashing lights on a black-and-white. In that case, you might want to consider taking the car out on an automobile race track near you for a track day.

These events are held at nearly every race track in the country, sponsored by local automobile clubs, commercial groups or, occasionally, local MINI dealerships. Generally held on weekdays or off-weekends, they offer a chance to take your MINI out on a real track for some serious practice.

Track days are somewhere between formal driving schools and actual auto racing events. On the one hand, instruction is available, but optional and you have the opportunity to take things at your own speed. On the other hand, nobody is going to be waving a green flag except to tell you that the track is open, or a checkered flag except to tell you that your session is over.

At these events, competitive racing is discouraged and aggressive driving can even be reason to ask a driver to leave. In fact, passing is generally only allowed on specific portions of the track and then only so that slower drivers won't be hounded by faster drivers on their bumpers. But you do have the opportunity to really wind the car out well beyond public road speed limits, and take it through the corner fast with no fear that anyone is going to be coming the other way.

At most track days, drivers are divided into individual groups by level of skill and experience. For example, one group will consist of drivers who have never been on a track before; one group will be for drivers who have some experience but don't want to drive at very high speeds; and one group for drivers who have significant experience and want to practice racing and car control techniques. During the day, these three groups will alternate, typically with each on the track for 20 minutes of every hour, with the remaining time spent checking their cars or sharing information and experiences in a classroom setting.

At many of these events, very experienced drivers will be available as coaches, especially for the novice group, to ride along and offer advice on how the driver can improve his or her driving technique. Typically, novices will spend the first few sessions learning the safe "line" around the track and will be accompanied by an instructor until they are comfortable with the track, their car, and their driving ability and are ready to solo.

Track days are a great way to have fun with other MINI owners, add a little excitement to your enjoyment of your MINI, and improve your driving skills at the same time. Track days are sponsored by some dealers—this event at Thunderhill Park in northern California was sponsored by MINIs of Mountain View—as well as by regional BMW clubs and independent organizations.

Though these events are certainly fun and exciting, they have a very practical side. Track days are the best possible opportunity for individual drivers to gain more experience with their cars and develop their own driving and car control capability in a safe and legal setting.

There will be a participation fee, since the club or organization has to pay for the use of the track, as well as for the cost of staffing the track with corner workers and having a safety truck with trained safety personnel and ambulance staffed with paramedics on hand, and for the insurance required by the track. Typically these fees range from $150 for a subsidized event up to $500 for a full club day with catered lunch and professional instructors.

The few other requirements, intended primarily for the safety of all participants, are quite simple. Cars must pass a basic technical inspection, focusing on the condition of the tires, the reliability of the suspension, and the capabilities of the car's steering and brakes.

Cars must be equipped with standard seat belts, which must be used, and the participant typically must wear a helmet that meets current auto or motorcycle safety standards. Organizers also require that all loose objects be removed from the car to prevent injury. That's all. Aside from the helmet, the car simply has to be as safe and well-maintained as you would want it to be for highway driving.

Finding these track days isn't too difficult. The race track websites will have schedules of all their events, with links to the organizations that are renting the track for specific events. Local sports car clubs, such as the Lotus, BMW, and Porsche clubs, sponsor track days in many parts of the country and are happy to have other enthusiasts share the costs of the event. And since the first MINI track day was sponsored at Thunderhill Racetrack in northern California by MINI of Mountain View, other MINI dealers are starting to organize their own events around the country.

Casual Autocrossing

Autocrossing has been a popular competitive sports car activity since the earliest days of sports car driving in the United States. Offering a competitive atmosphere and the opportunity to challenge your own driving ability and the car's capabilities, these events provide adrenalin-boosting excitement and the chance to improve your driving skills under very safe conditions.

An autocross is a race against the clock over a course laid out in a large open, paved area, such as a stadium parking lot, or occasionally on an auto racing track. The course is marked out by plastic traffic cones, and typically will include one or two longer straightaways, often ending in abrupt turns, tight and loose curves, and at least one section that requires the driver to weave in and out of a straight line of cones. Because the cones are plastic, if the driver strays off course, no damage will be done to anything except the driver's score and ego.

Typically at an autocross, all participants will have the opportunity to walk through the course before their runs to figure out how best to navigate the turns and curves in the most rapid means possible. Then, running one at a time, each participant will have two or three opportunities to drive the course. Times are generally taken to a tenth or hundredth of a second by automatic timing devices. A typical run will last from 30 seconds to two minutes, depending on the length and complexity of the course that has

Autocrossing is an inexpensive means to have fun with your car, make some new friends, and improve your driving skills. You even get to put numbers on the door.

been laid out. Time will be added to the recorded time for each cone that is displaced during the run.

Even though the courses are quite short, limited by the confines of the size of the parking lot where the course is laid out, and top speeds don't often exceed 40 miles per hour, autocrossing is an excellent way to learn to drive better. Since the basic skills of driving consist of controlling a car while accelerating, braking, and turning, and an autocross consists of nothing except accelerating, braking, and turning, every second on the course helps improve driving skills.

There is a hard-core group of serious competitors participating in these autocross competitions, but the majority of participants simply want to enjoy the fun of revving engines and squealing tires. For these hobbyists the opportunity to learn to drive better, have some fun with other car nuts, and enjoy a pleasant day outside is sufficient reason to participate. Since the organizations that sponsor these events thrive on attendance, every effort is made to make the first-time novice feel welcome, get adapted to the procedures, and learn how to drive their car better in this exciting activity.

The costs of autocross participation generally are quite low, often less than $25 for a full day's events. Safety requirements are similar to track day events, with each car passing a tech inspection before running, focusing on wheels, tires, steering, suspension, and brakes. For most events a safety helmet rated for automobile or motorcycle use is required.

A number of local sports car clubs sponsor autocross events, but the major organizer of these events is the Sports Car Club of America (SCCA). The SCCA is divided into individual regions and districts, so it's likely that there is a local SCCA organization near you that organizes autocross events.

Check the national SCCA website (www.scca.com) to find a local club near you, then look at their web site for information on activities and schedules. Find out when the next autocross is taking place in your area, and drive out to see what it's all about. You'll probably find at least one new Mini, and probably more, already actively involved in SCCA autocrossing, and the owner will be happy to tell you why he or she likes autocrossing and how to get involved yourself.

An autocross school is another way to sample the fun of autocrossing while improving your driving skills. Many of the regional SCCA clubs have organized autocross schools, and at least one commercial group—Evolution Performance Driving School—offers an excellent one-day school in conjunction with local clubs (www.autocross.com/evolution). As with the road-racing courses, we strongly recommend these schools whether you just want to learn a little more driving your MINI, or are thinking about becoming a serious autocrosser.

The nice thing about organized autocrossing is that cars are classed by their level of preparation, so you don't have to worry about competing directly against extensively-modified cars with your totally showroom-level MINI. In fact, SCCA currently offers four classes for street-legal cars, in addition to three classes for race-prepared cars. The "Stock" class is for cars that are equipped exactly as they came from the dealer (with a few exceptions such as allowing any tires and wheels of the same size as original equipment). For owners who wish to upgrade the performance of their MINIs, the "street-touring," "street-prepared," and "street-modified" classes permit nearly all the modifications discussed in the first three sections of this book at increasing levels of modification. You can check the SCCA regulations for exact information, and if you get serious about autocrossing, more experienced participants will be happy to explain the differences among the classes.

If you want to learn more about autocrossing, there is a variety of good information on autocrossing on the web for both novices and experienced drivers. A good place to start is www.autocross.com which includes both excellent information and great links to other websites on related topics. This is a good website for both the novice and the experienced autocrosser.

Just Do It

Regardless of which of these activities you choose, and you might choose to do all of them since many clubs have events in all three categories, you can count on the fact that you'll have fun, and you'll learn more about driving your car safely and fast under a variety of conditions.

Regional MINI gatherings, such as this picnic co-sponsored by one of the aftermarket suppliers and the northern California Mini clubs, are great ways to have a little driving fun, share information and admire one another's upgrades and modifications.

You might also discover that other MINIs are faster than yours and handle better. While much of that can be attributed to the owner's experience, some has to do with modifications that improve the car's performance. We'll discuss those in the next four chapters.

Chapter Ten

Making Your Mini More Responsive

We suggested earlier in the book that you could enhance the performance of your Mini by making a few changes to the engine, including upgrading the air intake, supercharger, engine control module, and exhaust. We think that any Mini on the street can benefit from the added horsepower and more satisfying engine response that these upgrades will supply.

In this chapter, we're assuming that, as you try out the various driving activities available to Mini enthusiasts—touring and rallying, track days, or autocross, you will start to think about making some additional improvements to your Mini. As your driving skills increase, you'll discover some limits to the street-stock car that can easily be addressed with readily available substitute parts and accessories.

Let's consider them in the order that we think makes sense. As you take a more active interest in your driving, and become more conscious of the car's behavior, you'll be ready to appreciate more responsiveness. Responsiveness is found in the feeling when you step on the brakes, shift gears, and accelerate. There are some really great ways you can improve that behavior.

Getting More Bite from Your Brakes

If you haven't already upgraded your brake pads, and have had the chance to spend a day out on the track, we suspect that towards the end of the day you were starting to smell a fragrance that was new to you: the odor of hot brakes. You may also have noticed that you were having to push harder on the brake pedal and your car was taking longer to slow down. And then there was the fine dirty dust that was coating those slick new wheels.

What you were learning was that brake pads intended for street use just don't cut it for a hard day of track use. So if you're thinking seriously about going back out on the track, and are already thinking about how you could go faster on some of the corners, it's time to switch to performance brake pads and to consider upgrading your brake rotors.

Upgraded Brake Pads

Switching brake pads is not an expensive or technically difficult chore. If you're thinking about going faster, then you'll want to be able to stop more quickly, and that means new brake pads.

Disc brakes seem like simple devices. When the brake pedal is pressed, the "brake master cylinder" behind the pedal forces brake fluid through the brake lines to the "brake slave cylinders" on each wheel. The slave cylinders in turn push against the backs of brake pads in the brake calipers on each wheel and these pads push against both sides of the brake discs (discs also are often referred to as "rotors").

Since the brake rotors are connected directly to the wheels, the friction created by the pressure of the pads against the rotors slows down the wheel, causing the car to slow down. The rubbing of the brake pads against the rotors generates heat as a byproduct of the process.

How well the brakes work, especially over a long period when they are being used frequently—such as descending a long hill on curving roads or when speed changes from very fast to very slow take place frequently, such as in racing—depends on two factors. The first is the co-efficient of friction between the material in the disc and the material in the pad. The second is the ability of the pad to maintain that friction as the heat generated by the friction causes the rotor to heat up.

> ### Brake Master Cylinder
> A cylinder connected to a reservoir of hydraulic fluid with a piston through it connected to the brake pedal. Pushing the brake pedal causes the piston to force fluid out of the cylinder and into the brake lines.
>
> ### Brake Slave Cylinder
> Smaller cylinders in the brake mechanisms at each wheel filled with hydraulic fluid that presses against pistons that in turn push the brake pads against the brake discs.

Both of these factors are determined by the material from which the brake pad is made. Brake pads are made of a variety of different materials, including organic, metallic, and ceramic materials, each with its own co-efficient of friction and ability to function effectively at varying temperatures.

On the street, you don't use your brakes very hard or very frequently. As a result, brake pads designed for street use are typically made of materials that are softer and have lower co-efficients of friction so that they will slow the car down gradually and progressively, rather than an abrupt or grabby manner.

However, when you're driving in a spirited manner at a track day or on the autocross course, you don't want to slow down gradually. If you're going to get good lap times on the autocross course, or be able to really drive at higher speeds on the track, you want the car to slow down in as short a distance as possible, something that the standard street pads aren't really designed to do.

Also, if you put the brakes to hard, continuous use—on a long section of curving roads, on an autocross course, or most definitely at a track day—the softer material on the street pads will become less effective in slowing the car down. As heat builds up in the disc from continuous use, the co-efficient of friction between the pad and the rotor decreases. In practical terms, that means you have to exert more and more pressure on the pedal to get the car to slow down, and stopping distances become longer and longer.

The easiest way to correct this is to substitute brake pads that have a higher co-efficient of friction and can stand up to heat for longer period of time. To meet these objectives, there are a wide range of alternative pads that you might buy. You can buy pads that are designed specifically for high-performance racing, and several gradations below that level.

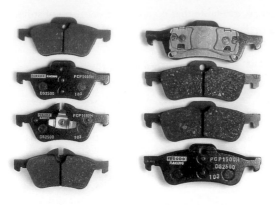

Ferodo DS2500 brake pads are a good example of "dual-use" pads that will provide solid braking performance with stock MINI brakes for a day of track driving or autocross, while improving pedal response and not reducing comfort or safety for daily street driving. Pad sets, as shown here, are available for both front and rear

Here, you don't want to go overboard. A set of pads that would be perfect for a driver at the SCCA national championships is not what you want to put on your car for the occasional track day. That additional bite that will slow a race car down quickly from high speeds would throw your maiden aunt into her seat belts, something she probably wouldn't appreciate.

In addition, racing brake pads that function very effectively at high temperatures don't work well when they are cold. These types of pads are excellent for racing conditions where they can be heated up before being used hard, but are totally unsafe for daily driving where brakes are used more infrequently and are almost never heated to any degree.

The good thing is that pads are available for all levels of use. If you do anticipate the occasional high-spirited outing, but normally use the car for more typical purposes, you can easily find an all-around brake pad that will perform better than the stock pads on the track or autocross course, and give you better responsiveness on the road, but still be safe and comfortable for daily use.

You want one that will give a better "bite" than stock street pads and handle higher temperatures so that it will continue to do its job under extended hard use, but not be a full-on race pad that only works effectively after it has had the chance to heat up. When selecting the pad, look at three factors: co-efficient of friction or "bite," ability to function at high temperatures, and price.

One example of a good choice is the Ferodo high performance brake pads which use their DS2500 compound for street and performance use. They wear less under heavy use, which means more time between pad replacement, have high friction performance at both high and low temperatures, so they are safe for street use as well as having good repeat use characteristics for an enthusiastic day on the track, and provide good pedal feel. A set of these for the MINI will cost around $150 for the front pair and slightly more for the rear pair.

Drilled and Slotted Rotors

Heat that causes deterioration of the brakes is not just a factor of the brake pads; it is also generated by the brake rotors, or brake discs, against which the brake pads rub. Build-up of brake pad residue on the rotors is a second source of deterioration of brake performance during a series of sessions during a track day.

Excellent replacement brake rotors are available that do a much better job of solving all of these problems than the original brake rotors with which the car comes equipped. Good upgrades are available at various prices.

The major advantage of the upgraded rotors is the way in which they are designed. These rotors are drilled through their surface at a number of points across the area where the pads rub against the rotor, and also have slots machined into them that extend diagonally across the disc from the inside to the outside.

Drilling the rotors has a major advantage in giving heat a place to dissipate, thus reducing the amount of heat build-up in spirited driving. Drilling has the secondary advantage of reducing the weight of the rotors, thus reducing the unsprung weight that has to be spun up and moved around when the car is in motion.

The grooves also help dissipate the heat from the rotors by creating a draft effect across the surface of the disc. In addition, they provide a channel through which the dust generated as the brake pads rub against the rotors can be removed from underneath the pads. By keeping the pads clean, the grooves increase the frictional efficiency of the brakes.

The increased efficiency and reduction in heat build-up can make a big difference in maintaining your brake performance throughout an entire track day, and they help make sure that the brakes are as good on your last run of the day as on the first. In addition, they are inexpensive insurance to keep your brakes operating efficiently on the road over a long day of enthusiastic back-roads touring as well as on steep hill descents.

The two metal plates of the front rotors are joined by braces in between the surfaces that create openings along the edge of the rotor. The openings created by the cross-drilling, and the openings on the edges of the rotor work together to help ventilate and cool the brake rotors. In addition, this construction strengthens the rigidity of the rotor, reducing the chance that the rotor will become distorted under heavy use.

A good quality pair of drilled and slotted front rotors is available from catalog suppliers for about $180, and the slightly smaller rotors that fit the rear brakes are available for about $150. Rear rotors differ in design from the front rotors. As with the stock Mini brake rotors, the rear rotors have a single surface, rather than having two surfaces with vents between like the front rotors.

Upgraded rotors have several advantages over stock rotors. Holes drilled through the rotors reduce weight while creating air flow to dissipate heat. Grooves across the rotors constantly sweep the brake pads to prevent brake dust build-up, and the grooves provide a channel through which the dust can escape.

Installation of these upgraded rotors is a bolt-on, bolt-off affair. Drilled brake rotors are permitted in BMW CCA spec class racing.

If you're a little more serious about improving your brake performance, but don't want to replace your entire brake system to get more brake surface area, there is a slightly pricier option. You might wish instead to consider a high-quality pair of cross-drilled brake rotors, such as those manufactured by Brembo Brakes.

These Brembo rotors have an attractive gold anti-corrosion finish that helps eliminate surface rust that can interfere with brake performance. The gold rotors also enhance the look of any road wheels, and give the MINI a more aggressive look. They are available for about $320 for the front brakes and about $220 for the rear brakes. They are quite simple to install in a bolt-off, bolt-on operation and fit all standard MINI wheels.

Getting Faster Response

For most drivers, driving performance is often synonomous with quick response from the car when shifting gears, letting out the clutch, and accelerating. These aspects of the car's behavior are directly affected by the gear shift lever, the clutch, and the flywheel, and all of these components can be upgraded to improve driving satisfaction.

Short Shifter for Shifting Satisfaction

One of the most satisfying aspects of performance driving is to run the car up through the gears with a series of crisp flicks of the shift lever. In the stock MINI, the transmission and gear shift linkage are designed to make this process fairly seamless, but the "throws" — the distance the shift lever has to be moved between gears — are fairly long.

The problem here is that while you are moving the shift lever from one gear position to the next, you have to have the clutch pedal in and the clutch disengaged. That means that the car is simply coasting. And coasting means you're wasting time.

If it was possible to shorten the distance that your hand has to move to shift gears, then the time lost coasting between gears would be reduced. And that means you can get

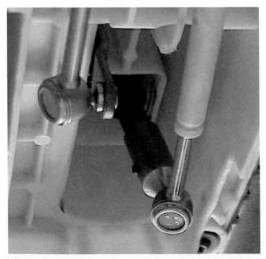

The Ultrik short-shift kit, consisting of an extension for the shift arm and a new dust cover plate for the shift linkage box, is shown below. At right, it is shown installed, looking up into the shift linkage box from under the car.

back on the throttle sooner during each shift of gears. It also means that your "heel and toe" will work more effectively on downshifts, because there will be a shorter period of time between blipping the throttle and actually changing down into the next lower gear.

Reducing the shifter distance is a straightforward improvement, taking advantage of the principles of leverage. All that is required is installation of an extension on the lower end of the shift lever. This changes the leverage between the shift lever and the rod that connects it to the transmission, so that you don't have to move your hand as far to make the gear change. This modified gear lever is often called a "short shifter."

Of course, if you do recall eighth-grade physics, you might remember that there is a trade-off between force and leverage. If you move the fulcrum closer to the side of the lever being pushed down, you do decrease the distance the lever has to be pushed to make the other end move the same distance, but you also increase the force required at that end. Changing to a short-shifter will mean that you have to push a little harder to make gear changes, but you should find that the change is barely noticeable.

One example of a short-shift kit is the The Ultrik Short Shift Kit, which is available for approximately $90. This kit consists of the extension to the shift lever and a modified dust cover plate for the box that encloses the shift lever mechanism under the car.

Working underneath the car, the mechanic removes the original dust cover plate, disconnects the shift rod, adds the extension (designed specifically so its extra length won't weaken the lever), makes some alterations to the shift lever case, and then installs the new dust cover plate. The mechanical work is not complicated, but it does involve raising the car, removing the exhaust system and modifying the case. Most owners will prefer to leave the work to an experienced modification shop.

Performance Clutch Kit

The clutch is that essential little component that uses a friction disk to transfer all that power being generated by the engine to the transmission and driveshaft to make the wheels go round. If the car didn't have a clutch, there would be no way of disconnecting the running engine from the transmission so that you could change gears or, for that matter, stop the car while keeping the engine going. For a quick primer in how a clutch operates, check out www.howstuffworks.com/clutch.htm.

It's surprising to think that all that power is transmitted through a disc pressed up against the flywheel: no chains, no gears, just pressure and friction. Yet, it's the contact between the two plates, the springs that hold the plates together, the friction material on the clutch plate, and the release mechanism that pulls the plates apart that can make all the difference. These parts determine how quickly and smoothly the plates separate to allow a quick gear change, and how quickly and tightly the plates go back together to put the power back to the wheels. And that speed and efficiency makes a big difference in performance and driving sensations when the car is pushed close to its limits on the track, in and out of the cones on an autocross course, or on the curves of a scenic backroad.

Like many other performance parts, clutches represent trade-offs between price and performance, and between speed and comfort. The clutch with which the car is equipped from the factory is a good component, but is built to a budget. More important, it is built with the average (or below-average) driver in mind, so its design

This is one example of a high performance clutch for the MINI. Included in the kit is the pressure plate (left), throw-out bearing (top center), alignment tool (bottom center), and pressure plate (right).

and choice of materials lean towards comfort and longevity, rather than towards performance and speed.

If you're thinking about using your MINI Cooper or Cooper S in a more enthusiastic way than that average driver, you may be willing to pay spend some money to improve the performance of your clutch. Of course, you should also be willing to accept the need to be more quick and precise with your gear changes than that average driver so that you don't start off, or go through gear changes, in neck-snapping fits and starts.

If you are willing to accept the trade-off, a performance clutch kit may be your ticket. But it isn't a simple, "either-or" choice, since there are several levels of upgrade available. One typical catalog, for example, offers a "high-performance street kit," a "casual autocross kit," a "casual drag race kit," a "race kit" and a top-of-the-line "high performance flywheel/clutch system."

Choosing the one that's right for you is largely determined by what you want to do with your car. Aside from the top-of-the-line system, the prices aren't significantly different for various applications. These kits sell in the range of $400 to $600, not including installation.

All of the kits consist of the clutch disc that is pressed against the flywheel when the clutch is engaged, the pressure plate that pushes the clutch against the flywheel, the throwout bearing which pushes the clutch disc away from the flywheel when the clutch pedal is depressed, and the alignment tool needed to install the parts.

It is the type of friction material that makes the difference among the clutches designed for different applications. In the "street kit" level, a steel-backed woven organic material is used, that allows a small amount of slippage before hooking up. This slippage, though less than that of the stock clutch disc, will smooth out the clutch engagement when starting off from a stop. Allowing the clutch to slip slightly can be important in situations such as starting from a stop on a hill.

The higher performance clutches will engage more positively, since the intention is to get off from a stop as quickly as possible, and spend as little time as possible with the flywheel spinning but not connected to the transmission while shifting gears. On these clutches, kevlar, carbon or ceramic materials are used on the clutch disc, which allow for less slippage than stock disc materials as the clutch is engaged.

At the level of performance and activities being discussed in this chapter, where you're using the car as a daily driver, but taking it out occasionally for a track day, autocross, or long-distance tour, you will probably be quite happy with a high-performance street kit. The organic disc material will provide more grip and quicker engagement and disengagement than the stock clutch, but still allows a little slippage.

Lightweight Flywheel

The flywheel is the other side of the clutch pick-up, but it has its own role to play in drivetrain performance. If you're looking for snappier response when you let out the clutch and push in the throttle pedal, you should consider substituting a lightweight flywheel for the same reasons, and at the same time, you consider upgrading your clutch.

The good thing is that upgrading either component will produce immediate and perceptible positive changes in the car's performance, so if your budget is limited or you're doing things one at a time, you can swap out them out one at a time. On the other hand, since the shop has to do all the same disassembly, pretty much, if you can afford to do both at the same time, you'll save money on the installation.

The flywheel on an automobile engine is a large disc at the rear of the engine that has a great deal to do with how smooth the engine runs. It is fastened to the end of the crankshaft, the shaft that is rotated as the pistons go up and down inside the cylinders. The momentum of the flywheel is used to smooth out the operation of the engine between cylinder firings and as engine speed changes.

As the engine builds up speed, part of its energy is used to spin the flywheel, which being large and heavy, requires some time to build up momentum. Once the flywheel is spinning, that momentum keeps it spinning for a short time, even after you let off on the gas and the engine is no longer producing as much power. The flywheel keeps the engine from speeding up or slowing down too abruptly, which in turn smooths out the car's changes in speed, keeping your passengers more comfortable as you shift gears.

Flywheel
A heavy disc connected to the crankshaft at the rear of the engine. Its weight and momentum smooth the power surges imparted to the crankshaft as each cylinder fires and smooth out changes in engine speed. It also provides balance to the crankshaft, works as part of the clutch in a manual transmission car and has a toothed gear that engages the starter.

Crankshaft
The engine's main power shaft, so-named because of the U-shaped cranks that connect to the pistons, and convert reciprocating piston motion to rotary drivershaft motion.

On most brands of automobile, the flywheel consists of a single metal disc with a center hub that clamps to the crankshaft. It also has a toothed gear around the outside edge against which the starter gears engage when you turn the ignition key to the start position.

For smoother performance in engine and clutch operation on the MINI Cooper S, BMW engineers have taken the basic flywheel design one step further. The MCS

Illustrated here is the Ultrik lightweight aluminum flywheel for the MINI Cooper S. It is considerably lighter than the stock flywheel because of the materials with which it is manufactured, and because it is a single-surface piece, rather than the stock "dual-mass" flywheel which was designed to smooth out clutch operation, but at the cost of slower engine response.

flywheel is what is known as a "dual-mass" flywheel. Instead of using just one disc, this flywheel consists of two discs with a spring mechanism in between. The spring mechanism allows the disc fastened to the crankshaft to rotate as much as 70 degrees, almost a quarter of a turn, before the disc that engages the clutch is put into motion.

This design is intended specifically to cause the clutch to disengage and engage more smoothly, making it easier for you to use that manual clutch as if you knew what you were doing. Here again, the designers have balanced comfort against performance, giving up a little performance to get a little comfort, which the average driver and passenger prefer.

Because there is a spring linkage between the two surfaces of the dual-mass flywheel, the noise and vibration is damped between the engine and drivetrain, reducing overall cabin noise, especially when the car is idling in neutral.

However, if you want to push the balance a little towards performance, and are willing to live with a bit more noise, especially when the car is not in gear, you can replace the stock flywheel with a lightweight single-disc flywheel. An aftermarket aluminum flywheel can weigh less than half the weight of the stock flywheel without risking engine longevity.

With that reduction in flywheel weight, you'll get perceptibly quicker acceleration and deceleration. These are two positive benefits if you're trying to get around an autocross course or track as quickly as possible, since best time of day will go the the car that can speed up on the straightaways faster, and slow down into the turns more quickly.

Since it seems as if every drivetrain modification in the typical tuner catalog promises increased horsepower, we want to make sure here that you understand we are not promising that a lightened flywheel will *create* more horsepower. Lightening the flywheel does not increase the amount of horsepower the engine generates, since it doesn't alter the engine operation.

The lightweight flywheel will increase the responsiveness of the car when you get on and off the throttle. Many drivers will mistake this responsiveness for added horsepower. Also, to a small degree it doesn't absorb horsepower as much as the heavier stock dual-mass flywheel, so more of your engine horsepower will be transmitted to the wheels. The lightened flywheel definitely will make driving more fun and can help reduce your lap times.

A lightweight aluminum flywheel will cost approximately $500. Since it is necessary to remove the clutch to replace the flywheel, if you're already substituting a high-performance clutch, it is considerably less expensive in the long run to change the flywheel at the same time.

Improvements in Responsiveness	
Street/Track Brake Pads (front & rear)	$300
Drilled and Slotted Brake Rotors	$330
Short Shifter	$90
Performance Clutch	$400-$600
Lightweight Flywheel	$500
Total	**$1,600 - $1,800**

Planning Your Improvements

In terms of priorities, upgrading your brake pads is well worth doing before your first track day, and they are a good upgrade for street use on any MINI. If you find that you enjoy your track outings, upgrading the brake rotors is a good step and should suffice for brake upgrades until the time when you begin doing regular track outings and begin thinking about upgrading the complete brake system.

The short shifter is a reasonable upgrade, even for cars that will only be driven for tours, and will definitely enhance enjoyment in track days. Upgrading the clutch and flywheel can wait until you have gotten experience driving your car at speed on the track or autocross course and want the added responsiveness that these upgrades will provide.

Chapter Eleven

Better Handling for Road, Track or Autocross

Discussing the MINI's handling in the second part of this book, we were particularly complimentary regarding the MINI's stock suspension, noting that it will reward a good driver and can be well down the priority list of things to work on for improved performance. Now, with some track time or autocross experience under your seatbelts, and lots of cornering practice in daily driving, you may be ready to consider tweaking the suspension a bit for better handling performance.

Once again we're back to trade-offs. For the average driver, with average passengers, the ability of the car to absorb bumps without rattling the dentures of gran'pa in the back seat is at least as important as how fast the car will get around corners.

As a result, when designing the shocks, springs, and suspension on any car, most engineeers are going to go more for a soft ride. The trade-off is that the car will lean more when going around corners.

In corners, as the car leans, that weight transfer is going to take weight off one of the powered wheels, and push the other wheel more firmly against the pavement, causing it to scrub off speed. Push that car too hard and you risk losing control. Either way, you're not going to go around the corner as fast as you would if the car didn't lean so much.

In the interests of improving your potential to get around corners, you may want to think about changing the trade-off, so that the car may not ride as softly going over bumps, but it will lean less going around corners. To do this, you'll want to consider replacing the springs, upgrading the shocks, adding a rear sway bar, and changing the rear control arms.

Each of the suspension modifications discussed here can be installed separately, if your budget is limited, and they can be installed in the order in which they're discussed. If you can swing the expense, you can save money and keep the handling completely balanced, by installing all the components at the same time.

Performance Spring and Shock Upgrades

Two suspension components have the most direct effect on ride quality and handling performance, the springs and the shocks. The length and resilience of the

The Mini can be lowered, spring rates can be stiffened, and handling made more responsive, all at the same time through the installation of an upgraded spring kit plus high-performance front and rear shocks. Springs and shocks are a required modifications for BMW CCA spec racing, and a very sensible upgrade for Minis that will be driven enthusiastically on backroads tours.

springs determines how easily and how far the body will move when the wheels hit a bump or when weight is transferred in acceleration, braking, or cornering. The shock absorbers reduce the amount of rebound on the springs, helping the body return to equilibrium after it bounces.

Let's start with the springs. Because most car owners put more emphasis on ride comfort than on cornering and acceleration performance, most cars are equipped with fairly soft springs that are designed with a good amount of spring travel. The basis Mini Cooper would be considered in this category.

The Mini Cooper S, with its sport suspension (optional on the Mini Cooper) does use heavier (less-resilient) springs that have a bit less up-and-down travel, so the car stays more level in turns and on acceleration and braking. However, the Mini engineers were still assuming you just want good street handling, and aren't going to want to go a little fast in the twisty bits or take the car on a track or autocross course, so they didn't make them too stiff or too hard.

If you do intend to take the car on the track or autocross course, a stiffer spring and lower ride height will be in order. With a stiffer spring, the car won't cushion you as much on the bumps, but on the other hand, it won't sway as much on corners, or shift back and forth as much on acceleration and braking. With a shorter spring, the center of gravity will be a little lower, also reducing the amount of side-to-side or front-to-rear body roll.

Good high-performance spring kits, that are effective in both street and track use, are readily available in the aftermarket. These improved spring kits will help your car maintain its stability when starting, stopping, and turning without wallowing around. These kits won't make your car ride so rough that your passengers will complain, but the kits will definitely increase the predictability of the car in the corners and help reduce your lap times. A typical upgraded spring kit sells for less than $250.

While most of the good performance spring kits will work with the original equipment shocks, to get optimal handling, you'll want to upgrade your shock absorbers at the same time. The shock absorbers work together with your springs so that the car doesn't just bounce up and down and up and down every time it sways or hits a bump.

Actually, the term "shock absorber" isn't quite accurate, since the springs actually absorb the shocks from uneven road surfaces, while the shock absorbers help counter the effect of the springs. The English call them "dampers," which is a more accurate term.

The shock absorbers in the MINI are long tubes that are installed between the wheel and the chassis in parallel with the springs. Inside the outer tube is a piston with a special valve that allows fluid to move from the main tube into the piston as the shock absorber compresses and then move back into the main tube at a slower rate when the shock absorber extends.

The shock absorber works by compressing easily when the spring compresses, but then reducing the rate at which the spring expands. So, instead of continuing to oscillate up and down as it would if only the spring were in between the chassis and wheel, the chassis comes back to a neutral position after only one or two movements.

Like original equipment springs, original equipment shocks are designed to do their job with emphasis on comfort, rather than performance. They damp the spring movement just enough to avoid making passengers seasick, but not enough to give a harder ride. To improve your handling, you'll want even less oscillation so that the car will return to a neutral position more quickly.

By installing performance shocks, you still get some springing action to absorb the bumps and weight changes, but the car will move less and return to neutral more quickly after acceleration or braking, or in between corners. A set of performance shocks designed specifically for the MINI, such as the one by Koni, is a good complement to shorter, stiffer performance springs. One MINI aftermarket catalog offers the Koni shocks for front and rear for a total of about $690, or the combination of performance springs and Koni shocks for a total of $875.

Incidentally, in the BMW CCA Spec-MINI class, stiffer springs and shocks are a required modification to assure that all cars will be competing with the same handling advantage and, with the improved handling, will be safer on the track.

"Coil-over" shocks are an alternative to replacing the springs and shocks separately. With these kits, performance springs are wrapped around the shocks, hence the name. The combined spring and shock is mounted after removing both the stock spring and

Coil-over shocks, such as these made by Spax, combine the functions of the spring and shock absorber into a single integrated component. Because the shocks are adjustable and springs are available in different rates, they can be used to tailor the car's handling to the specific type of event and the indvididual driver's preferences.

stock shock at each corner. Several different manufacturers, including Spax, KW, and Leda make coil-over kits, with prices ranging from $1300 to $1900.

Coil-over kits can certainly be used to improve the handling on street cars. However, they are more likely to be installed by owners who expect to use their MINI frequently on the track or autocross course, since they are available in different spring rates and do offer the means to adjust ride height at each corner.

Different spring rates will be appropriate, depending on the experience of the driver and the frequency with which the car will be used in competition. Springs that are closer to stock firmness will be appropriate for the person who doesn't compete too often, and also wants to use the car for street use. On the other hand, if the MINI is only going to be used for competition and the driver is quite experienced, the preference will be for a much firmer spring.

By adjusting the ride height at each corner, the owner can balance corner weights to compensate for other changes that have been made in the car, since balance is very important in tuning the car's handling for the race track.

Ride Height, Camber and Toe

When you change the ride height of your MINI with shorter springs and stiffer shocks, you will also change the angle of the wheels relative to the pavement and relative to their direction of travel. Since this will alter handling significantly, you should seriously consider making another suspension modification at the same time that you lower the car's ride height, to make sure that handling actually improves, rather than getting worse. Let us explain.

The angles of the wheels to the pavement and to the direction of travel are two important factors in suspension behavior, and consequently, in the way the car will handle. These factors generally are described with the technical terms of "camber" and "toe."

"Camber" is the angle of the wheel when compared with a vertical line, when the car is resting on its springs. If the top of the wheel leans in towards the car when the car is sitting still, we say that the wheel has "negative camber." On the other hand, if the top of the tire leans out when the car is sitting still, that would be "positive camber."

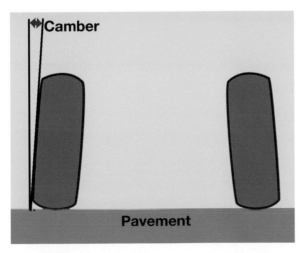

Camber
The inward or outward tilt of a wheel from vertical, measured in degrees. If the wheel tilts in at the top when viewed from the front or back, as shown here, camber is negative. If it tilts out at the top, camber is positive. Most cars have a slight negative camber to assure that the tires stay in full contact with the pavement in turns and when going over bumps.

The other angle is called "toe" and measures the extent to which the front edges of the tires point in, or point out, compared to the rear edges of the tires. If the fronts of the tires are closer together than the rear, the wheels are said to "toe in;" if the rear of the tires are further apart than the front, the tires are said to "toe out."

Camber and toe on both the front and the rear wheels will affect how your MINI handles. However, you can alter the handling by making changes to either the front or the rear wheels since one affects the other. Because the rear suspension of the car is considerably simpler than the front end (no steering or drive shafts to worry about), most tuners start there when making suspension modifications.

The camber angle is important because it will determine how much of the surface of the tire tread is in contact with the pavement when the car is going around corners. Remember we noted that the car will sway when it is turning, which puts more weight on the inside wheel and less weight on the outside wheel, reducing the contact of the outside wheel on the pavement.

Since we want as much of the tire to be in contact with the pavement as possible during the turn, we want the wheels to have a little bit of negative camber. That way, even if the weight over a particular wheel is decreased and the angle of the wheel changes as the car tilts in the corner, the full width of the tread will still be in contact with the pavement throughout the turn.

The extent to which the tires toe in or toe out determines how easy it is to get the car to turn. If the rear tires toe in, this will make the rear end of the car want to go straight, contributing to understeer. If the rear tires toe out, then it will be easier for the rear end to turn, contributing to oversteer.

Why is all this important? It's important because if you change the springs and shocks to lower the car, this will also change the toe and camber of the wheels. With the car squatting down, the rear wheels toe in even more than stock, and lean in more— more negative camber—as well.

If you lower the car without doing anything to compensate for changes in camber and toe, the result is that the car will understeer even more than it was designed to do.

Toe
The difference in the distance between the front of the tires and the rear of the tires, measured in inches. If the tires are closer together at the front than at the rear, as shown here, the wheels are said to be toed-in. If the fronts of the tires are further apart than the rears, the wheels are said to be toed-out.

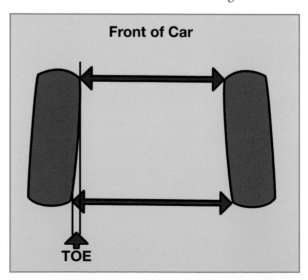

Front of Car

TOE

While the car may look cool, all tucked down around its wheels, it will actually handle worse, wanting to go straight even while you're trying to make it turn. This does not help your times on the autocross course or track.

For this reason, most MINI tuners will recommend that, at the same time that you lower the car and change its spring rates, you adjust the rear toe and camber in order to keep the car's handling neutral and to minimize tire wear.

At this stage in your driving, you really just want to get back to the limited understeer designed into the car. But as you gain more driving experience and can handle a car that is a little twitchy, you may wish to make changes yourself to increase the ease with which your MINI turns-in on corners.

Two methods exist to modify rear camber and toe-in: you can use a rear camber/toe kit to change the effective length of the stock rear control arms, or you can replace the stock control arms with adjustable control arms. The rear camber/toe kit is less expensive than the adjustable control arms, but the adjustable control arms allow you to adjust camber and toe separately, and are easier to adjust to meet the needs of different courses or race tracks.

Rear Camber/Toe Kit

One typical rear camber/toe adjustment kit consists of four adjustable bushings to replace the stock bushings in the rear control arms. The kit also includes an extraction tool to remove the stock bushings, and a spacer to maintain the gap within the control arm while removing and replacing the bushings.

As shown in the illustration, the bolts that attach the control arms are offset within the bushings, which allows variation in the effective length of the control arms. By varying the length of the lower control arm, you can change both the camber and toe.

The one limitation of this inexpensive design is that you change the camber and toe simultaneously. As a result, it isn't possible to make very fine adjustments of these two variables, but nevertheless, the design does compensate for the major problems that would be created by lowering the car without changing camber and toe.

The rear camber and toe-in can be made adjustable by replacing the control arm bushings with adjustable bushings, such as these at left. As shown below, the bolt through the bushing can be moved off-center, which will alter the length of the control arms.

Unless adjustable rear control arms are fitted, the camber/toe kit should be installed on any car that has been lowered through the use of shorter springs, so that the rear suspension can be corrected for the lowered height. They typically sell for around $300 and can be most easily installed when lowering hardware is installed.

Adjustable Rear Control Arm Kit

Adjustable rear control arms also accomplish the same objective of correcting rear toe and camber on lowered cars. Though more expensive than the camber/toe kit, they do offer a greater range of adjustment and are somewhat easier to adjust.

If you peek under the back of your MINI, you'll see four support arms, each about two feet long, two to a side, extending from the center of the chassis out to the rear wheels in sideways Vs. These are the control arms and they are there to make sure that the wheels stay vertical in hard cornering. Their positions also determine the extent to which the rear wheels toe-out or toe-in, and hence contribute to keeping the MINI going in a straight line and also to how easy it is to make the vehicle turn.

However, the stock control arms are not adjustable. The factory set-up can be changed by modifying the control arms mounting points, but the range of adjustment is limited, and adjustment isn't easy to do. To permit a wider range of adjustment in camber and toe, and to make the adjustment easier, aftermarket suppliers make adjustable control arms that replace the stock control arms on the rear suspension.

With these rear control arms installed, it is possible to adjust the camber and toe of the rear wheels after performance springs and shocks are installed. The control arms are adjusted so that the wheels will have a slight amount of toe-in and a slight amount of negative camber, as the car was originally engineered. The toe adjustment compensates for the increased understeer that resulted from lowering the car so that the car will still turn in fairly easily. Correcting the excessive negative camber that resulted from lowering the car assures that as much tire tread as possible is still in contact with the pavement during cornering.

Adjustable rear control arms are available for about $495. They can be installed easily and with little additional expense if they are installed at the same time that high-performance springs and shocks are installed. It doesn't make sense to install the control arms before installing modified springs and shocks, but they can also be installed at any time after the springs and shocks have been installed to allow additional suspension tuning.

Adjustable rear control arms are a slightly more effective way of adjusting camber and toe back to standard specifications after the car has been lowered. They have the advantage of allowing the camber and toe to be adjusted separately. Adjustable rear control arms are required for BMW CCA MINI Spec Racing.

Adjustable rear control arms are another handling modification that is required by the BMW CCA for MINIs racing in their spec class, so if you're thinking about going racing with that club, you might wish to check their rules regarding which make and supplier is accepted.

It is certainly possible for anyone with some jack stands and a wrench set to lower the MINI and install the camber/toe kit or adjustable rear control arms. However, because the adjustments need to be set accurately, tools are needed to measure camber and toe. Consequently, these modifications are best left to a shop that has experience in race-tuning MINIs.

Anti-Sway Bars to Reduce Understeer

In a front-wheel drive car, all of the steering and power comes from the front wheels. The usual result is that the typical front-wheel car has a tendency to understeer. If the car is going too fast, or turned too abruptly when entering a corner, the car will push ahead in a straight line, rather than turning to follow the direction of the front wheels.

Understeer is a good thing for the average driver turning the average corner, since the car is less likely to swerve or skid, should the driver turn the steering wheel too far or too fast. In fact, even most modern rear-wheel cars are engineered to have a little understeer.

However, since we want to get around the corners faster than the average driver, and we're willing to invest some time and practice in learning to drive the car better, reducing that understeer seems like a good idea. Though it seems counterintuitive we can reduce the understeer on the front wheels by altering one component of the rear suspension, the rear "anti-sway bar," also called an "anti-roll bar." (These components are also often referred to, inaccurately considering what they do, as "sway bars" or "roll bars.")

An anti-sway bar works by connecting the wheels on either side of the car to one another and to the chassis. The MINI Cooper S has an anti-sway bar on the rear for just this purpose, to help tune the suspension. The rear anti-sway bar keeps the rear wheels of the car more level as the car goes into corners.

As the inside corner of the chassis begins to move up when the car rolls toward the outside of the turn, the anti-sway bar transmits some of this motion to the outside rear corner. The net result is that the inside rear corner doesn't go up as much, and the outside rear corner goes up more, than they would without the sway bar.

Anti-Sway Bar
A bar extending across the chassis linking both sides of the suspension system. The bar's ends are connected to the wheels by lever arms at the ends and are fastened to the chassis by bushings that allow the bar to twist. When one wheel is pushed up or down, the bar twists, transmitting some of the motion to the opposite wheel, counteracting the initial movement of the wheel and helping the car stay level.

To see the value of this, again think of the car as if it is balanced on a pin at its center. If we can keep the back end flatter on the turns so that the inside rear corner of the chassis doesn't rise, less pressure is put on the outside front wheel and the car doesn't push, or understeer as much. Instead, the rear end of the car comes around more easily. Instead of resisting the turn, the car will follow the line of the turn more easily.

However, the stock anti-sway bar installed on the MINI represents a compromise,

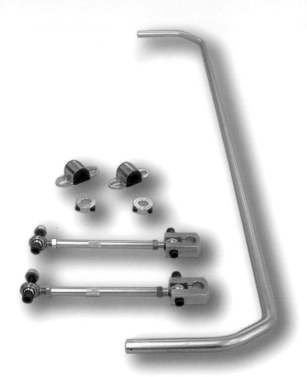

A good rear anti-sway bar for cars that will be used for active driving at track days, as well as for street use, is shown here. In addition to being heavier than the stock bar to help reduce the Mini's understeer, the Ultrik kit shown here has the added advantage of being adjustable. This anti-sway bar is clamped at its ends by the clamps on the connectors, which can be slid in and out on the bar to control the amount of control exerted by the bar. Consequently the suspension can be softened for street use, then tightened up for a track day or autocross competition.

between chassis roll and ride comfort, in favor of ride comfort. It is also fixed in place, so it doesn't allow any choice of response regardless of what you'll be using your Mini for.

To improve on that situation, aftermarket suppliers have developed stiffer rear anti-sway bars. The Ultrik adjustable rear sway bar kit shown on this page is 16mm thick compared to the original bar's 13mm thickness. The thicker bar is capable of transmitting more force from one side of the car to the other, helping the car stay level and balanced on tighter turns.

This upgraded sway bar also has sliding attachment points at each end, so that the range of movement can be changed to alter the responsiveness from softer to harder. With these adjustments, you can leave it on the soft setting for daily use, so that the car sways a little bit more, but doesn't ride quite so roughly. When you're getting the car ready for a track day or an autocross competition, you just release the tension bolts and slide the attachments to the hard setting to increase the car's cornering capability.

The Ultrik dual-use adjustable rear sway bar kit, including the sway bar, connecting arms, bushings, and fasteners is available for about $250. The installation is straightforward, but does require putting the car on jack stands, and then removing the old bar and getting the new bar to slide in around the rear suspension components and wiring harness, so you may wish to have an experienced professional shop do the job for you. It's usually about a one- to two-hour job

Even heavier rear anti-sway bars are available, but this is a case where more is not necessarily better. We suggest you leave the really heavy-duty bars to drivers who expect to plan to spend all or most of their driving time on the track or autocross course, since these heavier bars can make the car a handful to control in normal driving. In any case, it is important suspension modifications be balanced, using springs, shocks, and anti-sway bars that are compatible with one another. If there's any doubt, get the advice of a specialist before making major changes.

Front and Rear Strut Brace Kits

The chassis of the MINI Cooper and Cooper S is well-designed and pretty stiff just as it comes from the factory, which is one of the reasons why your MINI felt satisfying to drive when you first drove it away from the dealer. Several reviewers have remarked that the car felt "as if it had been carved from one block of steel."

However, as you start to drive the car harder, on track days or around the autocross cones, or just like tossing it around backroads corners, you might want to stiffen up the chassis just a bit more. This upgrade is one of the easiest in this book. It is accomplished simply by bolting a "strut brace" across the front of the car in the engine compartment, to connect the tops of the two front strut towers to one another.

This brace is designed to stiffen the front of the car to reduce flex in the suspension. Where the stock MINI feels pretty stiff and strong in corners, the added strut brace makes it feel really solid so that the car turns into the corners more easily without hesitation. Of course, since the brace is visible to anyone looking in the engine compartment and is an attractive accessory, it certainly will impress the spectators and may give you a little psychological edge against the competition.

A stiff, well-constructed strut brace is desirable on a car that is running with low-profile, high-performance tires and especially desirable when installed in conjunction with a lowered suspension. A typical well-engineered strut brace will cost about $325, and can easily be installed by anyone with the right-sized wrenches in less than an afternoon.

Chassis stiffness becomes increasingly important as the MINI is used more often for serious autocrossing, and is an important element in suspension tuning. For this reason, many tuners also prefer to add a rear strut brace to the MINI before making

A front strut brace helps to improve handling by stiffening the front of the car to reduce flex in the suspension. The brace is shown at left by itself and in the center as it looks when installed and connecting the shock towers. At right, the fasteners are shown in detail. Made of titanium, this one not only helps handling, but also improves the appearance of the engine compartment.

The rear strut brace functions in the same way at the rear of the car, providing a stronger connection from side to side to stiffen suspension and improve handling responsiveness. the kit is shown at left, including the strut bar and fasteners, and the fasteners are shown in detail at right.

other changes to the rear suspension of the car. Like the front suspension, this additional component is bolted on to the rear suspension mounts and extends across the car. A good rear strut brace can be purchased for about $200 and is easily installed.

One at a Time or All at Once

In the above discussion of suspension improvements, we've discussed each of the upgrades in terms of what they will contribute to handling. If you're working to a budget, there's no reason why you shouldn't buy the upgrades one at a time, as you can afford them, in the order in which we've discussed them.

However, if possible, we recommend that you install springs, shocks, and adjustable rear control arms or rear camber toe kit, at the same time to keep your handling in balance. It is also less expensive to install all of these modications at the same time.

As you get more experience with the changes in the handling of your MINI you can then move on to installing the rear anti-sway bar and the strut braces, since these will accentuate the handling responsiveness of your MINI and a little more driving practice may be in order before you're ready for the improvements.

Typical Suspension Upgrade Prices

Stiffer, shorter springs	$240
Koni front shocks	$360
Koni rear shocks	$330
Adjustable rear control arms kit	$500
Adjustable rear anti-sway bar kit	$250
Front strut brace	$325
Rear strut brace	$200
Total	**$2205**

(Cost savings of approximately 10 percent are available from many suppliers if all components are purchased at the same time.)

Chapter Twelve

Finding a Few More Horses

With the modifications to the engine that were suggested in Part Two of this book, it is possible to bring the engine's power to comfortably over 200 horsepower. But there's more where that came from.

By getting deeper into the engine, we can add even more horsepower and increase torque in the rpm mid-range, improving the car's performance getting off the line, overtaking other cars, and powering out of the corners. Horsepower-enhancing aftermarket parts that would be appropriate to consider at this stage include spark plug wires or a Plasma Booster to improve spark plug performance, an upgraded throttle body to increase fuel flow to the engine, and a water-to-air intercooler to improve horsepower.

Getting More Bang for Your Buck

Some increases in horsepower can be found by making changes in very small things, such as increasing the power and duration of the spark at the tip of the spark plug. With a better spark, you get more complete fuel burn and the power created by the expansion of the air/fuel mixture will come at a more optimal point in the engine revolutions.

We assume you've already put in performance spark plugs, but there is more you can do in this departtment. Two different devices are recommended to improve spark, one that works by changing the spark plug wires from being simple connectors to actually contributing to spark enhancement, and the other by adding some additional electronics to the ignition circuit.

High-Tech Spark Plug Wires

The intensity of the spark that is delivered to the cylinder by the spark plug determines how efficiently the air/fuel mixture in the cylinder will be ignited. The efficiency of the ignition in turn affects the engine's power output, mileage, and smoothness of operation.

The Nology company has engineering a set of spark plug wires that increase the intensity of the spark produced by the spark plug, to increase ignition efficiency. The Nology spark plug wires each incorporate a capacitor and separate ground connection.

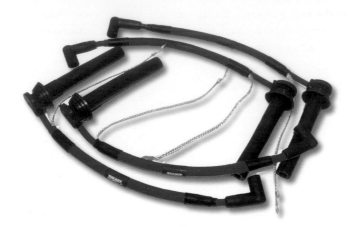

The Nology spark plug wires can be ordered in red, blue, yellow or black for that added eye appeal in the engine. The set sells for $199 and is very easy to install.

With this addition, the spark plug wire itself stores up the energy of the spark until it reaches a high intensity level, then releases it in a shortened burst that provides a quick, clean ignition of the fuel/air mixture.

The manufacturer claims an increase in spark intensity of over 300 percent, which measurably increases horsepower and mileage, and reduces emissions by providing more complete burn of fuel. One nice aspect of using upgraded spark plug wires to increase spark intensity is that spark plug wires are "free"—that is, any brand or type may be used—in the SCCA autocross stock classes.

An added benefit is that the substitution of the high-tech spark plug wires is legal under California Air Resources Board regulations. The wires sell for $199 for the set. Even better, they can be installed without any special tools.

Plasma Booster Ignition Upgrade

A simple "black box" can be added to the ignition system to achieve these benefits. Called a Plasma Booster, it is a power amplifier that increases the power of the primary and secondary spark circuit by nearly 100 percent to deliver a much "hotter" (more powerful) spark to the cylinder. A more powerful spark will ignite the air/fuel mixture more easily, and cause the mixture to burn more quickly. The result is more power from the fuel, more efficient use of fuel, and more consistent power from each individual firing for smoother engine operation.

Individual measurements before and after the addition of the Plasma Booster indicate an additional four horsepower from the engine, and ten percent better fuel economy. The Plasma Booster costs about

The Plasma Booster is an electronic component—a "black box"—that can easily be wired into the ignition wiring to provide a strong increase to the intensity of the ignition spark and thus achieve more effective fuel burn to add horsepower.

$270, and can be added to the engine in just a few minutes without any special tools. As a nice plus, it is certified for use in MINIs by the California Air Resources Board because of its benefits in reduced emissions and better fuel mileage.

Throttle Body Upgrade

When discussing basic engine operations, we noted that the amount of air and fuel that can be provided to the cylinders is a major factor in determining how much power the engine will produce. Changing the cold air intake box and filter increases the potential to provide more air into the engine, but the other side of the equation is how much fuel is added to the air, and how fast the fuel-air mixture can be fed into the cylinders.

As with most modern fuel-injected engines, the MINI uses a component called a throttle body to control the amount of air flowing into the engine. When you push the gas pedal, the electronic throttle connection causes a butterfly valve, sometimes called a "throttle plate" to open in the throttle body, increasing the flow of air into the engine.

Several types of upgraded throttle bodies are available for the MINI that have openings that are larger than the stock 58mm opening, so that more air can flow into the engine across the full range of throttle openings. With increased air flow comes increased horsepower and torque. The increased air flow also gives better throttle response, improving drivability across the rpm range.

The better quality throttle body upgrades incorporate precision machining of the nozzle, which helps increase air flow. By angle machining the throttle plate, the better quality products also prevent air from flowing into the engine when the throttle is closed, providing more precise response when you lift off the throttle.

One high-quality upgraded throttle body sells for about $460 plus a core charge of $250 that is refunded when the original throttle body is shipped back to the supplier. Replacement of the throttle body is a straightforward installation for an experienced mechanical shop.

An upgraded throttle body provides a larger opening and improved butterfly valve (the circular portion at upper right), to increase fuel flow into the engine.

Improving the Intercooler

As we discussed in an earlier chapter, performance of the supercharger on the MINI Cooper S is enhanced by the presence of an intercooler. If the supercharger was used without an intercooler, as the engine heat increased intake air would be heated, as well. And as we know, hot air is thinner than cool air. The result would be that as the engine heated up, it would produce less horsepower than when it had first been started up.

To solve this problem, the intercooler—which looks like a big flat radiator laying on top of the engine—surrounds the air duct between the air intake box and the supercharger. Air coming in through the hood scoop and blowing across this radiator helps cool the incoming air to make the supercharger work more efficiently. This type of design is called an "air-to-air" intercooler.

However, the limited space available within the engine compartment imposes some design constraints that limit the performance of the intercooler. In particular, there is very little space underneath the intercooler, limiting air flow around the intercooler.

To improve on this design, several suppliers have designed their own air-to-air intercoolers that can be substituted for the factory intercooler. These improved designs will improve the intercooler's ability to cool intake air. They don't actually increase horsepower, but they do reduce the loss of horsepower due to heat, so a MINI equipped with one of these devices will give better performance than a MINI equipped with the stock intercooler.

Some other sources have taken one more step, and created a water misting system, which sprays water on the intercooler. These systems take advantage of the same principle of water evaporation that causes you to feel cool when you first come out of the water in the summer. These systems help the intercooler work more efficiently by taking advantage of the water evaporating off the intercooler's radiator.

However, at least one designer, Ultrik, has taken a completely different approach to the problem. Ultrik makes a "water-to-air" intercooler, which has shown significantly better performance, not only when compared to the factory intercooler, but also when compared to aftermarket air-to-air intercoolers.

The new Ultrik water-to-air intercooler uses a radiator and flow of water to cool and help compress the air coming into the engine. Because it doesn't rely on air flowing across the intercooler, it is more efficient than the stock intercooler.

The Ultrik water-to-air intercooler works by using water as the cooling medium from the start, piping water around the intake passage, and then circulating that water through an auxiliary radiator to dissipate the heat from the air intake. In tests as the engine heats up, or is pushed hard in performance driving, this system has been shown to significantly reduce the loss of engine horsepower when compared to the stock system or any of the other aftermarket air-to-air or water-spray intercoolers. This water-to-air intercooler is available for about $1800.

What to Do When

Changing the spark plug wires will provide some additional performance, and since they are permitted in SCCA autocross, they are worth considering for anyone getting involved in the tiered competition programs. No use leaving any horsepower laying on the table. The plasma booster is a good alternative to obtain the same results, especially for a car being used in track day activities without limitations on ignition enhancement.

For anyone serious about upgrading the Mini to its limits, especially for serious track day use, throttle body upgrade and the water-to-air intercooler are worth considering after other horsepower improvements have been exploited.

Engine Performance Improvements	
Plasma Booster or Spark Plug Wires	$250
Throttle Body Upgrade	$460
Water-to-air intercooler	$1800
Total	**$2600**
(prices are for components only, and don't include core or installation charges)	

Chapter Thirteen

Increasing Reliability and Safety

If you are thinking seriously about extensive touring, perhaps on less-than-smooth backroads, or you're going to be doing much track time, sooner or later you will probably find yourself hitting a bump in a road, or taking an unintended off-track excursion. To insure that you don't do any serious damage, you may want to think about protecting mechanical components under the car that are vulnerable to damage from uneven road surfaces. This protection will be even more important if you have lowered the car by installing high-performance springs and shocks. If you're going to be driving the car hard, you'll also want to consider upgrading the cooling hoses.

Inside the car, you'll definitely want to think about protecting the single most valuable component in the car on the race course or road. That's your head, of course. In this chapter we'll give you some tips on buying a good helmet to protect your noggin, and we'll also make some suggestions about seat belts that can help improve your autocross lap times.

Protecting the Soft Underbelly of Your MINI

In the days when Paddy Hopkirk was racing the original Minis on long-distance European road rallies, one of the first modifications that was made by the factory was the addition of a sump guard—sometimes called a skid plate—under the car. The sump guard, as you might expect from its name, was primarily intended to protect the oil sump, the lowest portion of the engine, from being damaged. Such protection was critical, since the original Minis had their transmission under the engine, in the sump, with lubrication coming from the engine oil.

Even though new MINIs don't have their transmissions under the engine, if you were to run over a large rock in the road, or some other obstruction when sliding off the road, it is just as important to protect the underside of the engine, including the oil pan, wiring, and fluid pipes. Stock MINIs do have a plastic sump guard, but those are largely designed to deflect stones thrown up by the wheels, rather than providing heavy-duty protection against large obstructions.

At least one supplier makes a solid steel sump protector that replaces the stock plastic guard. The design is also improved, extending further under the engine than the stock plastic piece. This piece essentially acts like the skid plate on a rally car, protecting the underside of the engine and transmission from damage, if you run over a rock or debris in the road, or a high-center section on a bad backroad.

In particular, the steel sump protector guards the power steering cooling fan which, on pre-2004 cars, is exposed under the car. On these early models, any kind of obstruction that gets into the fan can stop it, which will blow a fuse that protects the fan's circuitry from overheating. However, when the fuse blows, it effectively shuts down the power steering, leaving the driver to wrestle the car back under control with only manual control.

We should note that the 2004 models and later have been modified so that the cooling fan circuit is separate from the power steering circuit, so you won't lose the steering assist should the fan be damaged. In addition, a plastic guard was added to protect the power steering fan, which is certainly better than nothing.

The steel sump protector skid plate sells for approximately $120 and is straightforward to install, though it does require that the car be jacked up or placed on a lift to provide access to the underside of the engine.

Should you decide not to install the sump protector, it is still a good idea to protect the fan on any of these models. To do this, a drilled stainless steel guard has been developed by aftermarket suppliers that can be attached on earlier models to protect the fan, or used to replace the plastic guard on later models. The power steering fan shield sells for less then $50 and is very easy to install.

Making Sure the Engine Stays Cool

Like most standard engines, the MINI engines are equipped from the factory with synthetic rubber radiator and heater hoses. With some attention to make sure they're not wearing out, these hoses are fine in normal use. However, they will deteriorate over time, and wear out faster if the car is driven aggressively. Unfortunately, since the deterioration is caused by chemical reaction between the coolant and the metal in the engine, it occurs from the inside out. As a result, this wear is generally not apparent on visual inspection. You can spot potential failure by squeezing the hoses. If they seem soft, they're prone to failure, which can allow the engine to overheat, with potentially catastrophic effects.

The alternative is to fit the car with silicone hoses, which are easy to install, and look good in the engine compartment. The advantage of silicone hoses is that they are not prone to electrolytic deterioration

Silicone radiator and heater hoses are not subject to electrolytic deterioration as are stock hoses. They're easy to install, and available in several colors, so they can add a nice accent touch to the look of the engine compartment.

like the stock hoses, which is why they're the type that is generally preferred by racing competitors. A set of hoses, which will pretty much last the lifetime of the engine, will cost less than $250.

Protecting the Old Noggin

Under the heading of protecting vital components, you've discovered by now that a safety helmet is required for most track days and autocross competitions. If you're getting tired of grabbing a smelly, old beat-up driving helmet from the pile on the pit wall, or using that motorcycle helmet you borrowed from your neighbor, you might want to think about getting a decent driving helmet of your own.

There are two types of helmets that are generally accepted for casual autocrossing and track days: motorcycle helmets and automobile racing helmets. The major difference is that motorcycle helmets are not made of fireproof materials and consequently are not accepted in most sanctioned auto racing activities.

Within both categories of helmets, there are open-face and full-face helmets. Full-face helmets are designed to provide full protection in open cars, and are somewhat safer for all applications, but are heavier and less comfortable. Open-face helmets are legal for use in closed cars in most sanctioned events, and will be lighter and more comfortable, but don't offer as much protection against facial burns in the event of a car fire.

A general factor to consider when selecting a racing helmet is the material with which the helmet is made. Basic helmet shells are generally made of fiberglass, which is perfectly safe, but is heavier than high-tech composite materials. Generally, the lighter the helmet, the more expensive it will be. If you don't expect to use the helmet often or won't be wearing it for very long at any one time—such as in autocrossing—the cheaper one may be just fine.

Another factor to evaluate in picking out the helmet is the size of the facial opening. This is largely a matter of personal preference, though helmets with smaller openings will be slightly safer. If you always wear glasses with your helmet, or get a little claustrophobic, you may prefer one with a larger opening.

No matter what style of helmet you prefer, you should check the "Snell Rating" that is required by virtually all santioned racing organizations. A Snell-rated helmet is certified for compliance with accepted safety standards by the Snell Institute and carries a cetification sticker on the inside of the helmet under the lining. The sticker will have an S, followed by an A for automobile or M for motorcycle, followed by two digits, indicating the rating year.

The Snell Institute is an independent, non-profit group that tests driving and riding helmets for safety, giving its rating to those that pass. The standards are changed periodically, and it is generally accepted that helmets become less safe as they get older, so the Snell rating number is changed every five years. Most organizations accept a helmet that was certified within the last ten years.

To be sure that you have an acceptable helmet, the last two digits of the number on the sticker inside the helmet should be 00 or 05, indicating the helmet was certified after 2000 or after 2005. Be sure to check this rating if you get an opportunity to buy a second-hand helmet from someone else.

A Snell-approved safety helmet is a requirement in nearly every autocross and track day event. You may not need to wear it while checking your tires, but on the course it will prevent a sore head or worse.

Keep in mind that the protection in a safety helmet comes from compressible foam between the shell and the liner, and that foam can only be compressed once before it looses its protective capability. If you do buy a used helmet, make sure that there is absolutely no indication of any damage. A helmet can look all right, but if it's been dropped, then the inside foam may have been compressed to the point where it will no longer offer adequate protection.

When you're buying your helmet, you want one that is Goldilocks-right: not too tight and not too loose. For this reason, you should consider buying one in person, rather than just ordering through a catalog. The correct size should be very snug and actually a little tight to get on, but you shouldn't feel any uncomfortable pressure points that would give you a headache in a long on-track session. Once the helmet is on, you should try pulling the back up. A correct helmet shouldn't move much, certainly not enough so that your vision is obscured. Similarly, grasp it under the chin (or above your face if it's an open helmet) and pull up. It shouldn't move unless your head moves. To find the correct helmet, you may need to try several brands.

Typical helmets that are perfectly safe can cost as little as $250, or as much as $1000, depending on material and design. Of course, the sky's the limit on costs for those fancy helmets you see the professional drivers wearing on the Speed Channel. But then, they have been custom-molded to fit the individual driver's head, fitted with radio equipment, and given that trick paint job. (And some pro drivers still toss their helmet into the crowd after a significant win!)

When you consider which helmet to buy, keep in mind that the cost of brain surgery has gone up recently. Whatever helmet you decide to buy, make sure that it is certified, and that it gives you a snug but comfortable fit, so that you do get your money's worth.

Safety Belts

For autocrossing and casual track-day events, you will need only the standard three-point safety belts with which your MINI is equipped. However, for added safety and better times, you may want to seriously consider purchasing a supplementary belt system with shoulder straps as well as lap belts that can be clipped into your regular safety belt system.

One good example of such a belt system is the Schroth Profi II Flexi Competition Belt, which is available through racing and MINI aftermarket suppliers. The biggest advantage of this system is that it will give you much more stability in active autocrossing. Instead of having to brace yourself with your hands on the steering wheel and your legs against the interior panels, the safety belt system itself will help keep you positively anchored into your seat.

The nice thing about this system is that the lap belts fasten to the same points as the stock front belts, and the shoulder belts snap into the regular stock belts in the back seat. One drawback is that the shoulder belts come up at a pretty steep angle from the rear clips. This won't be a major issue in keeping you in place, and won't even make much difference in a slow-speed collision.

However, we wouldn't recommend these belts by themselves for highway use. In the event of a high-speed collision, the force of your body against the shoulder belts would likely result in severe spine compression, probably causing a more serious injury than you might sustain with the stock three-point belt.

There is a fix for this problem, however. Most of the same suppliers from which the Schroth belts can be purchased can also supply a harness guide bar from Stable Energies that will fit the MINI. This bar fastens across the car and attaches to the clips of the shoulder portion of the standard three-point seat belt. Then the shoulder portion of the auxiliary belts is fastened to the guide bar to prevent spinal compression in the event of a high-speed collision.

The four-point auxiliary harnesses are available for under $250, and the guide bar can be purchased for about $100. They are legal in all SCCA autocross classes and will probably contribute as much to lowering your lap times during your first year of competition as any piece of speed equipment that you might buy.

For the person who participates in occasional track days and time trials, the combination of the four-point clip-in system and a guide bar would probably be marginally safer, and also help maintain car control. However, we should note that this system probably wouldn't be accepted for most wheel-to-wheel competition use on the track. When you're ready to get involved in motorsports at that level, you'll want to install a roll bar or roll cage set-up, with a full five- or six-point racing harness.

Chapter Fourteen

Track Day Driving Techniques

With some practice on the track, or on the autocross course, or preferably both, and some focused attention to your driving techniques while on the road, you should be getting a feeling for driving a high-performance automobile well.

Track days, sponsored by local car clubs, professional groups, or occasionally MINI dealers are a great place to improve your driving skills and have a lot of fun. In this chapter we'll discuss some of the ins and outs of track days.

Before You Come to the Track

When you decide you're going to take your MINI to a track day, the first thing to do is put the car through a careful safety check. Check under the hood to make sure you've got the proper amount of engine oil on the dipstick and the proper amount of coolant in the coolant tank. Make sure the engine belt and hoses are in good shape.

Check your tires and wheels. You'll want a little more air in the tires than you might normally carry for daily driving, but if you bring a tire gauge and portable air pump to

Track days, often shared by several sports car clubs, are a great way to practice driving techniques and have a lot of fun at the same time. Corners are the places where the real practice goes on, and where the ultimate benefits are realized, even if going fast on the straights is exciting.
Photo by Fred Voit ActionPhotos.

the track, you can add the right amount once you get there. You'll be removing the hub caps if your wheels have them, so make sure you've got the little hook tool in your tool kit. Check to make sure that the lug nuts are tight all the way around. Minis have been know to shed their wheels if the lug nuts come loose, which you don't want to happen, so use the lug wrench to tighten them all securely. A torque wrench to check tightness is a good idea, but you can usually borrow one at the track.

Remove everything from the car that you won't need at the track, then when you get to the track, take out everything that's not welded in or bolted down. For yourself, you'll want your helmet, if you have one (they can usually be rented at the track if you don't), comfortable clothing and decent driving shoes. Athletic shoes are just fine, as long as they aren't so wide they'll get in the way of the pedals. Sunglasses will be important, since the sun will be in your eyes somewhere on the track at the beginning or end of the day.

All set? Let's start with practising corners.

Types of Corners

We've discussed the basics of turning corners, but once you're on the track, you'll discover there is a little more to the theory.

The first point to consider, once you get out of the artificial blocks of city streets, is that very few corners occur as neat 90-degree angles with the same width from curb to curb on the exit as on the entry. Curves can consist of long, gentle sweeps that allow high speeds but reward patience, tight turns that require heavy braking and a very slow entry to avoid running out of road, or combinations of the two that start out tight and then open into sweepers, or worst of all, corners that start out as fairly high-speed sweepers and then surprise you by tightening up. Add to that corners where the pavement slope helps your turn, or at the opposite extreme, seems to slope the wrong way especially just when you want to increase your speed, and you've got a fistful of new concepts to learn.

But don't despair. The second point to remember is that the concepts you've already been working on mastering, including controlled weight transfer, slow-in and fast-out, braking and downshifting, selecting your turn-in point, apex, and exit, will continue to apply. The exceptions we've just mentioned, and will now discuss in more detail, are actually just variations on what you've been doing.

Sweepers

Let's start with the corner that is potentially the most fun, the long sweeper. The major difference between this and the basic corner we discussed earlier in the book is that you don't have a specific apex point where you get off the brake and then roll hard on the throttle. Instead, after completing your braking and making your initial turn, you will find yourself holding the wheel at one angle for what can seem like a long time.

The important aspect of this turn is that you are need to keep your car balanced through the turn by using the throttle. Instead of immediately accelerating as you unwind the steering wheel, as you hold the car through the turn, you'll hold the throttle at close to one point, and try to keep the car balanced from front to rear without accelerating or decelerating.

On a long, sweeping curve, the apex is likely to be well around the corner. Turn-in is made late, and the car is balanced on the throttle as the car is held at the turning angle until you can see past the apex and down the track.

Actually, there generally is an apex to this type of sweeping curve, but it is typically a long way after the turn-in point. You can tell when you've reached the actual apex, because you realize that the track or road is starting to straighten out. At that point, you can start to straighten out the wheel while beginning to press the throttle harder to start accelerating.

So the key thing to remember on a long sweeping curve is that there is a fourth segment: the period when you are balancing the car using the throttle, maintaining more or less the same speed as you come around the curve. One tip on these corners is to continue to look as far around the curve as possible. This will help you keep a continuous turning radius, and will also give you the opportunity to see when you can begin to straighten out the car.

Tight Corners and Hairpins

At the opposite end of the spectrum is the very tight, continuous-radius corner, which might vary from something greater than 90 degrees to a tight 180-degree "hairpin" where you will be completely reversing your direction within a fairly short distance.

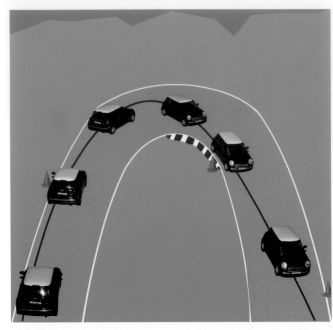

A hairpin turn is approached at a slow speed. Because the key to success in this type of turn is the exit speed, it is important to downshift to provide maximum torque for acceleration out of the corner. For the same reason, it is usually a good idea to make a late turn-in and late apex so that the car is straightening out and maximum acceleration is possible as soon as possible in the turn. Here the turn is completed well before the apex and the car is already accelerating at the point that it passes the apex.

In tight corners, all the aspects of the standard 90-degree corner apply, but must be performed to an extreme. You need to slow down significantly and will probably drop two or even three gears in order to be in the right gear for maximum torque when you complete the turn-in and get back on the accelerator; you need to wait to make your turn-in until you can exit the corner on almost a straight line; and you need to make a very late apex on the corner.

We can take the aspects of the turn one at a time. The first step will be to brake hard to reduce speed, while at the same time downshifting. On many racetracks, hairpins are often found at the ends of long straights, so that a period when the car is at its maximum speed in its highest gear is followed immediately by a turn that requires that the car be moving at a very low speed in its lowest practical gear.

Needless to say, this transition takes a lot of practice, but these types of corners reward the good driver who has excellent equipment and solid driving experience. At almost any track, this corner will see the greatest number of changes of position, since the corner is often almost a game of "chicken," with the drivers seeing who can wait the longest before hitting the brakes, each knowing that the driver who brakes last will be the first out of the corner, provided he or she has left enough room to slow the car sufficiently to be able to get around the corner.

Typically in these corners, the turn-in point will be almost even with the apex point, and the apex point itself will be well past the geometric turning-point of the corner. All of this is necessary so that the driver has the maximum distance over which to accelerate. The drivers who turn in early have to wait until they are completely around the corner before they can begin that drag race to the next corner. Such drivers are generally passed by the driver who turns later, but gets back up to speed earlier.

On these turns, the trick is to look around the corner, and wait until you can see well around the track before making your turn. It is not unusual to feel as if you're looking over your shoulder in an open car before you can see your line out of the corner and begin your turn. In a closed car, you'll probably be looking out the side window for your cornering line before beginning the turn.

Once you've slowed down and made your turn, then all that's left is to begin accelerating and wind the car up through the gears. In a normal rear-wheel car you might actually induce a little rear-end slide to bring the rear end around. In a MINI, by lifting off the throttle for an instant once you've begun your turn, you may be able to release the rear end. Then when you get back on the throttle you can use your speed to pull you around the corner.

Changing Radius Corners

In our modern world of carefully-engineered highways and geometric city streets, most corners have the same curve from the beginning to the end. For these corners, once you've turned the steering wheel, you can usually hold it at the same angle until you are through the corner. However, on back roads which were probably laid out to follow the contours of land or the boundaries of some farmer's property, it is not unusual to encounter a corner that surprises you half-way through by changing its curvature.

On road tracks, such corners are much more common. Track designers delight in making things difficult for the driver who is new to the track, or new to track driving, and the folks who lay out autocross courses positively delight in making things as difficult as possible. Two such corners are typical, ones that become more open as you go around them, and ones that become tighter as you go around them. The diagram below illustrates both as you might see them on a public road.

> ### Increasing Radius Corner
> A corner that gets progressively more open towards the exit of the corner, permitting the turn to be finished at a higher speed than the entry.
>
> ### Decreasing Radius Corner
> A corner that gets progressively tighter towards the exit of the corner, requiring that the speed be reduced as the car gets nearer the exit.

The first types are called "increasing radius" corners. On public roads, these are usually a positive surprise, since you find that you can get on the accelerator earlier and harder than you had expected when you entered the corner. On the track, they can be disconcerting because it usually means that you didn't need to have slowed down as much as you did on the entry and could have been going even faster on the exit.

But in general, they're not of too much concern for safe driving since it isn't likely that you're going to find yourself in an unexpected precarious situation coming out of the corner.

By contrast, corners that become tighter, with progressively smaller curvature as you go around them, can be quite dangerous. These corners, called "decreasing radius" corners, can deceive you into carrying too much speed on the entry. As the corner begins to become sharper, you realize you are going to have to turn the steering wheel tighter in order to keep from running off the road, but realize that if you do you may lose control of the car.

When driving an unfamiliar road, the best way to avoid this situation is to go more slowly, of course, and particularly wait until you are further into the corner before making your turn. That way you can see more of the exit and be able to gauge your speed more accurately.

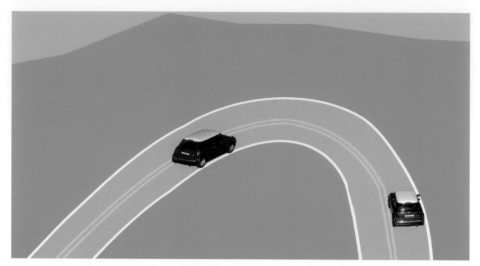

On this corner, the red car is encountering a "decreasing radius" corner and soon will have to tighten the steering wheel and probably slow down to complete the corner. The blue car, on the other hand, is encountering an "increasing radius" corner and will be able to gradually unwind the steering and increase speed to complete the corner.

However, if you do find yourself in the situation of having to turn the wheel more tightly after entering the corner, the worse thing to do is to follow your instinct and try to slow down by abruptly letting off the gas and hitting the brakes. If you do this, the car's nose will go down, making it even harder to get the car to turn, and you may very well find yourself going straight off the outside of the curve.

Instead, you need to try to keep the car as balanced as possible. Try to keep the car going at the same speed while as gradually as possible turning the steering wheel more sharply. If the situation was serious, you'll be rewarded by hearing your tires squeal as they start to slip a bit, but 99 times out of 100, you'll be all right.

Few people outside the realm of professional high-speed driving ever push their cars anywhere near their limits of adhesion or roll-over potential and all that will happen is that the car will scrub off speed as the tires slip a little. The car will make it around the corner without any problem, though you and your passengers may find your hearts beating a little faster when you're through.

It's the alternative where the trouble usually arises. When you see a car off the road, or worse on its side or top on the side of the road, you can pretty much assume that the driver got into a difficult situation, started to slide off the road, then either jerked the steering wheel hard or jammed on the brakes, or both, and wound up putting the car into a skid or roll.

It's worth remembering as you mentally prepare for decreasing-radius corners, that you are driving a MINI with its front-wheel drive. On the positive side, you can usually power your way around a decreasing radius corner by using the throttle and front wheels to pull you through. On the negative side, the MINI is more likely to bite you if you take your foot off the throttle, or worse, hit the brakes. This action will cause the car's weight to transfer to the front wheels and off the rear wheels, and it's very likely the rear end will skid out to the outside of the corner, leaving you facing the wrong way or worse.

Learning to handle tight and decreasing radius corners is where some practice in advance can pay dividends, and one of the reasons why some track time or autocrossing is a good idea even if you never expect to do any competitive racing. The first time your tires start to squeal, you'll be startled, but you'll begin to get some confidence in the car's ability to hold on to the pavement at speeds well beyond what you would have expected. You will also get a little more confidence in your ability to catch and correct a difficult situation without panicking and making it worse.

Of course, if you're working on improving your line around a track, and you're going to be taking the same decreasing radius corner again in two or three minutes, it is a simple factor to adjust your speed and turn-in point so that you start your turn a little later, and a little more slowly the next time around so that you can take the corner without scrubbing off speed and be able to accelerate more quickly coming out of the corner.

Stitching the Corners Together

If driving fast were a simple matter of braking, downshifting, turning in, hitting the apex and accelerating out as you released the wheel, then speeding down the straightaway until you got to the braking point of the next corner, racing and autocrossing would be a lot easier—and probably not nearly so much fun—as they are.

In fact, most race courses and nearly all autocross courses have only two or three corners where you will simply be able to drive straight down the course, while accelerating and up-shifting, after exiting the corner. Instead, most corners come in groups. No sooner are you out of one corner than you have to prepare for the next one. In fact, in many situations you may find that you need to begin preparing for a corner before you've had the chance to properly complete the last turn.

It's in these combinations of corners that less powerful cars can often overtake more powerful cars, and where the better drivers can improve on their lap times and overtake the less-skillful drivers. What's necessary is to be able to think of the entire series of corners together. Your choice of entrance line into the first corner should be determined by where you want to be when you come out of the last corner, and each of the in-between transitions in speed and direction should be made as smoothly as possible.

Two-Corner Combinations

We can start with the most obvious situation first, where a right-hand corner is followed immediately by a left-hand corner, or where the opposite is true. To drive this two-corner sequence effectively, two principles need to be kept in mind. First, you should "use all the track" as your instructor no doubt will remind you. Second, you will need to make your weight transition—from leaning in one direction to leaning in the other direction—as smooth as possible.

When discussing how to go around a corner earlier in this book, we stressed going to the very outside of the track before beginning the turn, and then touching the inside curb at the apex of the curve, and finally going to the very outside of the track on the exit. Generally, this principle will continue to be true on most right-left and left-right sequences.

Where there is sufficient space between turns, it is important to complete the initial turn by going to the outside of the track, then set up for the second turn. Since you can

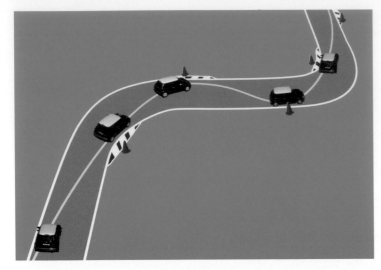

Where possible, it is important to set up properly for the second corner after completing the first corner. By using all the track, you can rebalance the car before entering the second corner. If you just drove down the center of the track, you'd take both corners too slowly and have less speed on the following straight.

maintain more speed on a larger-radius curve and you'll want as much speed as possible when exiting the second turn, you want to go out to the edge of the track to finish the first turn, then come back across the track to set up for the second turn. If you just drive down the center of the track around both corners, both turns will have to be sharper. If you don't take advantage of all the track on your first corner, you will be entering the second corner more slowly than necessary.

Even worse, if you start to make your turn into the second corner too soon, you'll find that you're carrying too much speed to make the corner cleanly. Instead of going around cleanly and smoothly, you'll find yourself scrubbing off speed, or even going off the track on the outside, as you attempt to get around the second corner.

In the situation where two right hand corners, or two left-hand corners, are taken in a row, the same rules apply. As usual, you go as wide as possible before making your turn-in, generally waiting until you can see your apex before turning. Then you complete the turn by going as wide to the outside as possible and stay on the outside of the track until you are ready to make your turn-in towards the second apex.

The second added factor in a combination turn is the weight balance of the car. Essentially, the principle here is that before you begin your turn-in for the second corner, you want your car upright and moving in a straight line. In the right-left and left-right sequence, the car must first tilt in one direction and then tilt in the opposite direction. If you attempt to begin the second turn before the car has finished its first turn, and before the car is again balanced at the center, it can be very easy to upset the car's equilibrium, causing it to push or spin.

Instead, try to be conscious of how the car's center of gravity first moves to the outside of the car as you begin the turn, then moves back over the center of the car as you unwind the steering wheel after passing the apex of the turn. As soon as the car's center of gravity is back over the wheels, and the car is no longer turning, you can begin making your second turn. This doesn't mean that you need to wait for the car to be stable after the first turn. Instead, if you do things properly, the movement of the center of gravity will be smooth, and your wheels will be straight at the instant the center of gravity is over the center of the car. At that point you simply continue to turn the wheel so the car goes in the other direction. The momentum of the shift in balance will simply continue across the car until the car is leaning in the opposite direction going into the second corner.

In the situation where two turns in the same direction follow one another, you still need to be aware of how the car's center of gravity is shifting. The car will progressively tilt away from the turn as you turn the wheel into the turn. Then as you gradually unwind the steering wheel coming out of the turn, the car will come back into balance, just as it did on the left-right and right-left sequence.

However, in this case, you need to avoid allowing the momentum of the weight transfer to cause the car to tilt too far in the opposite direction before you begin your second turn. By carefully controlling your acceleration out of the turn and the speed with which you allow the steering wheel to unwind you can begin the second turn just at the instant that the car is balanced, thus avoiding the problem of understeering and losing speed by plowing into the second curve.

Sequences of Corners

The corners on a track or autocross course that really show off a driver's skill and experience are those where several corners come in a row. In these circumstances, taking the optimum line around one corner may make it impossible to take the best line around the next corner.

For example, many tracks have a situation where if you go all the way to the outside of the track to prepare to enter the first corner in the sequence, the result is that you wind up exiting that corner way beyond the point where you can get a proper line into the second corner.

The key to these situations is to think about where you want to be when you come out the other end of the sequence of corners and are back on a straight section, whether that sequence is two corners, or five corners. As a general rule, the driver with the best lap time is not the person who goes through the corners fastest, but the one who gets from the beginnings of the straighter high-speed sections to their ends fastest.

Getting the highest speed on the straighter sections depends on coming off the last corner before that section on the best possible line. Sometimes this is impossible unless a less-than-optimal line is selected through one or more of the earlier curves in the sequence. This principle is sometimes called "sacrificing a corner" for speed.

Obviously, you aren't going to get this right the first time you drive the course. In fact, you have to find that line through the sequence of corners one step at a time, starting from the very last corner before the straight.

As you start to learn the track, or begin working to lower your times, start by driving relatively slowly through the sequence so that you can set up the last turn as effectively as possible in terms of how fast you're going when you exit. Once you've figured out where to begin your entry into that last corner, then you can do the same thing by determining where to turn in and how fast to enter the second-to-last corner in the sequence.

By following this process back to the first corner in the sequence, you may very well find yourself starting the first corner at a point that wouldn't make any sense at all if that corner were the only one, or you may find yourself going relatively wide and slow

On every track, there will be places where two or more corners will follow in close succession. Under these circumstances it often won't be possible to complete one turn before committing to the next corner, so the driver must be aware of weight transfer and braking opportunities in between the corners. The secret to finding the best line through a corner combination is to find the best exit into the straight at the end of the combination. This may mean, as illustrated here, that rather than taking the optimal line all the way through the first corner, the driver leaves the line early to get on the right line for the second corner.

around a corner in the middle of the sequence in order to finish the sequence at the highest possible speed.

For the near term, the main thing to remember is that when you confront a sequence of corners, you won't necessarily be able to follow the theories of correct lines through corners and find yourself going fast at the end. Instead, concentrate your attention on the last corner in the sequence, since that's where the greatest gains will be made in improving your lap times. Be willing to sacrifice speed around earlier corners in order to find that good line out of the last corner, and you'll be on your way to driving better.

Blind Corners

Whenever given the chance, those devious track designers will generally take advantage of terrain changes, or geographic characteristics to make the driver's task even more difficult. If they do very well, they will be rewarded by having their track called "technical." In our terms, a technical track is one that calls on all of the driver's skills to get good times.

One of the track designers' favorite strategies to do this is to use changes in elevation to create a blind corner. In a blind corner, the important elements of the corner, like the apex and exit point, can't be seen until the driver is already making the turn and is committed to a line. One of the best-known examples of a blind corner is the "Corkscrew" at Mazda Raceway Laguna Seca, but just about every good track has at least two or three examples of blind corners offering similar challenges.

To drive these blind corners well, two tips are in order. First, try to visualize the entire corner, including the part you can't actually see, in your mind's eye before entering it. Second, help yourself by finding visual landmarks that you *can* see in order to take the corner well.

Visualizing the corner in your mind is a trick that all good drivers use. It's often noted that an experienced driver can remember every foot of every corner of every track that he or she has mastered, and can drive the track in their mind so accurately that if you tell them to start, and they tell you when they've completed the mental lap, the elapsed time will be almost precisely the time it takes them to physically drive a lap. It's all visualization and it works very well for blind corners.

As you come up to a corner that is obscured by a rise in the terrain, or other barrier, you want to try to see through the barrier in your mind, picturing what the corner will look like as you clear the barrier. Do this several times as you begin driving a new track, each time getting a picture in your mind before the corner and then comparing it to what you see as you go through the corner. After a few laps, you'll have a clear picture in your mind of what the corner looks like. At that point you'll find that your confidence has been built up so that you can clear the barrier without slowing down more than is justified by the actual characteristics of the corner.

Another tip is to select a physical landmark that you can see as you make your turn, to give you a guide point to tell you where to aim the car as you go over the rise, or around the barrier that obscures the corner. For example, drivers who have mastered Laguna Seca will tell you that they aim for the top of the first oak tree as they make their turn and prepare to dive over that blind crest into the Corkscrew.

On other courses, the landmark might be a particular lamppost, or water tank, or other physical landmark in the distance that you can aim for when you round that blind corner or crest that blind rise into the next corner.

If you use the combination of creating a mental picture of the corner, coupled with a physical reference point to help you find your line, you'll be able to take the corner almost as if you had x-ray vision.

Corner Workers and Safety Flags

This is probably a good point to discuss one of the important roles that corner workers play at race tracks. All sanctioned race tracks will have a corner-worker station at each blind corner. Two workers will be posted at each of these corners. They use a set of flags of different colors to signal drivers.

During a practice session or race, one of the workers will face towards oncoming traffic to watch for unsafe situations that require drivers to be warned with a flag. If there is a faster car overtaking you, he'll wave a blue flag with a yellow stripe to warn you. If there is debris or fluids on the track, he'll wave a red and yellow striped flag, and if there is a safety vehicle on the course up ahead, he'll wave or show a white flag.

He also watches the cars for mechanical problems. If he sees something amiss, such as a loose part, oil leak, or smoke, that might endanger the safety of the driver or other drivers on the track he'll radio the other corner works and the driver will be signalled, with a black flag that has an orange circle (or roundel) in the middle, to return to the paddock at the next opportunity.

The other worker will be standing with his back to the first worker, looking further down the track. That worker is your eyes into the area that you can't see, but which you are about to drive into at high speed. He has only one flag under his arm, the yellow one.

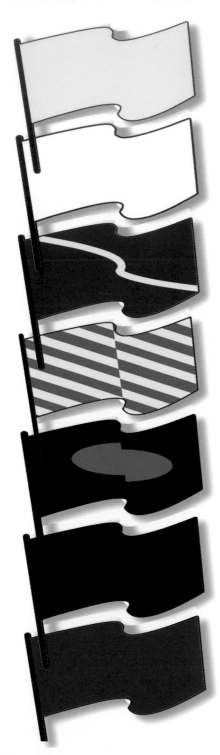

Yellow Flag

Waving yellow flag indicates a serious safety hazard is immediately ahead. Slow way down and be prepared to stop. No passing (depending on the organization) until the next flag station not displaying a yellow flag, or until green flag is displayed at start-finish. If stationary, means there is a safety hazard at a corner further ahead. Watch for waving yellow flag.

White Flag

When used by a corner worker, indicates that a safety vehicle (ambulance, fire, or tow truck) is immediately ahead. Slow down to a safe speed, and be prepared to stop, if necessary, until past the safety vehicle. At start-finish, may indicates that a safety vehicle is on the track.

Blue Flag with Yellow Stripe

A faster vehicle is immediately behind you and will be overtaking you. Stay on your line and expect the faster vehicle to pass you.

Yellow and Orange Striped Flag

There is debris, oil, or other hazard on the track surface immediately ahead. Be aware and be prepared to take a different line to avoid the hazard.

Black Flag with Orange Roundel

("Meatball flag") If displayed to you, or accompanied by a sign with your number, indicates you have a potentially serious mechanical problem. Slow down, move off the racing line, and proceed immediately to pit and go to steward's station.

Black Flag

If displayed to you, or accompanied by a sign with your number, proceed immediately to the hot pit and report to the steward's station. If black flag at all stations, track is being cleared; proceed to hot pits, but stay in car, ready to restart.

Red Flag

Serious situation on track. Slow down, don't pass, and safely pull off track at next flag station; track is being cleared immediately to allow clearance for safety vehicles.

If he sees something around the corner or over the rise that you need to be concerned about, such as a car spinning sideways or off the track in an unsafe place, he will turn around to face the oncoming cars, and wave that yellow flag to let you know that it isn't safe for you to drive around the corner at high speed.

When you see a waving yellow flag, you should slow down immediately and be ready to avoid the obstacle or hazard ahead. If the course worker is holding up the yellow flag but not waving it, this generally means that he or she has been told that there is a hazard further down the track that you should be ready for.

(Incidentally, when the yellow flag worker turns to flag down oncoming traffic, his partner on the corner will then turn around and face down the track to watch the incident and notify the stewards if a crash truck or ambulance is needed, and when the incident is clear.)

Any time the yellow flag is displayed, no passing is allowed. In some organizations, you can't pass until you see a green flag displayed at the start-finish line; in other organizations you can pass as soon as you go by a flag station with no flag displayed.

If both flag workers are standing there with their flags tucked under their arms, you can safely pick your line into the corner and take it with all the speed that's appropriate, even if you can't see around the corner.

We can't emphasize too much that you must look at each flag station on every lap before you drive into the corner they're watching. Also, though we've illustrated each of the standard safety flags and their generally-accepted meanings, be aware that flag policies differ among racing organizations; these are usually explained at the drivers' meeting, so be alert to what you are expected to do when you see each of the flags.

Wet Tracks and Slippery Pavement

Whenever we imagine ourselves driving on a racetrack, the sun is always shining, and the temperature is comfortable, but not too hot or too cold. Unfortunately, this isn't always the situation. It can be rainy and it can be cold and the track day will still take place.

With the high costs of track rentals these days, and the complicated logistics involved in putting together a track day, cancellation due to bad weather is just not an

Races take place rain or shine, just as does your everyday driving. Rain on a track day is a great opportunity to practice your slippery pavement driving techniques. The key is to be as smooth as you can be, as slow as necessary, and as alert to imminent problems as is humanly possible.
Photo by Walt & Louiseann Pietrowicz

option. It's only at the Indianapolis 500 and in NASCAR that they wait for the rain to stop before running.

Consequently, a few words are in order about techniques for running in the wet. Most of the following tips are also relevant for driving on highways in the rain or where glare ice may be a possibility.

Obvious point number one: slow down. You'll have more time to react to unexpected situations should they arise, and be carrying less momentum should you find yourself in trouble. Leave more room than normal between yourself and the vehicle ahead, and look well down the road for developing problems such as a car skidding out of control.

Obvious point number two: be alert. When you find yourself driving in the wet, or in the middle of that unexpected shower, clear your mind of all distractions and focus on your driving. Make sure you've got both hands on the wheel in the proper eight or nine o'clock and three or four o'clock positions. Use your hands to feel for any loss of traction in the front wheels. If the steering wheel starts to feel as if it isn't quite connected with the wheels, then you may be hydroplaning on top of the water, instead of moving through it with your wheels in contact with the pavement.

In the wet, it is critical to be smooth in your response. Any slickness in the pavement is going to multiply your reactions. You want to be even smoother with your direction corrections, acceleration and braking that you would otherwise be. Be sure that you are going straight before making any braking or acceleration changes. If you do need to make any changes in direction, do it slowly and carefully rather than abruptly.

Also, keep in mind in the wet that you are driving a front-wheel drive car. As long as your foot is on the throttle, your wheels will help you handle the situation, just so long as you are very smooth with your inputs. On the other hand, if the pavement is wet or slippery, if you release the throttle or hit the brake in the middle of the corner, the rear end of your car is going to get loose and spin out even more quickly.

On the track or highway in the wet, try to stay away from the most-traveled portion of the pavement. On the track the standard fast line around the corners is often called the "dry line." Because most of the cars travel on this line most of the time, that pavement will be impregnated with oil and rubber, which will rise to the surface first in a light rain. Instead, take the "rain line," typically about one car length in from the edge of the track.

On the highway, your best bet is to stay in the slow lane which will be slightly less slick, will keep you out of the way of those who think that rain can be ignored, and will give you run-off space if you need to avoid a problem.

Track Day Safety

Track days can be an excellent way to improve your driving skills and become more familiar with your MINI under reasonably safe circumstances. However, there are some good rules to keep in mind whenever you are out on the track with other drivers.

Be Aware of What's Going On Around You

It is critical to be aware of other drivers. One characteristic of nearly all track days is that the capabilities and experience of the drivers, and their desire to drive fast, will vary significantly. Unfortunately, abilities and need for speed also often vary in inverse relationship to each other.

You always need to be very aware of the drivers around you. Those in front may create situations to which you will have to react, and those behind you can startle you in unexpected places. Try to concentrate on everything immediately around you, but focus only on what is going on at the moment. This is no time to be thinking about where you're going for dinner after the event.

Watch your mirrors. Even more than in everyday traffic, you need to check your mirrors frequently to be aware of cars behind you, especially those that are overtaking you. Try to develop a habit of checking your mirrors at least once and preferably twice on each straight portion of the track.

Check your mirrors first just as soon as you complete the corner to see if there may be a car behind you that will want to take advantage of the straight portion to go past you. Check again just before you commit yourself to the next corner to make sure that no one is going to try to get around you just at the point when you are coming across the track to apex the corner.

Pay Attention to the Safety Rules

It may seem obvious, but we'll say it anyway: Follow the track safety rules. The track day supervisors will have specific rules for you to follow that will be determined by the nature of the group you are driving with and the characteristics of the specific track.

For example, when the driving group on the track isn't experienced, areas of the track where you can pass, and where you can not pass, are likely to be specified. Procedures for passing, such as that the overtaking car is always to go to the driver's right or driver's left of the car being passed, are also likely to be specified. These rules are not suggestions or simple courtesies. They are mandatory, and if the supervisors are doing their job, breaking a rule will bring a strong warning, followed on a second occurrence by immediate expulsion from the event.

Allow others to pass safely. During your first few track days, when you're feeling a little tentative about your car and your driving ability, and getting to know the track, it will seem as if everyone in the world is going faster than you are and is crowding your bumpers.

Safety on the track starts at the drivers' meeting, where passing and no-passing zones, flag signals, safety procedures for that track, the location of the track entry and exit areas, and other critical factors will be presented and discussed.

Typically, you'll find that you're being crowded on the corners, since you're likely to be slowest in those areas. Don't let that worry you, but be ready to let the faster cars go around you as soon as you're in an area where passing is permitted.

When you're aware that there is a faster car behind you, don't try to move over, or move off the line that you would otherwise be traveling. The driver overtaking you needs to know that you aren't going to turn abruptly in one direction or the other as they're trying to pass. It is up to them to make the pass safely.

As soon as you're in a safe passing area, point in the direction you expect the driver to go as he passes you. The point lets the driver behind know that you know he or she is there and that they can pass you without causing you to do anything unexpected.

It doesn't hurt to slow down just a bit to allow the car behind to get completely around you before the next corner. Typically at a MINI track day, the cars will be fairly evenly matched, but driving abilities will vary. As a result, you might be able to hold your own on the straight, or even out-drag the overtaking driver, but that proves nothing. If he or she can stay on your bumpers through the corners, then they're probably driving better than you and should have the right to practice their cornering without having to slow up for you.

Remember that there may be more than one car behind you waiting to pass. They will often assume that if you're letting one car pass, that you will be letting anyone behind them around as well.

Just don't be disconcerted by being passed. If you're courteous and predictable in your driving style, no one will mind that you're driving more slowly than they are.

Passing Safely

As you gain a little experience, you may find that you are overtaking other drivers. In this case, it is your responsibility to make the pass safely. At track days, especially in the novice groups, passing generally will be limited to the straights, which is the safest place to pass.

After you've gotten near the car ahead, wait for the next safe passing zone and look for their signal to pass. If you are not sure the driver ahead knows you're there, or not sure there is enough room to make a clean pass in the safe passing area, then wait until you can make the pass safely.

Be careful to completely pass the car ahead before you begin your turn. If you don't think you can pass them before the turn-in point for the next corner, then wait until the next passing zone to make your pass.

If you're the overtaking driver, it is up to you to make sure that the pass is made safely. There are no ifs, ands, or buts about this. The safe pass is solely the responsibility of the overtaking driver. We'll repeat that, since it is a fundamental principle of amateur racing: the overtaking driver is completely and solely responsible for passing safely.

To say it another way: Any doubts; back out. If you're the overtaking driver, you almost always can slow down and not make the pass. If there is any possibility that the other driver hasn't seen you, or that you won't be able to make the pass in a safe manner, then back out of the pass.

If you find that you simply can't safely get around a driver on the straights, even though you know you're faster on the corners, then the best thing to do is to slow down and give them a little space. Track days aren't races, and there are no prizes for proving you're faster than someone else. You might even pull into pit lane and then go back out on the track to give the slow car as much room as possible. Pausing for even thirty seconds is usually enough to get sufficient track space for yourself so you can go back to practicing at the speed that suits you.

Take Advantage of all Available Instruction

Here's another good tip: If the program in which you're participating offers to provide a coach or instructor to ride with you on your hot laps, take them up on it. This is no time for a macho "I'd rather do it myself" attitude. Once you're out on the track, you're going to discover that there is about twice as much going on as your mind can process and your memory can store.

Having an instructor or coach in the car will make sure that if something starts to happen that is beyond your power to control, there will be an experienced driver in the car to help you avoid the problem. Often, just having a quiet voice next to you saying, "brake now" or "turn in here" can help you stay focused.

Best of all, the instructor/coach can store up all the little data that you might miss or forget in the sensory overload on the track, and help you put it all in perspective once you get off the track. Having someone who can tell you , for example, "You're coasting into the corners by pausing between brake and throttle," can make everything suddenly make sense.

When You Get in Trouble

Sooner or later on the track, everyone has that moment when they believe they have just exceeded their ability to drive the car, or the car has just been pushed beyond its limits. On a fast corner, you may find that you're going faster than you expected, and it looks as if you're going to run off the outside of the track before you complete the corner. Or in the middle of a turn you may find that your front or rear end is sliding and you're not sure you can get the car under control. What do you do now?

Dropping a Wheel Off the Edge

If you do "go in too hot and overcook the corner" as drivers say, especially if you turn in too early, you may find that you can't turn the car enough to stay completely on the track. Getting too close to the edge of the track at the exit, you may have one or both of your outside wheels go off the track.

Dropping one or two wheels off the track can be fairly benign, or the prelude to disaster. Usually you'll have a pretty good idea that this is going to happen before it actually does, so you can prepare yourself for it.

Just as soon as a wheel goes off, the car is going to get pretty squirrelly. The wheels in the dirt are going to have very different traction than the wheels that are still on the track. At that point, the worst thing you can do is try to wrench the car back on the track. If you do try to do that, just as soon as the off wheels grab the pavement again, the car will start to spin with a vengeance, generally sliding across the track and off again on the opposite side. That is, if you don't encounter other cars as you slide across the track.

Instead, when you realize you're about to drop wheels off, you're better off continuing in a straight line until you either drive completely off the track, or slow down to the point where you can consider driving back on to the track.

When you do get the car back under control, before you drive back onto the track be sure you look behind you to make sure that there aren't any other cars coming up on you. Only after you're absolutely sure you can get back on the track without getting in anyone else's way, should you actually turn back on the track.

Spinning Out

The other possibility in a corner is that you lose your nerve after the car has started to turn. Instead of keeping your foot on the throttle and using both your steering and your power to pull you through the corner, you let off the throttle or worse, hit the brakes.

As you release the throttle or hit the brakes, the car will unweight at the rear and that understeer will immediately become oversteer. Pretty much the same thing can happen if you overcorrect after you drop a wheel off the outside of the track.

Either way, you can find your car losing traction completely and spinning. What do you do then? To answer this question, a little rhyme is often quoted in driver instruction: "In a spin, both feet in."

(You'll probably hear the first half of this rhyme, too: "When in doubt, both feet out," but as we've discussed before, that doesn't work on front-wheel drive cars, so just keep the second half in mind.)

Once the car has gone into a spin, and you realize you're just along for the ride, you need to get your right foot off the gas and use it to push the brake pedal in as hard as possible in order to lock up the wheels. At the same time, your left foot should push in the clutch so that the engine won't die.

Locking up the wheels will generally keep the car spinning in a reasonably small area. Having the clutch in means that no power will get to the wheels that could cause the car to go shooting off in a different direction as soon as it regains traction.

In addition, the engine should still be running when you finally come to a stop. That will allow you to immediately shift into a lower gear and get the car to a point where you're safe or where you can get back on track and into the flow of traffic.

Completely Off the Track

What do you do if you do go off the track? In the event you do slide or drive off the track, the first thing to do is to come to a full stop to make sure that the car is still running all right and you haven't broken something or sprung a leak.

Before doing anything else, wave your hand out the window to let the corner workers know *you're* all right. If they don't see any movement, they're probably going to assume the worst and call out the ambulance.

Once you're sure that everything on the car is still connected to everything else, and you've had time to catch your breath, then you can consider getting back on track. Before you do that, however, be very sure that you are entering at a point where oncoming traffic can see you, and be very sure that there isn't any oncoming traffic.

Then, and only then, should you move back on to the track. Remember that you're going to be moving slowly at first and allow for that when gauging how much space will be needed. Remember, there's no rush. This isn't Sebring and your racing contract doesn't hang in the balance if you lose a few minutes.

Once you do get back on the track, most track day organizations will expect you to come back into pit lane immediately and check in with the chief steward. At the least, the official will want to check to make sure that there's nothing hanging off or stuck to your car. They also may want to have a few words with you about why the car wound up off the track to make sure that you can be counted on not to be a hazard to yourself or others when you go back out again.

If you've gone off and you think something may be wrong with the car, you'll need to wait for the crash truck to come and get you into the pits where you can figure out what's wrong. If the car is in a safe place, well off the track, the best thing to do is wait in the car until the truck comes. Keep your helmet on and your seat belts fastened. That way you'll be as safe as possible while you're sitting there, and ready to have the car towed in when the truck arrives.

Even if the car isn't in a safe position, you are still likely to be safer if you are in it, belted securely and with your helmet on. You wouldn't want to be half in and half out of the car and then get hit by another car. Wave an arm and flip up the faceplate of your helmet so they'll know you're all right and don't require immediate medical attention.

Stay in the car until the corner workers tell you to get out. Most likely, they will push it out of harm's way, or keep the flags waving until the safety crew can get to you and move the car. Either way, they'll need to have you at the wheel to steer the car.

Only in the event of a fire should you make the decision on your own to get out of the car before the corner workers or safety crew tell you to do so. In that case, don't waste any time; just get out as quickly as you can and then move away from the car and over the wall off the track.

Once the truck comes, you need to have your helmet on and your seat belts fastened before they can tow you in. Then follow their instructions as they hook your car up to the truck and tow you back to the pits. No, it isn't fun, and it will be embarrassing, but getting yourself and the car back to the pits safely with no further damage is better than turning a small annoyance into a major disaster.

If It's Risky, Why Go to a Track Day?

We've talked about what you'll do in the on-track portion of a driving class, or at a track day, and we've talked about what can go wrong. Since things can go wrong, why would you want to go out on the track? The answer is simple: Sooner or later when you're driving, something *will* go wrong.

The main point of track days isn't that you get the thrill of driving fast. Instead, it is that you will get the opportunity to practice coping with problems in a relatively safe situation. There won't be anyone coming the other way, and you'll generally have enough space so that, even if something does go wrong, you'll be able to cope withthe problem, and practice your response without putting yourself or anyone else at risk.

Chapter Fifteen

Basic Autocross Techniques

Competitive autocrossing is a great alternative or supplement to track days. In autocross events, yours is the only car on the course while you're running, so you don't need to worry about anyone else getting in your way, or worse. Speeds are typically slower than on the track, so if something should go wrong, you are more likely to be able to deal with it than you might on the track.

Under the worst of circumstances, much less damage is likely to be done should the car get out of control on the autocross course. Typically, only a few cones will get knocked around, and your pride might suffer a blow, but that's about it.

Autocross events generally cost much less to enter than full-blown track days. While you'll get less seat time, when you're in the car you'll be learning as much about driving and car control as you would on the track, generally in a much more concentrated manner.

Principles of Autocrossing

Autocross techniques are pretty much the same as track driving techniques. They're just done on tighter courses and in lower gears, but the same principles apply.

Autocrossing is as much fun as you can have in your MINI without spending a lot of money, and the skills you learn will make you a safer driver on the highway as well.

Look Ahead, Think Ahead

The first rule for all types of driving is to look ahead of where you are and look in the direction you want to go. In autocross, this means that as you make your turn, you should already be looking at the next turn, or often the turns after that.

By the time your car is coming around a pylon (also just called a cone), there is little you can do to make any difference, so your eyes should be on the next turn, and your mind should be planning the turns beyond that. Remember that your car will go where your eyes are looking, so look ahead and look where you want to go.

Look for the Straightest Lines

The second principle of autocrossing is to find the line that allows you to go as straight as possible. The straighter the line, the faster you'll go. In autocrossing as in track racing, you need to look for every opportunity to point the car in a straight line so you can get hard on the throttle. Typically in autocross, this means looking for the straightest line through the corners, rather than turning every time the course turns.

Don't be deceived by the cones. They define the edges of the course, but have little to do with finding the fast line. This is not a game of connect the dots; instead it is a game of turning square corners into smooth curves.

Be Smooth

When you watch other drivers going through the autocross, they can often be divided into two camps. There's the noisy, almost out-of-control driver whose car seems to be skidding and squealing around each corner, with abrupt changes in direction.

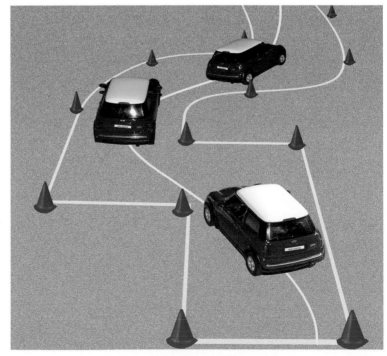

Shown is a typical section of an autocross course, including two 90-degree corners leading to a curve. Finding the straightest line in this section (marked here in yellow) means cutting across the square corners, but then staying in the middle of the course to be prepared for the next curve. Being fast in autocross means planning your line two or three corners ahead.

Walking the course is the first step in getting a fast lap time. Go with an experienced friend, if possible, and compare your ideas with theirs. Take your time, try to look at each corner as you want to approach it, and get a general picture of the overall course.

Then there's the smooth driver who seems to be fluid all the way through, with the car rolling easily from one turn to the next.

If you were sitting inside the car, you'd see the first driver's hands moving rapidly on the wheel, so fast they almost seem a blur. The second driver's hands wouldn't seem to move much at all. His hands generally would be on opposite sides of the wheel and not leave the wheel nearly as often.

Which one do you think will come in with the faster lap time? If you guessed the smooth driver, you'd be right. The really fast drivers know where they need to go, plan ahead, rarely get caught off-guard, and almost never look as if they're out of control.

Finding the Fast Line

Walking the course ahead of time can make a big difference. Since most autocross events only allow the drivers two or at most three runs, there really isn't enough time to develop a strategy for the course and figure out the best line while driving it. Instead, serious competitors will arrive early enough so they can walk the course and scope it out.

When you do walk the course, try to ignore the rest of the crowd. Don't just walk around to see where it goes; instead look at each corner, or sequence of corners and pause long enough to figure out how to go through that portion most quickly.

As you walk the course, divide it into cornering sequences and straightaways. You want to be in a position to get on the throttle quickly going into a straightaway, so that may sometimes mean planning your line through several corners in such a way that you can come out of the last corner at the right point and pointed in the right direction to burn up the straight.

The best strategy to deal with a sequence of turns leading up to a straight is to work backwards. Start with the straight, looking at where the car will be straightened out and

Traffic cones, often called "pylons" in autocross, are used to mark out the autocross course. A standing cone marks the edge of the course. In a slalom, a cone on its side indicates that you are expected to go past the standing cone on the opposite side. Each cone is outlined in chalk. You can touch a cone as long as you don't knock it completely out of its box.

pointed in the proper direction, then figure out how to take the previous corner so that the car winds up at the right point, facing in the right direction. Then evaluate the next previous corner and so on until you've figured out where you need to enter the sequence and how you should take it.

Autocross courses are typically made up of standard right and left turns, plus some ingenious obstacles that will be incorporated into every course. These include slaloms, chicanes, 360-degree turns, and sweeping turns. For each of these, we can offer some tips to take them as fast as possible.

Slalom Segments

Slaloms are an important part of every autocross course. This segment of the course will consist of a straight line of cones, typically placed at equal distances from one another. The task is to go from right to left to right again, weaving through the line while maintaining as high a speed as possible.

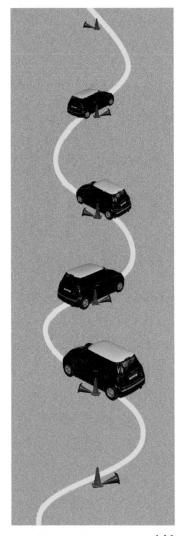

To run a slalom sequence quickly, you definitely need to be looking two to three cones ahead, rather than simply concentrating on turning around the next cone. Drivers who focus on the cones one at a time typically start fast, then find themselves going wider and wider with each turn until they finally reach a point where they have gone too wide and can't get turned without going off course or hitting a cone.

Instead, you should choose your turning point outside the line of cones, so that you just brush past each cone on the way to the point where you turn to line up to pass the next cone. If anything, you should start the sequence more slowly than you think will be necessary. That way you can gradually gain speed as you go through, rather than having to slide around and scrub off speed in order to stay on course.

Chicanes

Most courses you encounter are likely to have at least one section where the cones extend across your direct line of travel, on an otherwise straight section, forcing you to make a set of three tight turns, for example first right, then left, then right, to stay on course. These obstacles, a favorite of the fiends who lay out autocross courses, are called "chicanes." (A good term, since the word is the root of the word chicanery, meaning trickery or deception.)

A typical slalom segment is shown here, illustrating the principle that you turn outside the line of cones, and cross the line next to the cone, coming as close as possible to it. The tricks to quick times here are to look way ahead, and enter the slalom slow, then gradually speed up if possible.

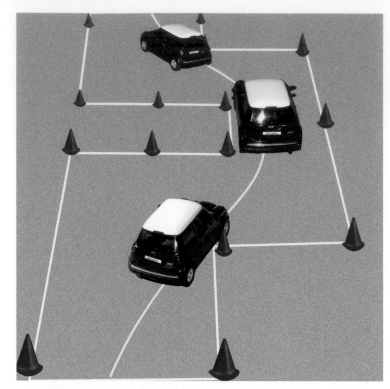

The chicane is proof that in autocross, you don't always drive the way the course looks. Instead, you want to find the smoothest, fastest line through the obstacle. In the chicane, that means a smooth curve that focuses only on the inside cones. Looking down the course will help make this a fast transition, like a slalom, rather than being four right angle turns.

Often the chicane is enclosed in a box of cones to make the problem a little more difficult. A few tips will help you negotiate this obstacle as quickly as possible. First, remember that the main trick to autocrossing well is to turn series of straight lines into smooth curves. Don't think of the chicane as a set of separate turns, but rather as a sort of slalom, where you want to take as straight a line as possible through the box.

Second, plan ahead to figure out where you want the car to be pointed when you exit the chicane. Then work your line back to determine how you want to enter the chicane.

Third, as you go through the chicane, don't be tricked into dropping your sight line. Instead, look across and out towards the next turn as you enter the chicane. This will help you find the quickest way through.

Finally, don't be timid, and don't be tricked into making your turns sharper than they need to be. Be aggressive at the entrance and make your turns early. On most chicanes, you will be able to get on a straight line and back on the accelerator well before you're actually through the obstacle, turning what could be four turns into only two turns.

Hairpins and 360 Turns

Another typical element of many autocross courses is the tight hairpin around a cone. Sometimes, the course may even require a 360-degree turn. This turn will be marked a single pylon sitting in the center of the path of travel with some large open space around it. Your challenge is to go around the pylon, executing a 180- or 360-degree turn and then continuing on the course.

This type of obstacle is tailor-made for the Mini's front-drive capabilities and easily-reached handbrake. The trick to this is to use the handbrake or your left foot to release the grip of the rear tires on the pavement, then use the powered front wheels to pull you around in a controlled skid.

To manage this, you'll drive close to the pylon, and when you're even with it, turn the steering wheel to put the car in a sharp turn around the pylon. Holding the wheel turned with your left hand, you'll give a quick pull on the handbrake, holding the button down and then immediately release the brake. You can also accomplish the same effect by using your left foot to stamp on the brake pedal and immediately release it, while keeping your right foot on the gas.

Either way, the quick braking should break the rear end loose so you can bring the car around with the nose almost touching the pylon. Once you're about three-quarters of the way through the turn, you get hard on the accelerator to pull you back into a straight line and on down the course, and allow the steering wheel to unwind.

High-Speed Straights and Sweepers

Autocross courses are great places to find the limits of your car. In particular, most courses will include at least one high-speed sweeper. Most of the same principles for sweepers that we discussed in the last chapter will apply, including taking a late apex and balancing the car on the throttle until you've got a straight exit line to the next corner entry.

On these corners, you'll want to get your car right at the edge of adhesion. You'll be able to tell where that is by the squeal that the tires make as they struggle to hold on. Some drivers say, "A squealing tire is a happy tire." You'll learn what that means when you turn your car into a long curve then accelerate until the car is right at its limits, and use the throttle as much as the steering wheel to keep the car on course.

Starts and Finishes

Nearly all autocross courses are timed electronically, with a beam of light and electric eye at the start and at the finish. As you make your start and cross the finish, your car breaks the beam of light, starting and stopping the timer.

For safety purposes, the SCCA has had a long-standing rule that there must be a right-angle turn before the start line, and another right-angle turn before the finish line. The cones that mark the turn before the start line, and after the finish line count just as much any other cone on the course, so you have to be careful in your start and finish. These rules help assure that cars don't enter the course or leave the course at unsafe rates of speed.

You will want to be going as fast as possible when you cross the starting line, so that you begin the course with as much momentum as possible. Similarly at the finish, you don't want to slow down until you've crossed the line and are off the course.

But you don't want to be faster off the mark than the course permits. On many courses, the person setting the course will set up the first obstacle, for example with a decreasing radius corner, so that the real hotshoes will find themselves in trouble as soon as they're across the starting line.

When you walk the course, and as you sit at the start line waiting for your signal to begin, have a plan of attack on how you should negotiate the corner into the start line,

At the start, a flagger will signal you when it's safe to start. However, you don't have to start as soon as he drops the green flag, since the time clock doesn't start until you break the light beam between the green cones that mark the starting line. The start will almost always incorporate a set of two 90-degree corners, but your fast line (marked here in yellow) will curve between the corners and should set you up up for the first corner on the course.

based upon the direction you need to be going for the next two or three corners.

Similarly, there may be a complicated set of turns going into the finish that can trip up the unwary, causing them to be off the throttle just when they need a fast finish. Keep these possibilities in mind as you walk the course, and plan your strategies accordingly.

You won't need to worry about shifting gears. With the MINI, your best bet on most courses is to start off in first, and then shift up into second as soon as you can. For the rest of the course, you can then just stay in second, confident that you're well up in the rev range where you've got good torque for maneuvering.

Occasionally an event may be able to set a course that does include one or perhaps two very long straight sections, where an upshift into third is needed towards the end to keep on the power band or avoid exceeding the rev limits. Even on these courses, you'll need to downshift again almost immediately to be ready to power through the next corner, so you won't lose much if you just run the car up to the top of the rev range without shifting.

Setting Up the Car

During your first season of autocrossing, you don't need to make many changes to the car. Most of your improvements in time will come through improvements in your own driving skill. In fact, the SCCA stock class places significant limits on what you can do to the car. In these classes, you can make only a few changes to the engine. You can substitute a more efficient air filter, and replace the exhaust system behind the catalytic converter, but that's about it on the power side.

On the suspension, you are allowed to substitute adjustable shocks and a front sway bar to reduce the car's tendency to understeer. However, with the MINI's excellent stock handling capabilities, it may take a season of experience before you would notice the difference in your time by these modifications.

What you can do within the limitations of the stock class is to replace the wheels and tires, so long as you stay within the stock sizes. Here you can make a great deal of difference in your lap times. As we've discussed previously, by replacing the stock wheels with a lighter-weight set you give the engine less mass to move. By mounting some good-performing tires to replace the run-flat tires that came with the car, you can get much better traction, and reduce the unsprung weight to boot.

These Kumho Ecstas mounted on lightweight wheels provide a definite advantage over stock MINI tires and wheels on the autocross course. These already have done a few hot autocross laps but are not used on the street. The driver has marked them with a chalk line at the base of the tread to help confirm that tire pressure is right. If the chalk isn't touched, pressure is too high; if it is completely rubbed off, pressure is too low.

If you get serious about autocrossing, you might consider buying tires with a softer compound that are designed specifically for racing. However, these tires won't last long at all if they're also used on the street, and their tread pattern won't be very good in the rain. You'll want to mount them on a separate set of wheels and put them on the car after you arrive at the event. (Yes, there's room in your MINI for four wheels and tires, and a floor jack.) Making this investment can certainly wait until you've worn out your first set of street tires and have gained the skill to take advantage of the improved tires.

But even if you decide to use the original run-flats for your first few events, experienced MINI autocrossers suggest that you can accomplish a lot by adjusting your tire pressures. You'll probably want to increase the pressure on the tires so that they are less likely to roll off the wheels on hard turns. Inflate the fronts with about four pounds less pressure than the rear and you'll do a lot to reduce the MINI's basic understeering tendencies.

Another tip to find the right pressures is to make a mark with chalk or white shoe polish on the tire at the point where the tread joins the sidewall. If the mark is worn off after a run, then the tire is rolling over too far and you should increase the pressure that you're running. Experiment with different pressures over the course of several sessions until you find a level that works best for you.

Be sure to check that the lug nuts are tight while you're adjusting tire pressure and before going out on the track before every run. To be absolutely sure that they're tight, you'll need a "torque wrench" which measures the pound-feet of pressure required to twist the lug nut. You don't need the best quality, since you won't be using it every day, but a good one can be purchased at any auto supply store for about $50. Tighten the lug

nuts individually to 80 pound-feet and you'll be sure that you won't be singing in the middle of your run, "You picked a fine time to leave me, loose wheel."

You Can Learn a Lot by Watching

Most regional SCCA autocross events also include a track walk for novices (and anyone else who wants to tag along) in between sessions. These track walks will be conducted by a fast and experienced driver, who will be happy to show the fast line on the course and share some of his or her secrets to gaining fastest time of day.

In between your runs, you also need to use your time effectively. After your first run, you may have some idea of which corners are toughest, or where you seemed to be slowing down too much. Watch the other competitors to see what line they're taking through that portion, and watch where everyone seems to be having the greatest difficulty. As you watch, try to visualize in your mind what the course looks like from the driver's windshield so you'll have an idea of where to go when you're on the course.

If you plan to do more autocross or track day events, consider getting an inexpensive torque wrench and the appropriate socket to fit your lug nuts. With a "click" torque wrench as shown here, you set the desired torque setting on the shaft of the wrench, and then tighten the lug nut until the wrench clicks.

Many autocross events will require competitors to act as corner marshals on the course during a session when their group isn't running. The primary task of the corner marshals is to replace cones that are knocked over and they help the starter make sure the corner is clear before each run. Working as a corner marshal is an excellent opportunity to get up-close-and-personal as other drivers run the course since you're in a safe area out on the course. Check out the techniques of the fast drivers and see how they are taking specific corners. Their experience may help you take seconds off your own time.

We encourage you to try at least one autocross event. We can guarantee you'll be made to feel welcome. The experience should be fun and exciting and will definitely help you improve your driving skills as well as getting a better understanding of the capabilities and behavior of your MINI.

When you're starting to autocross, take advantage of all the opportunities to learn from the experts. At most SCCA autocross events, a "novice" course walk is scheduled in between sessions, when an experienced autocrosser takes newbies around the course and offers some tips on how he or she makes fastest time of day.

Chapter Sixteen

Touring the Back Roads

Even if there aren't any opportunities for track days or autocrossing in your local area, or you just don't feel comfortable putting your new Mini through that kind of ordeal, touring can be a great way to enjoy time with friends, see the scenery and sights in your region, and have some fun with your Mini.

But even on pleasant grand tours, there are some advanced driving tips that can make your time on the road safer and more fun.

When The Route is Brand-new

One major difference between driving on a track or autocross course, and driving on a tour on public roads is that you can't learn the course in the same way. Even if you've driven a section of road frequently, you still can't memorize the turn-in points and apexes of each corner the way you might on the track. So your mind-set must be different for touring. When you can't be sure what the rest of the corner will look like, the major goal is to keep your car under control, rather than attempting to push its limits.

Take your Mini out of the big city and enjoy the views on the backroads. Just keep the basics of safe driving in mind, and keep your Mini properly maintained, and prepared for any emergencies that may arise.

In particular, on roads that are new to you, you need to be aware that the curvature of the corner may change as you come around it or come over the crest of the hill. You may find that the easy corner is followed, right around the bend or just over the next rise, by a much tighter corner that you aren't ready for.

Old hands at road rallying suggest a trick to deal with blind crests that can help a little bit. If you're coming up a rise or hill, and can't see where the road goes after the crest, look at the telephone poles or tree line. Generally they'll give you a clue to whether the road curves over the crest, and in which direction, or continues to go straight.

What was a reasonable speed when you entered the corner may be too fast for the radius of the curve on the other side. Remember from racing, this is a "decreasing radius" corner. Generally, the possibility of circumstances like that means staying well within the limits established by the road and geography, rather than those determined by the car.

Nonetheless, whenever traffic permits, the twists and turns of a good backroads route can still allow you to enjoy the handling and power of your MINI. Generally, it can be more challenging to drive a two-lane back road near the 45 mph speed limit, than it is to drive a divided highway at 70 mph.

Be Ready for the Unexpected

Unlike the race track, out on the road you don't have a person with a yellow flag standing at the apex to warn you if there's an obstruction right around the bend. Instead, you need to keep your speed limited to the level where you can use your reflexes and brakes to bring the car to a safe stop, or steer around the obstacle, if you do encounter an unexpected problem.

To be safe, you need to be aware of those times when you can't see around the corner, and so need to slow down to the speed noted on the caution sign and be alert to what's on the road as you go round that blind corner.

Don't forget that you can drive around many obstacles rather than trying to stop to avoid hitting them. Often the safest course is to make a quick, slight direction change, rather than trying to stop.

As you drive, try to be conscious of what the sides of the road look like, as well as the road itself. If you do encounter that recreational vehicle stalled in the middle of the road, you need to know whether your only option is to slam on your brakes, or if you can safely go off on to the shoulder to avoid hitting the RV.

Passing on the Backroads

Because we are so blessed in this country with freeways and limited-access highways, the old techniques of passing have largely been forgotten. They're rarely taught in driving courses, except to emphasize not to cross a double-yellow line, and there aren't many opportunities to practice the technique.

However, the more time you spend exploring the two-lane byways, the more often you'll find yourself in a situation where you really do want to pass that slow-moving vehicle up ahead. To make a pass safely on a two-lane road just requires keeping a few guidelines in mind, then cultivating your ability to gauge the "closing speed" of your vehicle and the one coming at you from the other direction.

Obviously, there can never be any passing across a double-yellow line, or when there is a solid yellow line in your lane. To emphasize this, in most states there will also be a roadside sign stating "No Passing Zone" wherever visibility ahead is too limited to permit safe passing, and "End No Passing Zone" when there is sufficient visibility ahead to permit safe passing.

The first point to keep in mind in passing safely is that you need enough room to accelerate to a speed faster than the car immediately ahead of you before leaving your lane. Then you need to get far enough ahead of them to be able to safely return to your lane without forcing the car you just passed to slow up abruptly. You could work out the math, but a typical pass will require a minimum of half a mile, so you must be able to see at least that far down the road to make sure traffic is clear and there is enough space to complete your pass.

It is possible to pass even when you can see a vehicle coming toward you from the other direction, if the road is straight ahead of you and the oncoming vehicle is far off. However, the best strategy is to wait until the oncoming vehicle has passed you, at least until you are confident of your ability to determine the passing distance required, and to estimate how fast the oncoming vehicle is approaching you.

Here a second tip applies. When getting ready to pass, you don't want to be right on the bumper of the car ahead. Instead, you want to have enough room so that you reach your maximum passing speed *before* you leave your lane to pass. That way, you will spend as little time as possible in the opposite lane before returning safely to your own lane. To do that, you should be at least two to three car lengths behind the car in front of you when you begin your pass.

If there is a vehicle coming from the other direction, and you can see far enough up the road to make sure that there will be space to pass after the oncoming vehicle passes you, then you should prepare to make your pass before the oncoming vehicle gets to your point. To maximize the amount of time you have to complete your pass, you should begin to accelerate as the oncoming vehicle approaches the car ahead of you. If you've timed things properly, you will be at your maximum speed and ready to move into the opposite lane just as the oncoming vehicle passes you.

When passing, it is worth keeping in mind that it is illegal in all states to exceed the posted speed limit on any road or highway *under any circumstances*. In other words, if the speed limit is 65 mph, and you come up behind a farm truck going 45 mph, you're permitted to go up to 65 in order to pass it, which isn't a difficult pass. On the other hand, on that same road, if you find yourself behind a cautious driver doing 60, you are allowed to accelerate to 65 to pass him, if space permits. However, you can be ticketed if, as would be more likely, you have to accelerate to 75 mph in order to pass the slower vehicle.

Bad Weather Conditions

When you're a long way from home and the weather turns bad, you may not have much choice except to deal with it. Rain, fog, snow, or ice can happen at the most unexpected times and places, and you should be mentally ready for the possibility.

Just as on the track under wet conditions, as soon as it starts to rain even a little bit, you need to slow down. Especially during the first rain of the season, oil and rubber that has sunk into the pavement will float back up to the surface very soon after the rain begins. Oily, wet pavement can be every bit as slippery as icy pavement and caution must be your first rule.

The same rules apply for highway driving in the wet as on the track. Make your changes in speed and direction as smooth as possible. Try to stay off the most heavily traveled section of pavement. Staying in the slow lane will allow less sensible drivers to get past you, as well as giving you a better chance of avoiding trouble if the problem arises.

If the rain gets very heavy, your best bet is to tuck under an underpass or preferably get off the highway completely to wait for it to let up. Visibility can go to zero almost instantly and the wet pavement can make it difficult to stop if someone in front of you skids sideways or stops without warning.

Fog is also a hazard that is underrated by many drivers. The moisture can make the pavement slippery, and visibility can be erratic. Because fog can gather in low-lying areas, you can easily drive into a space where visibility is only a few feet or less. Be aware of this, and if you see an area of thick fog ahead, slow down to a crawl before going into the foggy area.

The Mini's optional fog lights are helpful, but are not a cure-all. They do focus the light beams on the pavement immediately ahead, rather than reflecting it off the fog, but do not penetrate the fog any more than regular beams. In any case, make sure you've turned off your high beams. If your Mini is equipped with the optional high-intensity taillights, turn them on so the cars behind you can see you better.

In snow and ice conditions, caution is critical. Not only is it easier to lose control of the car, but if you slide off the road in cold weather, even survival can become a challenge. One of the most dangerous times to be driving is when the temperature hovers right around zero. Melted snow or rain on the pavement can easily turn to ice, especially on bridges and overpasses. Keep your speed down, and be very sensitive to any feeling of loss of control.

Again, make changes in speed and direction cautiously and smoothly. If there is snow on the road, you are generally better off driving with at least one front wheel in the snow because the grip will be better there than on the portion of the pavement cleared by the wheels of other vehicles. If you do need to put on chains, of course they go on your front wheels, since these are both your power and your steering wheels.

Above all, don't be in too much of a hurry to complete your journey if the weather turns unexpectedly bad. Be willing to get off the highway and hold up in a restaurant or motel until things get better.

Just be aware that you don't want to get off the main highway unless you are sure you'll be able to find your way to a safe and secure place to stop. In bad weather, the back roads are likely to be less well patrolled than the main highways and the worst place to be is in an uninhabited and unpatrolled area.

Emergency Equipment for your Mini

Even if you're never going to be more than a few miles from home, but especially if you're venturing out on longer tours, you should equip your Mini with some basic equipment to cope with the unexpected. Your stash should include a basic set of repair equipment, and emergency supplies that can be readily assembled and packed where they'll be handy. Put the small equipment in the glove compartment and bigger stuff in one of the rear stowage areas and leave it there. Always check to make sure that everything is in place whenever you head out on the highway. Your basic kit should include the following items.

Never leave home without your cell phone. Buy an extra charger for it that you can leave in the car all the time so you never have to worry about being low on power. Subscribing to an emergency road service, such as available through most major auto insurance companies, and having their telephone number in the car will take care of most roadside emergencies, especially in or near urban centers.

A major credit card, an ATM card, and a telephone credit card are also absolute necessities so that you can pay for a tow or emergency repairs, or make a phone call in rural areas where you can't get cell phone service. In addition, tuck some money in five dollar bills and some

> ### Safety Kit for Your Mini
>
> Cell phone and charger
>
> Emergency road service card
>
> Major credit card and phone card
>
> Small stash of cash and coins
>
> Emergency flashlight and batteries
>
> Highway safety flares or reflectors
>
> Tire pressure gauge
>
> Emergency tool kit, including: multi-point screwdriver, combination pliers, and lineman's pliers, repair wire, duct tape, electrical tape, assorted zip-ties
>
> Tire repair kit and electric air pump
>
> Jumper cables or emergency battery
>
> Work gloves and latex gloves
>
> First aid kit
>
> Emergency blanket
>
> Gallon of drinkable water
>
> High-protein energy bars
>
> Small notebook and pen or pencil
>
> Disposable camera
>
> Emergency CB radio

quarters for the phone in an envelope in the glove compartment. Cash money may be all that's accepted if you need to have your chains installed on the highway or convince a tow truck driver to help you out.

A flashlight is essential for many applications. An emergency light that can plug into your car's power source, plus a handheld flashlight that can be used to check a map, wave at oncoming traffic, or shine into the engine compartment, are both good pieces of equipment to have. Get a flashlight with a plastic case so it won't rust. Those emergency lights that plug into the car are nice, but won't work if your battery runs down.

To protect yourself if you break down in high-traffic situations, you should also have some highway flares or tripod reflectors that can be placed behind the car to warn oncoming drivers of your presence. Any major hardware store or auto supply store will stock a neat kit with these kinds of supplies for your car.

You should have a good tire pressure gauge, available from any auto parts store, in the glove compartment. Check the tires each morning and any time you suspect a tire may be low to make sure the pressure is at, or slightly above, the level shown on the tire safety decal on the driver's door sill of your car.

Even if you are a complete klutz at auto repairs, it's a good idea to have a set of basic tools and some emergency repair supplies tucked in a plastic or canvas tool kit to supplement your standard Mini tool kit.

At the very least, the kit should include combination pliers, lineman's wire-cutting pliers, a flat-head and a cross-head or multi-tip screwdriver, and a medium-size adjustable "crescent" wrench. Supplies including a coil of repair wire, a roll of duct tape, a roll of electrical tape, and a package of various-sized plastic "zip-ties" can be very useful. With these few tools, you—or a helpful good Samaritan with some mechanical ability—can make a variety of stopgap repairs that will at least get you off the highway and to the next point where you can get cellphone service to call for emergency assistance.

A tire repair kit in a pressurized can, and a 12-volt tire inflator should also be part of your emergency kit. These kits are easy to find in catalogs, or at hardware, or auto supply stores. Incidentally, if you do get a flat tire on any heavily-traveled highway or road, don't attempt to repair the flat on the shoulder. Instead, drive to the next exit and get completely out of traffic before attempting a repair. The tire inflator also will be very handy around the race course, where you can use it to pump up your tires to racing pressure.

Jumper cables have long been a staple in emergency kits and probably should be in yours as well. Even at the track or on the show field it is easy to leave a door open all day long when you're in and out of the car frequently, with the interior lights running down the battery. The combination of cold weather and a low battery can mean a car that won't start.

However, if you do include jumper cables in your kit, make sure that you use them properly and with care. With modern electrical systems and the car's various onboard computers, it's possible to do serious harm to the car when trying to jump-start it. Even worse, a bad battery can literally become a bomb, with acid vapor ready to explode with a little spark. If you have to use the cables to start your car or that of a friend, carefully follow the instructions in your owner's manual and on the jumper cable package. If you've got the space, an emergency battery kit, available for about $50 from most parts stores or accessory catalogs, is a better idea and should be a standard piece of equipment in your garage.

If you do have to work on the car in an emergency, whether it's just to put on the tire chains or fix a small problem, it's never especially pleasant. Things you have to grab are often greasy and dirty, not to mention cold and wet. Putting a pair of work gloves and a couple pairs of latex mechanics' gloves, as well as some hand cleaner, in the emergency kit is always a good idea.

Even in high summer, a blanket is a useful piece of emergency equipment, and in winter weather it is critical. You can lay on it to check under the car, wrap up in it to keep yourself warm, or rig a shelter to keep off the sun. A standard wool or polyprop blanket in the car also can serve a variety of non-emergency uses, like that impromptu picnic, as well as being available for the more desperate survival challenges.

A small first aid kit is also a good idea. You can't do major surgery, but you can prevent it by treating small cuts and scrapes properly so that they don't get infected. Add headache remedies and suntan lotion for comfort on long days at the track.

If you're going to be driving outside of urban areas, and especially if you're driving in very hot or very cold conditions, a gallon of water that can be used for drinking or put in the radiator is worth having in the car. A day's worth of calories for every passenger in the form of high-protein energy bars is worth tucking in. Even if you're not stranded, hunger or thirst can ruin an otherwise nice trip.

You should have a small notebook, a pen or pencil, and an accident check list tucked in your glove compartment. In case of an accident, you'll need to get the name, address, driver's license number, tag number, and insurance contact information for any other drivers involved with you in an accident, as well as the names, addresses, and phone numbers of witnesses. Keeping a small disposable camera in the glove compartment also is a good idea so you can shoot pictures of the accident scene and the cars involved for use if any legal or insurance claims arise later.

If you're going to be out in the boondocks or up in the mountains, you might also want to get an emergency CB radio, usually less than $50 at electronics stores, for when you're out of cell phone service areas. A CB radio can be used to radio the state highway patrol, which monitors channel 9, or truckers on the road, who monitor channel 19, in areas where a cell phone won't pick up a signal.

Get Off the Beaten Track

We spend way too much time on the main roads and limited-access highways. Use the capabilities of your MINI to get off the beaten track once in awhile. Take a look at a map and figure out if there is any other way to get to your destination besides the main highway, or just take a map and lay out an interesting route for a Sunday drive. There is lots of scenary out there, small towns that still reward the adventurous traveler, and curving back roads that will make you happy you own a MINI. Life's too short to waste it on the interstate.

Part Four

Competitive Motoring

We hope by this point, you've discovered how much fun it can be to drive your MINI fast and well on backroad tours, on autocross courses, or at track days. Either that, or you are interested enough in learning how to improve and drive the new MINI that you're reading the book all the way through before you actually go out and play with your car.

Either way, in this section we will describe the various types of competitive activities that will allow you to really challenge yourself as a MINI driver.

In addition, we will suggest upgrades to your car to make it perform even better, especially in competitive events. Though the upgrades we'll be suggesting may provide better handling and performance at the expense of a little comfort, none of them will make the car less usable or less safe on the street.

We'll also build on what you've already learned about driving well by offering some further tips in this part of the book on autocrossing, and on racing wheel-to-wheel with MINIs and other cars on the race track.

Chapter Seventeen

When Going Faster Becomes a Passion

*T*aking your MINI out on a road race course for club track days, or going autocrossing as a novice, as we've noted, is a great way to learn more about your car's capabilities and improve your own driving skills. If you've done it, you've probably discovered how much fun the MINI is to drive harder than you can safely do on the street.

But now, perhaps you're starting to wonder just how good you are compared to other drivers. If you're on the autocross course, you're starting to look at your lap times in comparison to other drivers, rather than just using your times to see if you're improving. If you've been out for track days, perhaps you're starting to enjoy overtaking other cars, and beginning to wonder how you would fare in a real race.

If so, you should consider moving up to the next level of MINI motoring. Maybe you're ready to start competing, rather than just participating.

Class Competition in SCCA Autocross

Running in the street stock class at SCCA regional autocross events is certainly a great way to spend a weekend day and burn off a little rubber. But there's much more to this sport than just seeing how fast you can get your street car around a set course in one of the local parking lots.

If you discover you enjoy autocross competition, national SCCA autocross events, such as this one at Beaverrun Motorsports Park in Pennsylvania in 2004, bring drivers from all over the country to compete for national points. *Picture by Fred Voit ActionPhotos*

Part of the fun of competition is to tailor your car to your own preferences, exploring the differences that modifications can make within the limits of the rules. If you're getting to the point where you're doing about as well as the other newbies in their street cars, then perhaps you're ready to consider modifying your MINI to run in the street touring, or even the street prepared or street modified, classes.

If you've already gone autocrossing, you probably ran in the "stock" or "street" class, which only allowed changes to the air filter, front sway bar, shocks, the exhaust system back of the catalytic converter, and wheels and tires. That doesn't begin to scratch the surface of modifications available to you, and doesn't even allow many of those that we've discussed so far.

If you're prepared to move up into the recently-introduced SCCA "street touring" (STS for the Cooper and STX for the Cooper S) class, there are a number of other things that you can do to your car that will not only give you better handling and power on the track, but also improve the car's performance on the street, without giving up much in terms of driving ease or riding comfort.

For example, in streeet touring you're still required to run street tires with a 140 or higher tread wear rating, but you can mount wheels up to 7.5 inches wide. You can also install the improved air intake discussed in Part Three of this book. In addition you can make all the changes to the chassis discussed in that section, including replacing springs, shocks, sway bars, and camber plates (which we'll discuss in here in Part Four). You can also install a high-performance header—which we'll also discuss in this section—as long as it's emission-legal (which means on the MINI that it must include a catalytic converter). Finally, you can even remove some of the interior appointments, including the radio and air-conditioning system, and you can substitute race seats, and install a lighter battery.

If you want to go further than that, the street-prepared class for Coopers and street-modified class for Cooper Ss allow almost unlimited modifications. However, be forewarned, these classes are terrific opportunities for pushing a highly-modified MINI close to its limits, so winning a trophy can be an expensive proposition. Many owners in this class spend several times the value of their original car on modifications and don't expect to also be able to use them on the street.

If you're going to be spending money on your MINI mods, then it's probably also the right time to get serious about improving your technique, which means taking a good autocross class. Many of the regional SCCA clubs offer autocrossing training, especially during the months between the official season. Check with your own SCCA club to see what may be available in your region.

There is also at least one commercial company, the Evolution Performance Driving School (www.autocross.com/evolution/) that offers multiple-day classes at tracks all over North America during the year. They teach basic and advanced autocross techniques using specialized equipment and professional instructors and get great reviews from experienced autocrossers.

On-Track Time Trials

If you enjoy running your car on a set course against the clock and feel like three or four one-minute autocross runs in a day isn't enough, but don't relish the thought of putting your shiny MINI at risk by racing against other cars, then the SCCA program of Solo I time trials may be just the thing for you. A similar time-trial program has recently been introduced by the National Auto Sports Association (NASA), called the NASA TT (for Time Trials) program.

These events are run on regular race courses throughout North America during the year. They're like Solo II autocrosses in that you run by yourself against the time clock, and the class winners are determined by the best lap times achieved. However, they're like track racing in that the course is actually a complete race track, which might be as long as two to three miles. In Solo I and NASA TT, a typical lap time will be in the range of two to three minutes but the cars reach considerably higher speeds during a circuit of the track than are possible on a Solo II parking lot course.

On the downside, time trials are more expensive and involve more risk to you and the car than Solo II, but the experience makes a good stepping-stone to full road racing. In most organizations, you'll need all the safety equipment required in road racing.

Required safety equipment for SCCA Solo I typically includes a protective roll cage and five-point seat belts for both driver and passenger in the car, and some organizations will require a fuel cell in place of the gas tank. In addition, to race in Solo I you'll need a flameproof racing suit as well as flameproof shoes and gloves, and an automobile racing helmet. NASA TT safety requirements are somewhat less stringent, but nevertheless emphasize safe car preparation.

Because of the costs of renting road-racing tracks, entry fees are substantially higher than for Solo II autocross events, though the cost per minute of racing isn't that much different; you just get many more minutes at speed in these events. To the entry fees, you need to add the cost of fuel, an oil change after every second weekend, and a new set of tires every five or so weekends.

But there's little to replace the adrenaline rush of keeping focused at speeds well over legal highway limits while trying to hit the apex of each corner exactly right so that you can beat your competition by that elusive tenth of a second. Time trials definitely take track days to a completely new level.

For more information on SCCA Solo I activities, check the national SCCA website www.scca.com and your regional SCCA organization. For more information on NASA TT programs, check www.NASA-TT.com.

Organized Track Day Programs

Track days can be a fun and relatively safe way to enjoy your car's speed and handling capabilities. Driving around a race track, at speeds sometimes in excess of legal road limits, is a pretty cool thing to do.

However, if you continue to do it with no real goals in mind, and no help in meeting those goals, it's as if you were out by yourself simply whacking a ball around a golf course, without worrying about whether it got into the holes, much less how many strokes you took each round. You'd never do that if you wanted to master the game of golf. You'd get a pro to give you lessons, critique your swing, and help you learn which club to use.

By the same token, you wouldn't expect to become a better driver, much less a competitive race driver, without any more help than following other people around a race course? But there is help available, even after you've completed an advanced driving skills course.

At least one organization, the National Auto Sports Association (NASA), offers an excellent program called the High Performance Driving Events (HPDE) at tracks in northern and southern California, Arizona, and Nevada. These programs offer opportunities for novice drivers to work with experienced racers to improve their driving skills on the track.

The HPDE program divides drivers into four groups, ranging from first-timers through experienced track drivers, with the instructors deciding when you're ready to move up to the next class.

In Group One, you have an instructor riding with you, or you are following an instructor, with lots of off-track time with the instructor to discuss finding the fast line, getting through corners, shifting and braking. Passing on track is very limited.

In Group Two, you drive without direct supervision, but are still given critiques on your technique, and passing is permitted in specified areas of the track. In Group Three, speeds increase, the number of cars on the track increases, and passing is permitted in most areas.

By the time you are judged to be capable of driving in the top level, Group Four, your skills are at nearly at the point of racing. Passing is permitted everywhere on the track, but under the standard practices of any amateur racing group. The only difference between Group Four driving and actual racing is that you aren't trying to beat anyone over a specified number of laps, so there are no grouped starts, or sprints for the finish line.

Progress from Group One to Group Four typically occurs over a number of track events, so each driver can move ahead at his or her own pace as the driver acquires more experience and skill. NASA also sponsors the International Touring Car Series, and is currently working with BMW CCA on racing events with classes that include the MINI Cooper S, so graduates of the HPDE activities can move up to wheel-to-wheel racing within NASA if they wish.

For more information about NASA HPDE, check the NASA website: www.NASAProRacing.com. Also, check with race tracks in your region to find out if similar programs are offered at their tracks by other organizations.

Club Racing—Almost the Real Thing

When you're ready to get really serious and want to find out what it's like to cope with the added variable of other cars on the track with you at the same time, each trying to hit the same apex that you want, you'll be ready for wheel-to-wheel racing. MINIs are regularly raced in Sports Car Club of America, and BMW Car Club of America Club Racing. MINIs are even professionally raced in the Grand Am Cup Series.

Each of these organizations has defined classes that allow you to race with a MINI that is close to its original showroom specifications, or modify your MINI to run in relatively more unlimited classes. The Spec Classes are a great place to start racing without finding a deep-pockets sponsor or breaking your piggy bank. In the words of the BMW CCA rules, spec racing places "the emphasis on driving skills while offering a finite capital expenditure" by racing cars with strictly limited modifications that are still street legal and very close to stock condition.

BMW CCA Club Racing

The BMW Car Club of America runs an excellent club racing program that includes specific classes for the MINI Cooper and MINI Cooper S. This program offers competitive wheel-to-wheel racing with cars grouped by their performance capabilities so it can be a great way to experience real track racing.

To make it as easy as possible to get your feet wet, BMW CCA runs organized race driving schools all over the country. All you need to participate in one of the schools is a driver's helmet and a safe street MINI (or other BMW). (For more information click on "Getting Started" on www.bmwccaclubracing.com.)

In the Club Racing program, the BMWCCA has established Spec Classes for both MINI Cooper and MINI Cooper S models. These classes allow MINI owners to race against other MINIs in an active racing schedule at race tracks in all regions of North America.

In the MINI Spec Classes, relatively few items must be, or in fact can be, changed from the car as it came from the showroom, so racing preparation can be done for much less than most owners spend to modify their cars for the street.

Safety preparations are mandatory. The car must be equipped with a bolt-in roll cage, five-point safety harness, headlamp covers and window net. Though gauges can be added, nothing in the interior can be removed, including the rear seat and carpeting. As a result, there's no reason why a car can't be used for street transportation and racing.

Drivers are also required to have full safety clothing to race, including a Snell-

Brad Davis races his MINI Cooper S in SCCA Show-room Stock and BMW CCA MINI Spec events on East Coast tracks. In these classes, it is the skills of the driver that provides the competitive edge, since there are very strict limits on car preparation. *Photo by Henry Kowalski.*

approved auto racing helmet, and fireproof racing suit, gloves, and shoes.

Tires, wheels, shocks, springs, rear sway bar, and rear control arms must be changed to race-grade products, and the brands, types, and sources for these modification components are specified in the rules.

The car can be mechanically upgraded to improve performance, but only with the addition or substitution of specific components. These allowed (but not required) modifications include drilled brake rotors, cold air intake, cat-back exhaust system, and power steering pump heat shield. The stock front seats also can be replaced with racing seats.

Owners are permitted to overhaul the engine, but boring and machining can only be done within specified tolerances. To insure that racing advantage comes from driving skills, rather than from the size of the owner's check book, no other changes can be made to the car. The supercharger pulley can not be changed, nor can the ECU be remapped, and exhaust headers can not be replaced.

By agreement between BMW CCA and series sponsors Tire Rack and MiniMania, all required modifications and some of the optional modifications must be purchased from those vendors, but substantial refunds from the sponsors are available to racers as soon as they've had the car inspected by BMW CCA and a logbook has been issued for the car.

As a result of these strict limitations, it is quite possible to put a MINI on the track for BMW CCA Club Racing for just over $6000 in modifications. For that you get all the fun, excitement, and Monday morning bragging rights of taking your car on the track for wheel-to-wheel racing competition. and if you're willing to take the time to remove the roll cage in between events—driving a car with a roll cage without a helmet on isn't safe—you'll still be able to drive your MINI on a daily basis (with or without your competition numbers on the doors).

Short of having the engine rebuilt, no competitor can spend more than about $2200 to add the few permitted performance modifications that can be made to the car within the rules, and none of these modifications will make the car any less usable on the street.

To download a copy of the current BMW CCA Club Racing MINI Spec rules, go to the "Series Information" page at www.BMWCCAClubRacing.com and click on "Spec Mini rules."

If you find that you enjoy racing and want to devote more resources to the hobby, other BMW CCA racing classes, including stock, prepared, and modified classes, allow you to further upgrade the performance of your MINI and compete in faster and more challenging classes as your driving skills improve.

If this sounds like it may be your cup of tea, the best way to find out is to enroll in one of the many excellent BMW CCA Club Racing drivers' schools that are offered at tracks all over the United States and Canada. Completion of a BMW CCA racing school is the first prerequisite to racing with the BMW car club, so it's where everyone starts.

Once you've completed the school you can decide if you want to invest the money to upgrade your MINI to the club's standards for MINI spec racing or stock classes. More information on the BMWCCA club racing programs is at www.bwmccaclubracing.com.

BMW Car Club of America — MINI Spec Class
Required and optional components and approximate costs

Required Safety Modifications, Any Supplier

Bolt-in rollcage	$850
Driver's safety harness	200
Window net	60
Driver's safety wear	800
Approximate cost of required safety modifications	**$2000**

Required Modifications, MiniMania Components

Adjustable rear control arms	$500
Rear sway bar	250
Headlight covers	50
Total cost of required MiniMania package	**$800**

Required Modifications. Tire Rack Components

17x7.5 inch wheels	$1472
215/45-17 tires	920
Springs	160
Front and rear shocks	912
Total cost of required Tire Rack package	**$3522**
Approximate cost of required modifications	**$6105**

Permitted Performance Modifications

Cold air intake	$200
Cat-back exhaust	700
Drilled front brake rotors	360
Drilled rear brake rotors	300
Driver's race seat	500
Hood pins	50
Power steering pump heat shield	50
Approximate cost of permitted modifications	**$2160**

Note: Component lists are from 2004 MINI-Spec rules. Prices shown are retail, as of December 2004. Prices for Tire Rack components are discounted to racers by about 30 percent, with the rebate paid when the customer is issued a BMW CCA Club Racing Logbook. Prices for MiniMania-supplied components are discounted by about 20 percent, with rebate paid when the BMW CCA Logbook is issued.

Sports Car Club of America Club Racing

The Sports Car Club of America (SCCA) is the largest and oldest racing organization in the country with an amateur club racing program. It offers competition at major tracks in all parts of the United States in the same way as the BMW CCA does, but with cars of all manufacturers eligible to participate.

In the same manner as in BMW CCA club racing, cars are classed by their level of preparation and performance capability, so it is possible to compete at SCCA events in a car that is very close to showroom stock condition. SCCA racing classes and preparation rules are very similar to SCCA autocross classes. These classes, and preparation rules, are documented in the SCCA's General Competition Rules, known as the GCRs

Though many SCCA club racing competitors compete in purpose-built cars at a near-professional financial level, the entry-level Stock Class is designed to allow new racers to participate without making much more than safety changes to their car. It is certainly possible for you to compete in wheel-to-wheel races through the SCCA on a budget that doesn't require bottomless pockets or a wealthy sponsor.

Just as with the BMW CCA program, you have to go through a training and qualification program before you can venture out on the track for wheel-to-wheel competition. SCCA requires proof of good physical condition with a medical exam, and satisfactory completion of two school sessions in order to earn a provisional novice license that allows you to take part in your first race.

One difference between the SCCA program and the BMW CCA program is that you must have a race-prepared car to participate in an SCCA driving school. That means installing a roll cage, safety harness, and basic safety gear in your car, as well as buying full driver's safety gear before you can begin racing.

Consequently, you'll certainly want to find other means to decide whether wheel-to-wheel racing is for you before making this investment. You can do this by taking part in a BMW CCA driving school or one of the commercial race driving schools , or you may be able to arrange to rent a race car to take the SCCA school, before making the investment to turn your street MINI into a race-capable car.

You'll be classified as a novice until you have safely and satisfactorily completed two races. Complete those requirements and you earn your regional racing driver's license that qualifies you to continue racing in regional SCCA races.

More information on the SCCA programs is available at www.SCCA.com/club/.

Chapter Eighteen

Competition Upgrades for Your MINI

When you get to the point that you want to take your MINI driving to the next level and get seriously involved in autocrossing and track events, you'll need to add some safety gear to the car to meet the requirements of most organizations with which you might run. Also, as you reach a point in your driving ability where you're starting to reach your MINI's limits of acceleration, handling, or braking, you may also want to make some mechanical upgrades to improve the car's performance.

Either way, the aftermarket suppliers have just what you need. In this chapter, we'll discuss means of further increasing your engine's horsepower and response, gaining stopping power and improving the MINI's handling. We will also discuss how you can meet the safety requirements of your racing organization if you've decided you want to take your MINI out onto the track for some serious competitive motoring.

Finding Even More Horsepower

By now, in your desire for more power, you've changed out the air intake, remapped the ECU, replaced the cat-back exhaust system, and replaced the supercharger pulley if those changes are permitted by the group that organizes the events in which you participate. In addition, you may have replaced the spark plug wires, or added a spark booster, and installed a water-to-air intercooler to increase your net horsepower for enthusiastic driving.

Be assured, there are still more parts on the shelf that will help you get the maximum available horsepower out of that sturdy four-cylinder engine under your hood. You can substitute a high-performance camshaft and if you're really serious, replace the cylinder head to improve the engine's ability to breathe. If your car is going to be used just for track or autocross competition, or you're willing to do a little work before big weekends, a high-flow exhaust header and catalyst can give you a solid boost in performance.

High-Performance Camshaft

The M ini engine has what is called a "single overhead camshaft" (abbreviated SOHC). The camshaft is the component on the engine that is connected to the driveshaft by a roller timing chain (it looks like a bicycle chain) and rotates with the crankshaft to cause each of the intake and exhaust valves to open and close at the right times. The M ini uses a single camshaft to control both intake and exhaust valves on all the cylinders, and it is mounted in the top of the engine, so it is called a single overhead camshaft.

The actual camshaft consists of a shaft that runs from the front to the rear of the engine. On this shaft are mounted twelve cams, three for each cylinder. As these eccentrically shaped cams rotate with the shaft, they push on two rocker arms for the two intake valves and a dual rocker arm for the two exhaust valves on each cylinder, causing the intake and exhaust valves to open and close. A high spot on the cam pushes the valve open, and then as the cam continues to rotate, the lower spot allows the spring on that valve to push the valve closed.

As the intake valves open, they allow the air/fuel mixture to enter that cylinder. As the intake valves close, the exhaust valves open, allowing the combustion gases left after the explosion to escape from the cylinder.

By changing the size and shape of the cams, it is possible to change the points at which the valves open and close, how far they open, and the time during which they are open. Consequently, changing the camshaft is a standard way of upgrading the performance of an engine. A camshaft that causes the valves to stay open longer is said to be "hotter"—producing more power—than one that doesn't allow as much time for the fuel/air mixture to enter the cylinder, or the exhaust gases to escape.

The trade-off here is that additional horsepower can only be gained by negatively

affecting the smoothness of the engine operation, especially when idling, so a hot cam is often said to be "lumpy." To some extent, the design of the camshaft also has a negative effect on gas mileage, since more fuel is allowed to enter with each rotation of the engine.

As one might expect, there are several different variations of cams available, with the hottest being very good on the race track, but totally unsuitable for street use. However, there is a middle ground with several aftermarket camshafts that have been engineered to provide better engine

The camshaft for the M ini engine looks like this, with twelve cams machined into the shaft to actuate the intake and exhaust valves. Pictured here is a high-performance cam shaft which has a different cam profile to allow the valves to remain open longer, giving the engine more horsepower, especially at higher rpm.

performance without noticeable negative effects on the smoothness of the engine. These camshafts are ideal for the MINI that is used primarily for street use by an owner who would also like improved performance for occasional track days and autocross events.

To select the one that's right for you, rely on the advice of an established supplier and tell them what your objectives are in replacing the camshaft, as well as what else you've already done to the car. It's possible they may be able to recommend other changes that you can make to increase performance and horsepower before going to the expense of buying and installing a new camshaft. If they think a higher-performance camshaft is the right answer, they should be able to recommend one that will meet your goals.

Replacing the stock camshaft with a high-performance camshaft is an effective way of improving engine performance while still using stock valves and valve springs. This way, engine performance can be improved without the expense of disassembling the motor and changing the cylinder head.

A high-performance camshaft typically is available for the Cooper S for about $500 and for the Cooper for less than $600. In both cases, there is generally a core charge of about $100 which is refunded when the original camshaft is returned to the supplier. Installation should only be undertaken by an experienced professional shop.

High Performance Cylinder Head

The cylinder head is the portion of the engine that channels the fuel-air mixture into the cylinders and the exhaust gases out of the cylinders, and controls the flow of fuel and exhaust with the valves and valve springs that are installed in the cylinder head. The cylinder head also includes the upper portion of the cylinders where the fuel/air mixture is compressed and the explosion takes place that pushes the cylinder downward.

The design of the cylinder head, and the quality of its manufacture determine how easily air can enter the engine and how efficiently exhaust gases can be removed from the engine. The design also determines the pattern of the compression and combustion in the cylinders.

A high-performance cylinder head is illustrated here in two views. The view on the left is looking at the cylinder head from below, which shows the intake and exhaust valves for each of the MINI's four cylinders. The view on the right is the same cylinder head, this time looking at it from the top down, showing the valve springs and the cradles for the cam shaft. The difference between this head and the stock head is in the quality of the machining, and the shape of the passageways, all of which facilitate the flow of the fuel/air mixture and exhaust gases.

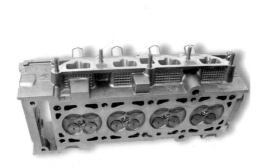

For the owners who want maximum performance from their MINIs while still using them primarily as daily drivers, additional increases in horsepower and torque can be achieved by substituting a high-performance cylinder head.

In high-performance cylinder heads, the passageways through which the air and gases flow are engineered so there is a minimum of obstruction. To further improve flow, the manufacturing process is as precise as possible, and then is finished off by hand-polishing, so that the surfaces of the air and exhaust passages are very smooth to reduce turbulence in the flow. Finally, the shape of the upper portion of the cylinders is altered to change the pattern of combustion in the cylinders and by doing so increase the power produced as the burning mixture expands.

One product that has proven its performance benefits is the Stage 1 Performance Cylinder Head, available through some aftermarket MINI suppliers. Because of the complexity of its design and intricacies of its manufacturing, this cylinder head isn't cheap, but it has been shown to add 20 to 30 horsepower to the engine's performance.

The Stage 1 head sells for about $1900, and there is a $1000 core charge, which is refunded if the original head is returned to the supplier within 30 days. Installation also requires a head gasket kit and new headbolts, which will add about $200 to the costs. Professional installation is required so the total cost will be around $2500.

Exhaust Header

Breathing is still the means to the biggest improvements in horsepower and torque. Air has to get into the engine, and the exhaust has to get out. Because of environmental protection requirements in many states, we've left until last one of the critical links in that path: the exhaust header.

The exhaust header is that set of curly pipes that connects the exhaust side of the cylinder head to the exhaust pipes and muffler. Four pipes coming off the exhaust side of the head, one for each cylinder, channel the exhaust gases from the cylinders into common pipes that flow into a single pipe and into the exhaust system.

On the MINI, the engineers have attached the catalytic converter directly to the bottom of the exhaust header. The cat then attaches to the "cat-back" portion of the system. (In many other cars, the cat may be further back in the system).

The Ultrik exhaust header is a good example of a high-performance aftermarket exhaust header. With its quality manufacturing and smooth-flow design, it measurably improves exhaust flow and consequently horsepower and torque. The Ultrik is built with an integral catalytic converter, but because it isn't stock, it isn't legal for street use in many states. However, since it can be installed fairly easily, it could be put on for track days, and then removed for street use.

The design of the exhaust header can make a big difference in how smoothly exhaust gases flow out of the cylinders. Any constraints on this flow and the pistons have to do more work as they push upward in the exhaust cycle, which means a drag on horspower and torque.

As with many other parts of the engine, manufacturing costs and engineering constraints have prevented MINI engineers from designing the high-quality system that would fully optimize exhaust flow. Fortunately, aftermarket manufacturers have jumped into that gap, making a stainless steel exhaust header that includes a catalytic converter which is a bolt-in replacement for the factory part.

Tests on one of the best versions of this performance component show that replacing the exhaust header can produce a significant increase in torque, especially in the higher rpm range. In practical terms, that can mean better acceleration out of corners and higher speeds on entrance into the straights, which means lower lap times.

Because the catalytic converter is an integral part of the emissions control system on modern cars, in most states it is illegal to remove that portion of the system or replace it with a non-factory substitute. As a result, it isn't legal to replace the exhaust header on MINIs that are going to be used on the street.

However, if you're building a car that is designed primarily for competitive events and isn't used on the street, putting on a high-flow exhaust header is a sensible and relatively inexpensive performance enhancer. If you only use the car occasionally for competition and don't mind doing a little wrench work before the big weekend, the bolt-in design of this system means that it can easily be swapped in for competition and then removed for street use.

Since many of the MINI aftermarket headers include a catalyst, you don't even have to fret about increased emissions. The aftermarket header won't produce any greater emissions out the tailpipe than the stock header.

With a catalytic converter attached, a high-performance exhaust header is available for about $750, and you can install it in your garage with standard tools. A new gasket, costing about $10, will be needed when you make the exchange.

Snappier Response

If you're really getting into doing track days or autocrossing, and haven't considered replacing the clutch and flywheel with a quick-reaction clutch and lightened flywheel as we discussed in the third part of this book, now is the time to consider doing that upgrade. If you can make your downshifts into corners quickly, losing as little time as possible coasting between gear changes, your lap times will improve.

A performance clutch and lightened flywheel is key to this aspect of your driving. For the same reason—improving your performance through the gears—a close-ratio gear kit can help reduce your lap times.

Tilton High-Performance Flywheel and Clutch

If you haven't yet made the change, and are serious about finding every tenth of second that you can, you may wish to consider doing what the pros do and replacing your MINI clutch and flywheel with a Tilton high-performance clutch and flywheel.

The Tilton clutch and flywheel system for the MINI is designed specifically for track use and combines light weight and fast response to reduce time between shifts and provide positive hook-up on acceleration. The parts you see here are, from top to bottom, the two parts of the pressure plate with the finger-like diaphragm springs that keep the clutch engaged, the clutch disc surfaced with high-friction material that connects to the driveshaft and is pushed against the flywheel when the clutch is engaged, and the lightweight flywheel that attaches to the engine crankshaft.

This substitution offers several advantages over stock components and less-expensive upgrades. Going from front to back, the system starts with a light, balanced flywheel weighing only 11 pounds, which means the minimum amount of inertia and quicker response. Behind the flywheel is a smaller-diameter lightweight clutch, which means less weight in the car and a reduction in rotational inertia as with the flywheel.

The clutch disc itself has a cera-metallic surface, which means quick pick-up with no clutch fade over a long race. Finally, manufactured to racing standards by a well-respected racing supplier, this whole system is guaranteed to stand up to racing demand and provide long-lasting performance.

There are some trade-offs with this competition clutch that make it better for track than for street use. First, the Tilton clutch does away with the dual-mass flywheel with which the stock engine is equipped. As a result, your Tilton-equipped MINI will be louder at idle than a stock MINI. But then quiet idling isn't the point on a race car, is it?

Second, the clutch has a much quicker on/off action, which is ideal for race use, but hardly what you would want when you're stuck in stop-and-go traffic. It also will wear out rapidly in normal use, when we often slip the clutch to smooth out driving, such as when parking, backing up, or starting off on an incline. Even in a race car, care must be taken not to slip the clutch when traveling at slow speed through the paddock or loading the car on the trailer.

As you might expect, the Tilton materials and manufacturing quality are going to cost a little more than typical clutch and flywheel upgrades, but the performance and especially the durability in race conditions make it the best choice when you're seeking to be the very best. The full kit, including flywheel, clutch disc, pressure plate, throwout bearing adapter and installation hardware costs about $1500.

Straight-Cut Close-Ratio Gear Kit

When the engineers are selecting gear ratios for a manual gear box, they're generally going for the best gas mileage possible. That means that gears are selected to produce

The Ultrik close-ratio gear set is a good example of the replacement gears that are available to upgrade a Mini for track use. The parts for the upgraded gear train are shown separately in the top image, and assembled in the bottom image. The gear ratios are different from stock, giving up top speeds that would be useful on the highway for the gear ranges that provide optimal torque on the race track. Straight-cut gear teeth provide a more positive engagement to handle higher horsepower, but will be noisier than stock helical gears.

reasonable torque at the lowest possible engine speed, which may not be what you're looking for in a track car. They're also assuming that the average driver may not be all that precise in shifting, so they'll use bevel-cut gears to reduce the possibility of grinding gears when shifting.

In racing, you'll sometimes hear drivers bragging about their "close-ratio" gearbox. They'll also talk about using "straight-cut" gears in the gear box. Ultrik makes a close-ratio straight-cut gear set for the Minis that is exactly the kind of upgrade they're talking about.

The first term—close-ratio gears—describes a gear set that has different ratios than the standard gears that are installed in stock Minis. The purpose of installing a close-ratio gear set is to keep the engine well up in the power band (which as you may remember really starts about 3500 rpm) at the range of speeds common on a road track. It is especially important so that you will have all the torque possible for that all-important part of the turn where you are accelerating, because the car that accelerates fastest out of the corner will be the one that's ahead at the end of the next straightaway.

With this gear box, the engine easily can be kept in the power band at normal racing speeds in all types of corners. To provide equal acceleration out of corners, the Mini with stock gearing would have to have considerably more torque, especially at low engine speeds.

The following table shows the ratios in the stock Cooper S gearbox and those in the Ultrik close-ratio box, and the speed the car is moving at the 7000 rpm redline in each gear. Quick review of this table illustrates the effects of a close-ratio box. With the close-ratio box, the car will be within its best power range across the full range of practical racing speeds, achieving higher speeds in lower gears.

Of course, the racing Mini won't be able to claim as high a top speed as the road Mini—which seems a little counterintuitive. But it's worth remembering that races are

Stock and Close-Ratio Gear Sets
Gear Ratios and Speeds

| | Gear Ratio | | Speed at 7000 rpm | |
	Stock S	Close-Ratio	Stock S	Close-ratio
First	11.418	9.370	43 mph	52 mph
Second	7.176	7.792	68 mph	63 mph
Third	5.399	6.516	91 mph	75 mph
Fourth	4.410	5.323	111 mph	92 mph
Fifth	3.652	4.344	134 mph	113 mph
Sixth	2.984	3.546	164 mph	138 mph

won and lost with acceleration out of the corners and there are few, if any, tracks in the country where a MINI is going to have the space to reach that fabled 160 mph top speed.

The second feature of this competition gear kit is the design of the gears. In a standard box, the gear teeth are cut at an angle to the gearshaft, so that two gear teeth are engaged at any one time. These are called "helical gears." By contrast, "straight-cut" gears have teeth edges that are parallel to the gearshaft. Because of their design, helical-cut gears make less clatter in operation and are smoother.

However, in racing the helical gear is slower to engage than the straight-cut gear. Also, it doesn't transmit power as effectively as a straight-cut gear. Since a race driver should be able to shift more precisely, and gear noise is not an issue, for competition the straight-cut design is preferred.

Because of the noise, most MINI owners who use their cars on the street as well as for competition probably wouldn't enjoy the straight-cut gears in daily use. Close-ratio gears also require higher rev levels for given speeds because of their ratios, so the competition box would deliver much lower mileage and greater engine wear. However, for MINIs that are being built up primarily for track use, competition gears are worth serious consideration because of the competitive edge they provide.

The Ultrik gear kit with the ratios listed above is available for about $3500. Since it requires removal of the gear box and replacement of the gears, installation is best left to a service shop that is experienced in MINI work.

More Stopping Power

"The longer you can go fast, the faster you'll go." If some grizzled old racing or autocross veteran didn't say that, someone should have. One of the basics of racing, whether on a road course or autocross course, is that brakes matter because they allow you to maintain higher speeds longer on the straights before you have to brake for the corner.

On a road course, one of the best ways of getting ahead of your competitor is by out-braking them on the corner. You stay door-handle to door-handle with them down the straight, then wait to hit your brakes until after they do and the corner is yours. On the autocross course, the longer you can stay at top speed before braking for the corner, the faster your time will be around the course.

You can have all the power you want, but if you can't make your car stop more quickly than your competitor, you'll have trouble gaining that competitive edge. It all comes down to having brakes that are better than those of your competitor.

Earlier in this book we recommended fitting your car with 17-inch wheels when you replace the stock wheels, so that you could install a set of competition-grade brakes when you were ready. We also recommended that you upgrade your brake pads and consider upgrading your rotors for both street and track use, so you've already gotten a taste of the difference made by having good, sustained stopping power.

As your driving gets faster, and you start probing the limits of your MINI's stopping ability even after installing upgraded brake rotors and pads, it's time to consider upgrading the brakes. Rest assured that there are a variety of options in the market for you to consider.

The easiest and least expensive brake upgrade is to install high-performance or racing brake pads for track use. Another excellent upgrade is to replace your brake lines for improved pressure. For better performance and quick recovery, you can replace your brake rotors with drilled and slottted brakes. And for the serious performance driver, there are several complete brake systems that incorporate upgraded versions of all these components.

Race-Grade Brake Pads

To gain that competitive edge in braking, the easiest conversion is to a set of high-performance brake pads. Upgrading your brake pads is one of the least expensive means of improving braking performance. Brake pads are an easy replacement to make, as well. Just remove the wheel, release the retainers, slide out the old pads and slide in the new ones. Then replace the retainers and wheel and you're ready to go.

As we discussed in the previous part of this book, Ferodo makes high-performance brake pads in various compounds that have a higher co-efficient of friction than typical street pads do, which means a more effective bite and quicker brake action when you press the brake pedal. Made of a denser compound, they also have less compressability, which improves pedal feel and reduces pedal travel.

Ferodo DS3000 racing brake pads are one example of pads that provide superior stopping power on the track, though not suitable for street use.

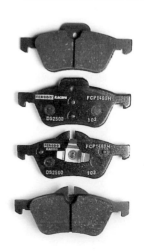

For street/track use we recommended Ferodo DS2500 pads. Engineered to perform well across a wide temperature range, they're suitable for street use, but give excellent performance for occasional track use.

On the track, you need to be able to use your brakes hard ten or fifteen times every lap. As the brakes convert your forward energy into friction and heat, they are going to heat up. Even on longer autocross courses, your brake pads will get hot. For these applications, it is good toknow that the material in your brake pads will maintain its high friction level even as the brakes really begin to heat up.

For the experienced driver who wants to take the next step up for track days and racing, racing-grade brake pads such as the DS3000 pads made by Ferodo, are available for the MINI's front wheels, where more of the braking action takes place.

These pads excel on all the criteria of good brakes: high friction levels, higher initial bite, better performance at high temperatures, and quicker pedal action.

The only drawback is that the DS3000 compound is intended for racing use only. The racing pads don't produce much friction until they are heated up, and then at performance temperatures they are quicker to bite than street pads, so we don't recommend them for street use.

However, all you need to do is upgrade the front and rear pads to a good dual-use level, then swap in the race pads on the front just before you're ready to go out on the course. Fifteen or twenty minutes after the end of the event is all that is required to swap them out, and you'll be ready to hit the road again. A set of excellent Ferodo racing-quality pads for the front wheels is available for about $200.

Stainless Steel Brake Hoses

When we first described how modern hydraulic brakes work, we noted that there is a master cylinder connected to the brake pedal, which pushes fluid down through the brake lines to the slave cylinders at each wheel, which in turn push the pads against the rotors. At the very last point before the fluid gets to the slave cylinders, it passes through four flexible hoses that link the slave cylinders to the solid lines on the chassis. These hoses have to be flexible so that the front wheels can turn for steering, and all wheels can go up and down over bumps and in corners.

These flexible brake hoses, each about 12 inches long, are one weak link in the whole braking system. Stock hoses are made of rubber. As the fluid is pressed into these hoses, under hard use the rubber will expand before the pressure of the fluid builds up in the slave cylinder and pushes the brake pad in.

The MINI engineers incorporated rubber hoses, despite these limitations, for the simple reason that most drivers never use their brakes very hard, and the rubber hoses are less expensive. However, any serious race car builder knows the opposite: the racing driver will use the brakes hard, over and over again, and good stopping power is never too costly.

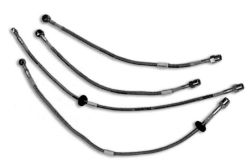

Stainless steel brake hoses, with high-performance polymer liners and braided steel sleeve assure that brake fluid pressure is completely transferred to the calipers.

The alternative for competition and active street use is a flexible brake line made of a high-performance polymer called PTFE in place of the rubber, which is in turn surrounded by braided stainless steel strands to prevent expansion. With these lines, all of the pressure from the master cylinder is transferred to the slave cylinder to apply the brakes.

Braided steel brake lines have become the standard in all racing applications. However, because of their durability and performance they should also be considered for street use by the enthusiastic driver; other than the purchase price and installation time there is no downside to making this substitution.

A set of braided stainless brake lines for all four wheels that fits the standard MINI brake calipers is available for less than $175. Installation is also straightforward and can be done by the home mechanic. However, since brakes are a critical item, and installation does require bleeding the brakes, the installation might be left to a professional brake shop.

Brake Conversion Kits

To make a car go, they say, there's no substitute for cubic inches. To coin another phrase, to make a car stop, there's no substitute for surface area. The bigger the brake rotors and pads, the more effective the brakes are going to be at reining in those horses you've been stuffing under the bonnet.

If you want to maximize your stopping power, you can opt for a complete conversion kit for the front disc brakes—the ones that do most of the stopping—that will meet your needs for high-performance touring and autocross use, for frequent track days, and full-on racing. Of course, the look of custom aftermarket brake calipers and discs peeking through the wheel spokes give your MINI that serious competitive look.

Conversion kits from three different manufacturers—Wilwood, Stoptech, and Brembo—illustrate the range of performance and prices that are available in the MINI aftermarket. All three of these kits incorporate larger-than-stock rotors for increased surface area and better stopping power.

One note that we should make upfront: Because of their larger diameters, these kits can't be used on 15- or 16-inch wheels and won't fit all types of 17-inch wheels. When you consider ordering an upgraded brake kit, check with your supplier to make sure the kit you buy will fit the wheels you have on your MINI.

The Wilwood Big Brake kit is probably the most versatile of these kits as well as being least expensive. The kit will fit the stock 17-inch MINI wheels, as well as most other 17-inch aftermarket wheels. It includes stress-flow forged brake calipers, The calipers on this upgraded system incorporate four pistons to provide more aggressive and consistent stopping power than the standard two-piston calipers on the stock MINI. The brake pads in this kit are "Q" compound polymatrix brake pads for reduced noise and dust levels while providing high resistance to fade, long wear, and low rotor abrasion.

Vented iron rotors of 12.19 inch diameter add stopping power because they have a larger surface area than the stock rotors. Drilled and slotted, they also dissipate heat more readily than stock rotors, as well as dispersing brake dust to avoid irregular build-up of dust on the rotor faces. The kit includes high-quality mounting brackets and fastening hardware and is available for about $900 on some websites.

Stoptech's Big Brake conversion kit is a very popular kit that is a good upgrade for enthusiastic road use, and is frequently seen at MINI track days. The 12.9 inch (328mm) diameter rotors in the Stoptech kit also provide more stopping surface than the stock MINI rotors. In addition, they are vented for cooling and slotted to facilitate removal of brake dust. High-performance brake pads, stainless steel brake hoses and all mounting hardware are included with the kit.

The Stoptech Big Brake conversion kit is available with anodized calipers for about $1700 and with vivid red calipers for about $1900.

At the top of the pecking order is the Gran Turismo Brake system made for MINIs by the Brembo company. Brembo is the brand most often seen on the most expensive performance cars on the road, including Aston Martin, Jaguar, and Ferrari, and this quality is obvious in the MINI kit.

The Stoptech brake kit is a good example of a medium-priced performance brake kit. The kit includes brake rotors, calipers, pads, stainless steel hoses, and mounting brackets, and installation is very straightforward.

The brake rotors on this kit are a two-piece design that employs an aluminum hat to create a "floating disc" to reduce heat transmission and improve stopping power and pedal feel. Rotors are 320x28mm and are both vented and cross-drilled for cooling. Calipers, available in black, red, or silver incorporate four pistons for efficient performance.

In spite of its larger size, the Brembo system is lighter than the stock factory system. The reduction in unsprung weight is important, since it means that the brakes can be upgraded without the loss in horsepower at the wheels that can result from installation of heavier upsized brake systems.

The Brembo Gran Turismo front-brake system is priced at about $2600 from suppliers. Installation can be done by a good tuning shop or an experienced amateur mechanic.

If you do opt to install one of these upgraded systems on your front brakes, we would recommend that you also upgrade the pads and rotors on your rear wheels to keep front-to-rear braking in balance. To complete the look, you can buy specialized spray paint to paint your rear brake calipers to match the front calipers.

Reducing Wheel Spin in Cornering

Perhaps the most important upgrade that we haven't yet suggested is the limited-slip differential. The main reason for not recommending the limited-slip diff until now is because it offers such a comparative advantage that it isn't allowed in any of the autocross stock or street or road-racing spec classes in SCCA or BMW CCA competition.

On the other hand, if you satisfy your urge for spirited driving primarily at open track days or on less-traveled back roads, you may very well want to consider this MINI modification. But let's start at the beginning with why a limited-slip diff is a good thing.

Why Do We Need a Differential, Anyway?

If you go back to basic geometry, you'll remember that the further you are from the center of a circle, the greater the distance around the circle. If you think about your front wheels, you can see that the same principle applies. When you drive around a corner, the outer wheel is going to have to travel further than the inner wheel. That means that the outer wheel has to revolve faster than the inner wheel as you turn.

To accomplish this feat through the power wheels requires some means to put the power to one front wheel while allowing the other wheel to spin freely so that it doesn't scuff and slow you down. This is done with a device that dates back almost as far as the first four-wheel automobile, the differential.

In the simplest terms, the differential is a set of gears that transmits the power from the drive shaft to the wheels. These gears are designed so that the internal "pinion" or "spider" gears attached to each wheel rotate together when the car is going straight and both powered wheels are spinning at the same rate. However, when the car goes around a corner, the spider gears can spin at different rates to allow one of the wheels to spin at a different speed than the other. (For more information on how a differential actually does this, www.howstuffworks.com/differential.htm provides an excellent animated explanation of the inner workings of the differential.)

> **Differential**
> A gear system between the drive shaft and powered wheels that permits the outer driving wheel to turn faster than the inside wheel when the car is turning, to prevent skidding and tire scrub.

The problem with this set-up is that the power is always divided equally between the wheels. However, since the gearing of the differential allows one wheel to rotate at a different speed than the other, the actual power applied to the pavement at each wheel depends on how much grip that wheel can get. If, for any reason, one of the wheels has less grip than the other, the torque may be too much for that wheel and it can break loose and begin to spin.

This can happen in regular driving conditions if one wheel hits an icy or slippery patch, especially when starting up, when a significant amount of torque is required to get the car underway. Under these circumstances, the wheel with the least grip starts to spin and you get nowhere. At that point, you'd be happier if the wheels were locked together, since some power would still get to the wheel with more grip and you'd be able to get out of the slippery spot.

In racing, a similar thing can happen on hard cornering. As the car leans away from the inside of the corner and the weight transfers to the outside wheel, the inside wheel doesn't press as hard on the pavement. This will have the same effect as if the pavement under that inside wheel was more slippery than the pavement under the outside wheel. Take enough weight off a powered wheel, and the wheel will begin to spin.

In racing, what this means is that with a regular open differential, the amount of torque that can be applied to the wheels will be limited by the cornering speed. Exceed the cornering limits and the inside wheel will start to spin.

Once the inside wheel starts to spin, all you can do is back out of the throttle until the car gets more weight on the wheel and the torque being applied to the wheel decreases. Then the spinning tire will regain its grip and get you around the corner, but much slower than you might have wanted.

Limited Slip Differentials

To overcome this limitation, racers first developed differentials with internal (spider) gears designed so that they could only spin at different rates for a short time before an internal mechanism caused them to lock together, putting power back to both wheels. These "locking differentials" or "lockers" were quite effective, but jarring in their operation and not particularly useful for anything except racing.

More recently, racing engineers have developed "limited-slip" differentials (LSD). Several types of LSDs are available for the MINI. The simplest is a device that can be installed in a regular differential, effectively converting it into an LSD. A second uses multiple floating spider gears to transfer power away from a spinning wheel. A third incorporates a hydraulically-actuated clutch mechanism operating on the spider gears.

The Phantom Grip is one example of the simple device that can be installed in the existing differential. This component consists of two disc plates with springs between them, constructed so that the faces of the plates press against the spider gears to constrain slippage under moderate acceleration. In racing and autocrossing, this action is increases exit speeds out of corners. Under hard straight-line acceleration, the disc plates pivot to lock the spiders completely, so that both wheels exert equal power on the road.

The Phantom Grip is available with standard springs that work effectively for occasional track or autocross events while still providing smooth operation for day-to-day driving. For the owner who uses his or her MINI primarily for racing, race-quality springs can be specified, though the race-quality version can be jerky in daily driving.

The Phantom Grip sells for about $400. The race springs add about $40.

The more common, though more expensive, approach is to replace the existing differential with a differential that incorporates an integral limited slip mechanism. The Quaife differential is perhaps the most well-known of these types among racing drivers.

The Quaife unit is a type called "automatic torque-biasing differential" (ATD). It incorporates a set of floating planetary gears that transmit varying torque to the wheel with traction depending on the difference in wheel spin between the two wheels. The result is smooth, pro-active operation that puts more continuous power to the pavement through the corners. One drawback of this style is that it weighs more

The Phantom Grip is a simple device made of two plates with springs in between that exert pressure against the pinion, or spider, gears inside the differential to assure that a portion of the power in high-speed turns is always transferred to the non-slipping wheel.

than other styles of LSD.

Quaife makes a differential specifically for the MINI Cooper S. Because of its smoothness, it is very effective for the MCS that is used as a daily driver, but still raced or autocrossed seriously. The Quaife LSD sells for about $1200.

For the serious racer who prefers less weight and inertia than the Quaife differential, a slightly more expensive Salisbury-clutch LSD is available. In a Salisbury clutch-type LSD, when one wheel tries to spin faster than the other, hydraulic action press the clutches against the spider gears, transmitting a portion of the power to the wheel with grip.

The Salisbury LSD can easily handle up to 300 horsepower, enough to satisfy the most serious MINI racer, though it isn't as appropriate as the Quaife for street use. This high-performance racing LSD sells for about $1400.

The Quaife limited-slip differential is a completely self-contained LSD that replaces the stock differential in the MINI Cooper S. It is an excellent, high-quality upgrade for the racer or autocrosser who plans to race at a level above the Mini Spec or Street Touring classes, but is still smooth enough for street driving.

For the racer or autocrosser who drives a MINI Cooper in a non-supercharged competition class, a limited-slip differential is manufactured for the five-speed transmission. This replacement is manufactured to racing-quality specifications, but offers smooth operation that makes it ideal for the dual-use driver.

An added benefit of this differential for the Cooper is that it can be supplied with a final drive of your choice, providing different choices for short- or long-track use. This LSD is supplied with a 3.71:1 final drive as stock, and is available in 4.29 and 4.54 ratios as well, though these changes require adding a spider (pinion) gear. This high-quality LSD for the MINI Cooper sells for around $2000.

Better Cornering Performance

If we haven't been clear enough up to this point, we'll emphasize the point again. Fast times on the track and autocross course, and satisfying jaunts down the backroads, are all about cornering. The faster you can get the car around the corners without losing control, the faster you'll be going when you enter the straights and the better your times will be. Your everyday driving will also be safer and more fun.

We've already discussed basic and advanced improvements to MINI handling to gain an advantage on the corners. These improvements have included better tires, lighter wheels, shorter and heavier springs, and more responsive shocks. We've also discussed changes to the rear suspension, including stiffer sway bars and adjustable rear control arms. Nevertheless, there are still a few other modifications that will provide

small but significant improvements in your MINI's handling. These components come under two categories: camber/caster plates, and suspension bushing kits.

Front Camber/Caster Plates

The MINI's ability to put power to the pavement through turns and its ability to steer and turn into corners responsively is determined by the "camber" and "caster" of the front wheels as well as the back wheels.

As we explained earlier, camber is the angle between the side of the wheel and a vertical line at right angles to the pavement. This angle determines how much of the tread will be in contact with the pavement, especially under cornering conditions when the weight of the car is pressing down on the wheel, or lifting up on it.

In racing, if you have the ability to change camber, you will want to set the front camber so that the tire leans in just a little bit. This is said to be negative camber, though the angle may be only a degree or less from vertical. With negative camber, the full width of the tread will still be in contact with the pavement when the wheel is unweighted.

Caster is the angle of the line around which the wheel turns, relative to a vertical line. Think of the fork on your old bicycle. If you remember, it slanted backwards from the bottom to the top, which kept the wheel going straight without much steering pressure. Since the angled front wheel was so effective in keeping your bike going in a straight line, you could even ride "no-hands" and still keep going straight.

Adjustable front camber/caster plates for the MINI, such as those shown here, replace the factory upper strut tops and allow accurate adjustment of the camber and caster of the front wheels in order to fine-tune suspension handling and steering response.

The principle is the same on your Mini. A slight caster angle is desirable for normal driving, because it causes the wheel to come back to straight after a turn while the steering wheel slips through your fingers. This also makes long-distance driving easier, since you don't have to be constantly adjusting the steering to keep the car going in a straight line.

If you think of your bicycle again, you can also visualize that when you turned the wheel, the tire tended to roll on to its side, producing what you now know should be called increased camber.

However, in racing it would be easier to steer your Mini into the turns if it had a smaller caster angle (the line about which the wheel turns would be more vertical) than would be desirable for road driving. This would also keep camber changes to a minimum when the wheel is turned.

Consequently, serious racers want to have the ability to adjust camber and caster in order to fine-tune suspension handling and steering response. If the car is likely to be used on the street, it would also be nice to be able to put the adjustments back to stock after track use. To meet these objectives, several aftermarket suppliers have introduced camber/caster plates that replace the factory strut tops and enable easy adjustment of both camber and caster.

The aftermarket camber/caster plates have two purposes: First, they allow you to fine-tune your suspension adjustment so the front wheels have exactly the right camber and caster for good cornering on the track. Second, they allow you to change back and forth between competitive caster/camber angles for racing and more comfortable caster/camber angles for street use.

These plates are installed in place of the tops of the strut towers, and hold the upper mounts of the kingpins to which the wheel is fastened and around which the wheel turns. All you need to do to adjust the camber and caster is place the wheels on alignment turntables so they can turn easily, loosen and readjust the camber and caster angles, then tighten up the plates. You don't even have to jack up the vehicle to make the adjustment.

Two versions of camber/caster plates are available, one version for use with coil-over shocks, and the other for use with the separate shock and spring set-up. Either way, the cost of the plates is about $500. Installation is pretty straightforward, but you will probably want the assistance of a good race tuning shop to help you get the correct camber and caster angles dialed in and marked for racing and street use.

High-Performance Suspension Bushings

There are a number of points at which the chassis of the car is connected to the wheels. These include the front wishbones, steering rack, trailing arms, control arms, and anti-roll bars. The problem is that at each of these points one part must move relative to another part as the car goes over bumps, as weight shifts in turns, and as the wheels turn relative to the body.

If the metal parts were simply connected to each other at these movement points, they would soon wear out and break. Even worse, every time they moved, the pieces would rub across one another, creating noisy rattles and squeaks, and transmitting road noise directly into the car.

To solve this problem, auto engineers put "bushings" in between the moving parts, so the metal pieces don't come directly in contact with one another. In the MINI that is designed for typical street and road use, these bushings are made of a fairly soft rubber-like material. This is a good thing, since the bushings soften the ride while effectively reducing sound transmission and shake. (Auto engineers collectively refer to these bad things as "noise, vibration, and harshness" or "NVH.")

However, as we've noticed, a soft, quiet ride is often the antithesis of good handling and speed on the track, and such is the case with the bushings. The soft bushings are very flexible, so the car's handling and turning aren't as precise as the competitive driver will want.

Bushing
A sleeve, usually removable, placed in a bore to act as a bearing surface. Suspension bushings use rubber or other compressible material to provide a cushion between mounting points and supports.

To reduce flex without compromising noise suppression, serious competitors usually replace the soft bushings with polyurethane bushings. The material in these bushings is significantly less flexible than the rubber that is normally used, providing a much greater feeling of control in steering and handling.

Powerflex polyurethane bushings, one excellent brand, are available to replace each of the rubber bushings in the suspension. Prices vary from around $30 for the anti-roll bar and steering rack mounts, to $40 for the rear trailing arms, $70 for the front wishbone, and $160 for the eight pieces required for the rear control arms.

If you want to completely control the flex in the rear suspension for racing and serious track activities, you may wish to go one step further and replace the rear trailing arm bushings, which control rear suspension movement, with high-performance solid rear trailing arm bushings. Solid bushings precision-machined to exacting tolerances aren't cheap, at $495 a pair, but they are the final step in upgrading the MINI suspension to racing quality.

Polyflex bushings, shown above, provide necessary suspension isolation, but aren't as soft as standard rubber bushings, so they improve the responsiveness of handling and steering on the MINI. Replacing the standard bushings on the rear trailing arms with machined bushings, shown below, is the final step in upgrading the MINI suspension for racing.

Safety Items for the MINI

If you're planning to race your MINI in one of the growing number of organizations that sanction specific classes for MINIs, then you'll be required to install some basic safety equipment. The minimum required in club racing includes roll-over protection, driver safety harness, window net, and headlamp covers.

Roll-over Protection

The starting point is a proper race roll bar to protect you, and your passenger, in the event of a roll-over. For complete protection, especially in a MINI that is being built specifically for racing, you may want to go to a full roll cage that provides greater roll-over protection and bars across the doors that protect against impact from the side. (BMW CCA requires a roll cage.)

Several alternatives are available. At a minimum for racing in most organizations, you'll want a basic bolt-in roll bar that can be installed using supplied back-up plates and grade-five mounting hardware. This set-up provides good protection in the event of a roll-over and can be removed when you're not actively campaigning the car. Even with this style installed, you still have access to the back seats for street use.

Two styles are available, one for cars with and one for cars without a sun-roof. The complete set-up is only about $350, which is a reasonable price for added roll-over protection, and wouldn't be out of place in a MINI that is used primarily as a street car. The bolt-in rear roll bar is approved for SCCA racing.

An upgraded version of the roll-bar style of protection includes a diagonal brace for better protection and a harness bar at shoulder height to which the shoulder harnesses are fastened. This version can be used only on cars without sun-roofs, but is available in a design that allows you to leave the roll bar installed but unbolt the diagonal and harness braces when you want to use the back seat. This is a desirable design for about $490.

A third style of roll bar has the rear diagonal brace and harness bar welded into the structure for better structural rigidity. The drawback of course is that the rear seat is not accessible when the roll bar is installed. Available for MINIs without sunroofs, this alternative costs about $500.

For complete protection, especially in serious racing competition, a full roll cage, with supports at the front and sides of the cabin and with bars that go across the doors for side-intrusion protection, is the best option. A well-designed roll cage providing full protection for the driver and co-driver, is available that can easily be bolted in without any welding required.

In this design, the diagonal cross brace and harness bar behind the front seats are welded in, so the back seat is pretty much unusable. However, the door bars do unbolt to provide easier entry when the car isn't being raced. The full roll cage is available for both sunroof and non-sunroof cars for about $850.

It's important to note, though it may seem counter-intuitive, that a roll cage is not

This is a good example of the bolt-in style roll cage which is legal for most racing organizations. The cross brace to which the safety harnesses are fastened, and the diagonal brace for structural integrity are welded in. Note the installation of a fire extinguisher system.

a good idea in a car that's being driven on the street. The reason is that the roll cage adds lots of hard surfaces on the interior of the car for you to hit in the event of an accident on the street.

When you're driving on the street, you're not going to be wearing your safety helmet, and you probably won't want to put up with fastening the five-point harness every time you get in, so you have nothing to protect your head from impact, or to hold your body firmly in the seat and keep it from being thrown against the bars.

Nevertheless, it is possible to install a bolt-in roll cage just for a few race weekends a year, and then remove it for street use, since installation and removal take less than half-a-day of work and no special mechanical skills.

Seat Harnesses

Pretty much every racing organization will require five-point seat harnesses for the driver. Not only do these harnesses provide protection in an accident, keeping the driver (and passenger if also belted in) from being thrown about the interior, or worse, being partially ejected from the car, but they also help stabilize you when you're driving enthusiastically.

The "five-point" term refers to the fact that these harnesses have a belt over each shoulder, generally fastened to the roll bar or cage, a seat belt fastened to the floor on both sides of the seat, and an anti-submarine belt that fastens to the buckle and to the

floor in the center front of the seat. This fifth belt prevent the lap belts from rising under heavy braking or collisions and prevents the wearer from sliding forward under the seat belts.

A full five-point seat harness from a manufacturer like Sparco, one of the best-known harness suppliers, sells for about $200, plus another $10 to $15 for installation hardware. It is worth emphasizing that seat belts should be installed by a specialist with racing experience, since a badly-installed harness system can be worse in some types of accidents than if the driver weren't belted in at all.

Finally, most race sanctioning organizations require that the car have a window safety net. When you're racing, you'll be required to have your windows down, so that in the event of accident you can get out quickly, or be removed from the car, even if the door is jammed shut. To keep any important body parts, like an arm, or your head, from going out the window in a serious accident, you'll need to have an easily-removable safety net covering the window. A good safety net for your MINI is available for about $60.

Five-point seat belts for racing include shoulder harnesses, a lower anti-submarining belt, and lap belts with a quick-release buckle.

In addition, you'll need clear protective headlight covers to keep glass from getting on the track in the event of a front-end collision. You can use racers' tape if you wish, but clear plastic covers are preferable and can be left on to protect against gravel and stone impact on the highway. These are available for your MINI for about $50.

Driver Safety Equipment

Autocross and track day events require only that the driver wear an automobile safety helmet with a current Snell approval rating. If you move up to wheel-to-wheel club racing, however, you'll need full safety gear. In addition to your "brain-bucket" you'll need a fireproof Nomex racing suit (consisting of either a three-layer suit or two-layer suit and Nomex underwear), fireproof driving gloves, and leather or Nomex-lined driving shoes.

Some of the racing equipment catalogs offer a packaged-deal for novice club racing including suit, gloves, and shoes and helmet for under $500. However, if you want a good-looking outfit so you can really look the part as envious friends watch you slide into your MINI in the paddock, you'll probably be looking at $750 to $1500 for your gear, in addition to your helmet.

Chapter Nineteen

A Primer for Novice Racers

No book can begin to give you all the information you need to be competitive on the race track, much less the experience that makes the real difference. You're going to need to attend several days of race driving school, with classroom sessions interspersed with on-track practice to begin to make any sense of how to get your car around the track safely when competing against several dozen other hotshoes.

Then you're going to need considerable "seat-time" to acquire experience with your car and hone your own skills before you'll consider yourself out of the novice class.

But we can cover the basics so that you've got some idea of what's going on before you get out on the track in competition for the first time. We hope this material will be useful as a review, as well, a year or two from now. And even if you have no intention of ever taking your shiny new MINI out "in anger" as the old-timers say, we might be able to give you a taste of what drivers deal with in competition. At the very least, perhaps we can make your own Sunday afternoon armchair racing a little more interesting.

Preparation is Half the Battle

Any experienced racer will tell you that what happens out on the track between the time the green flag drops and the checkered flag is waved is only a small part of the big picture of racing. In addition, there's the preparation of the car to go racing, things that should be checked before you leave for the track, and things that should be checked before and after every session. While this off-track work won't win you any races, even if well done, it can sure lose them in a hurry if any part of it is poorly done.

Car Preparation

We've reviewed all the go-fast items, and safety components that are required and permitted by most racing organizations, as well as some that may be great for track days and better street performance, but may not be permitted by the organization with which you expect to race. We strongly recommend, however, that while there is still time to make necessary changes, you get a copy of the rules for the club you'll be racing with to make sure that you've done everything that the rules require and haven't done anything that they don't allow.

MINIS race at all competitive levels. Don Racine races this MINI Cooper S in BMW, SCCA, and exhibition events such as the Pittsburgh Vintage Grand Prix, as a test bed to develop new MiniMania competition equipment. *Photo by Walt & Louiseann Pietrowicz.*

Our best advice in planning on how to set up your own MINI for racing is to become a new best-friend with someone who is actively racing with the group already, especially if they're racing a MINI. Amateur race drivers, by and large, are a generous group and will extend a helping hand to anyone crazy enough to join them in this exciting and demanding hobby.

There's no question that you'll need a proper roll cage, properly installed, and a safety harness, also properly installed, before any club will allow you out on the track for a race. Find out whether any other safety gear, such as catch tanks for your radiator, safety clips, or other equipment, is required to protect the track surface during the race.

Before you load up the car to go to the track, you'll want to go through it very carefully, or have an experienced race-prep shop do the work for you. Every nut and bolt that can be reached with a wrench needs to be checked to make sure it's tight. Seventy miles an hour at low rpm on the highway is very different from speeds that will go over 100 and revs that are going to be kept near the readline for half an hour or so, and it's amazing how easily a nut can get loosened under that kind of use.

Speaking of hard use, you should plan to change your oil frequently when you're racing the car. Changing your oil after every second or third weekend is not excessive on a race car. Fresh oil is probably the cheapest and most important single thing you can do to keep your car running well.

Check the condition of the engine belt. Since most of us will need the assistance of a shop or experienced mechanic to replace the MINI's serpentine belt, this is not something that can easily be done at the last minute or at the track.

Similarly, check the condition of all the hoses and make sure all the hose clamps are tight. This may be a good time to get your engine cleaned, as well, since it is much easier to spot leaks, worn spots, and loose clamps when the engine compartment is clean.

Check the thickness of the brake pads on each wheel. Once you start driving aggressively, you're going to be using up brake pads and changing them is another thing that's much easier done in the comfort of your own garage.

Check the tread on your tires while there is still time to buy a new set and get them installed. If you've gone through a few track days and a racing school, you may already be needing a new set of treads, at least on the front of the car.

It can be a very good idea to replace the lug bolts on your wheels with studs, and then use open lug nuts on the studs to attach the wheels. With studs and open nuts, it is very easy to see whether a lug nut is starting to loosen; with lug bolts they can be hanging on by a single thread and only a check with a torque wrench will actually make sure they are tight enough.

If you're driving a pre-2004 MINI and haven't had the coolant tank replaced, you might wish to do that. A number of instances of splits in the plastic tank have been reported, and dealers have a better quality plastic replacement tank available now. As an alternative, a good-quality polished aluminum tank is available as a replacement for about $225.

Check the rules of your racing organization; many tracks do not permit the use of antifreeze in the coolant of a car racing on the track because of how slippery spilled antifreeze can be. It's much easier to drain your radiator and replace the antifreeze with fresh water at home (distilled water may be preferable if your local water has a high mineral content) rather than trying to do it at the track.

A product from Red Line called "Water Wetter" is known to raise the effective boiling temperature of water as well as providing corrosion protection, so if you are running plain water it is a good idea to add a bottle of that to the radiator in place of the antifreeze. Just be sure you replace the water and antifreeze if you're going to be parking the car outside in freezing weather.

Before You Leave for the Track

During the week before your race, you should check and top up all fluids, including oil, water, and brake and clutch fluid. In teching cars at the track, it's amazing how often we find cars with insufficient water in the coolant tank.

Track racing doesn't stop if you have a problem with your car. Run into a problem and you're out of the running or out of the race, so careful preparation of the car and careful checking of all details before going out on the track are as critical to winning as good driving. This is Brad Davis racing in SCCA Nationals at Daytona. *Photo by Henry Kowalski.*

Check the torque on each lug nut. Most MINI racers like the lug nuts torqued to at least 80 pounds to make very sure there is no danger of losing a wheel in a corner. Tires should also be inflated to a higher pressure than you would normally keep them on the street.

You're going to check tire pressure before and after each session, of course, but if you inflate the tires a few days before loading up for the track and then check them just before you leave you'll be able to spot a slow leak or leaky valve while there is still time to get the tire repaired or replaced.

Make sure that you've got all the equipment that you'll need, including racing documentation, safety gear, tools, spare parts, fluid, and so forth. It is a very good idea to make yourself a list of everything you think you will need, or might need, from racing helmet to stopwatch, for the weekend. Put the list in a protective cover so that you can use it to load the car and support vehicle before leaving for the track. When you discover you need something else at the track, add that to the list so that next weekend you won't forget it. There's nothing worse than arriving at the track and discovering you're missing something basic that you need to race, like your racing gloves.

Before and After Each Session

Before each session, check the tire pressure on each tire. If the tires are cold, they should be about four pounds or so less than the pressure you like to race at. Tire pressure is the easiest and cheapest thing to modify that will change the handling of your car, and over time you'll find the tire pressure that you like best.

Check the torque on each lug nut before going out. This is also a good time to visually check the condition of the tread on each tire, and the condition of the brakes and brake lines. If the engine stops in the middle of the race, the worst that's likely to happen is that you have to be pushed off the track and towed into the pits. Lose a wheel or your brakes and much worse things can happen to the car and to you.

Check the oil level in the engine and transmission, the level of water in the radiator tank, and the brake and clutch fluid.

Before you go out on the track, it is a good idea to start the engine and do a visual check of the engine compartment. That way you can make sure that everything is hooked up and spinning around as it is supposed to be, and nothing is leaking that shouldn't be, while there's still time to do something about it.

The worst feeling in the world is to be belted into the car, in the middle of the grid, at the two-minute warning wondering if that funny noise you can hear, or smell that you've just noticed, is coming from your own engine. At that point, there's no way of jumping out and popping the hood just to make sure everything looks right without losing your place on the grid.

Get to the grid well before the time for your race. This is especially important during your first season of racing, for the simple reason that if you rush things, you're going to forget something. By the time the five-minute warning is given on the grid, you should be settled into your car, your seat belts should be fastened, and you should have your helmet and gloves on. Then sit quietly for the two minutes before the three-minute warning and focus your thoughts on the coming race.

When the three-minute warning goes up, start your engine and check your gauges. Then try to close out all thoughts of the outside world so that your entire universe is limited to you, your car, the cars around you and the track.

After your practice session or race, just as soon as you come in from the track, before you've taken your equipment off and starting explaining to anyone who will listen just exactly what was happening at that last corner, you should immediately check your tire temperatures to see if you're carrying too much or too little pressure in the tires.

You can do this with a relatively expensive pyrometer, checking and comparing the temperature at the center of each tire tread with the edges. If the edges are colder than the center, the tire is over-inflated. If the edges are warmer than the center, then the tire is under-inflated. If temperatures across the tire are the same, then you're in good shape.

You also can get most of the information you need by checking the pressure on each tire and using an old rule of thumb. If the tire pressures are about the same as they were cold, you've probably got too much pressure in the tires. If the pressure in the tires has gone up by much more than four pounds, then you've probably got too little pressure in them, and the flex of the tires is causing them to heat up and make the pressure increase. If the pressure when they're hot and you've just come off the track is about four pounds higher than when they were checked cold, you're probably just about right.

When the Green Flag Drops

Nothing that you've done in your previous track days or in racing school can prepare you for the experience that awaits you when the green flag drops in your first race. Nevertheless, we can offer a few suggestions so that the sensations of the moment don't completely overwhelm you.

At the start of the race, you really find out what makes racing different from driving around the track on track days. The difference is that, while you are trying to get your shift points right, brake and turn in on the right line, and accelerate out, on all the different corners of the particular race track you're on, there are 20 to 40 other cars out there trying to do the same things in the same place and frequently at the same time as you.

This is what's different about racing. The new variable that makes racing different from, say, golf, is that you're not alone; there are other cars on the track with you. Nowhere is this more obvious than at the start. So let's talk about what you'll encounter.

On the Pace Lap

While you were getting belted in on the hot grid, starting the car, checking the gauges and listening to the engine to make sure everything was running right, we'll bet that your pulse was beginning to race. It didn't slowed much as you swung out of the pit lane and on to the track, and took your place on the starting grid following the starter's instructions. Now you'll be taking one full lap behind the pace car before the race actually starts so the first thing you need to do is calm down.

The first thing you should do on the pace lap is concentrate on your breathing. Yes, it's a Zen thing. You need to get your pulse and respiration back under control. Sure

The pace lap is an excellent time to refresh your memory about the layout of the track, especially if it's unfamiliar. In Pittsburgh, this Vintage Grand Prix course through Schenley Park is only set up for racing once a year, and the obstacles, like this stone wall, are forbidding. All the more reason to use the time on the pace lap to focus on the track and your own race, rather than worrying about other cars. *Photo by Walt & Louiseann Pietrowicz.*

this is the most exciting thing you've ever done, you're all alone in the car, and you can't remember a thing that you were supposed to have learned in driving school. All the more reason to calm down and relax.

Breathe slowly and listen to your breathing in your helmet. Try to get your breathing into a long, slow pattern.

Now you can begin to attend to the other three things you should be doing on the pace lap: checking your car, locating the corner worker stations, and reviewing your memory of the track so that the key points are fresh in your mind.

The first thing to do is to check your gauges to make sure that water temperature is coming up to regular running heat, and that oil pressure is still under control. Speed up a little and touch your brakes to make sure that the car revs and slows the way it is supposed to.

It is a good idea to begin heating up your brake pads a bit by riding the brake pedal with your left foot to cause the brakes to drag slightly while continuing to maintain speed with your right foot on the throttle. This is particularly important if you're running racing pads, which don't work very well when they're cold.

Regardless of what you've seen on Speed Channel, one thing we don't recommend that you do is to turn the car back and forth to "heat up your tires." First, it really doesn't do much good unless you're driving on real race tires, which you're not. Second, there's always the potential of zigging when the guy next to you is zagging, which could lead to an exchange of paint. That's never a good thing, especially on the pace lap. Third, a combination of a little oil on the track and a little zig or zag, and you could find yourself spinning off the track before the race ever starts. That can be downright embarrassing.

As you go around the track, note the flag workers at each corner displaying the yellow flag. The yellow flag means that you shouldn't pass on the pace lap, but you already knew that. The main reason to notice the flaggers is so that you can fix in your mind the location of each flag station; the flag workers will be your eyes around the corner at each critical point on the track. It's a nice thing to do to acknowledge their presence with a little wave so they know you know they're there.

On the pace lap, you should also be checking for your cue points for each corner. Note where the braking point is, where your turn-in is, and where you'll be tracking out. This can be a little challenging since you will also be trying to keep even with the car gridded next to you, trying to keep from running over the bumper of the car in front of you, and trying not to delay the person behind you.

After the Pace Car Goes Off

We're going to assume that you've been diligent in your practice and have had the chance to develop a pretty good idea of the best line around the track. However, during the first couple corners of the first lap, you might as well forget everything you know about where you think you should be on the track.

We say this because your number one concern on the start is simply to make it around the track safely on that first lap. Of course, your number two concern is to do it as quickly as possible, but at no time in the race is the old racer saying more relevant: "To finish first, you must first finish."

As you round the last corner, and the pace car disappears into the pit lane, there will be a very short period of time when everything seems as calm as can be. Check to make sure that you're in second gear, take a deep breath, and then… All the fiends in hell will seem to have broken loose at the same instant.

When the green flag drops—probably quite a ways up ahead since you're going to be gridded pretty far to the back for your first race—every single one of the drivers will simultaneously shove their accelerators to the floor.

One tip here: watch your tachometer. Like most drivers, you probably shift by ear most of the time. However, at the start of the race, you're not going to be able to hear your own engine. In addition, with all the confusion around you, and your own excitement, it is very easy to get too enthusiastic with the accelerator. This is probably the easiest place in the race to blow an engine. So in the midst of everything else going on, we're telling you to watch your tachometer to select your shift points.

Forget everything you've ever thought about how neat it would be to gain a place or three on the start. Imagine instead the biggest freeway toll booth complex you've ever driven through, with all the drivers leaving their booths at the same time, and all aiming for the one or two lanes available ahead. That's about what the start will feel like.

Your goal should be just to try to maintain your place in the melee. Focus on what's happening ahead of you and simply try to drive in a straight line unless it is absolutely necessary to swerve around a very slow car ahead of you. With a little luck you may be able to get away from the start a little bit faster than the car next to you so you can claim your place in line ahead of them. In any case, you'll probably have to slow up a bit as all those cars that were going two abreast try to get into a single line to go around the first corner.

What really matters, however, is getting through the chaos of the start and around the first or second corner with your car intact. If you lose a few places, so what? If the cars were

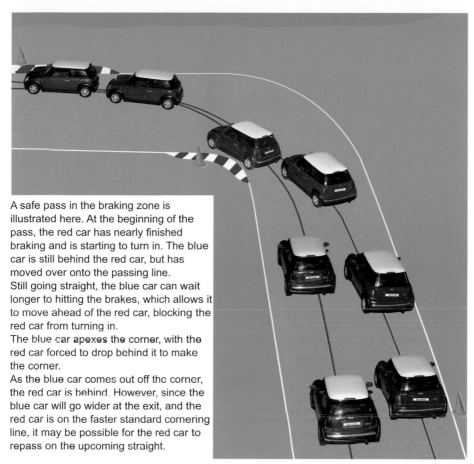

A safe pass in the braking zone is illustrated here. At the beginning of the pass, the red car has nearly finished braking and is starting to turn in. The blue car is still behind the red car, but has moved over onto the passing line.

Still going straight, the blue car can wait longer to hitting the brakes, which allows it to move ahead of the red car, blocking the red car from turning in.

The blue car apexes the corner, with the red car forced to drop behind it to make the corner.

As the blue car comes out off the corner, the red car is behind. However, since the blue car will go wider at the exit, and the red car is on the faster standard cornering line, it may be possible for the red car to repass on the upcoming straight.

faster than you (and there certainly will be a few fast cars behind you that, for one reason or another, didn't get gridded where they belonged in the pecking order of your grid) then they belong ahead anyhow. If they're slower than you, then you'll have the chance to prove that in the laps of the race to come. The main point is simply to get around the first two corners in good shape so that you can actually be a part of the real race.

Passing on Corners

Sure you've passed other cars when you were driving the circuit on club track days, in the High Performance Driving Events of NASA, or in driving school. Generally, however, passing was limited to straightaways only. There is a good reason for that. When two cars are going straight down the track, it's pretty obvious if one driver and car is faster than the other driver and car, and the faster one can easily go by the slower.

However, in racing those differences are pretty well resolved through the use of qualifying times and class grids. As a result, you will generally find yourself surrounded by other cars that are roughly the same speed as yours. It isn't very likely that you're going to get ahead of them by passing them on the straights.

Instead, your passing will have to be done on the corners. That's where the races are won or lost, because that's where driving skills really come into play. Becoming skilled at driving around the corners faster than other drivers, and then learning how to get around the same corner they're going around, at the same time, is what drivers spend their careers learning how to do.

Conditions for Passing in the Braking Zone

But even if we can't give you the secret tips in this book on how to beat other drivers through corners, at least we can tell you how to make a proper pass. Then you can practice, and at the least you'll know what's going on when another driver makes a pass on you. In a short while, with some practice, you too will be able to start passing other drivers on the corners.

In most amateur racing organizations, one rule is sacred: The driver who is making the pass is responsible for the safety of both cars and both drivers. No excuses, and no explanations can alter this fact. If two cars crash in a corner, the driver making the pass is always considered to be at fault.

A proper pass is done by entering the corner ahead of the other driver. Ahead, in this case, means that at the turn-in point a reasonable portion of the front of the passing car is ahead of the car being passed. The passing car will be on the "passing line" which is inside the normal cornering line.

If these two conditions are satisfied—the passing car has a slight lead on the car being passed, and is on the inside of the car being passed—then it isn't possible for the car being passed to get to the apex of the corner before the passing car, so the passing car can accelerate out of the corner ahead of the car being passed.

The most typical way that a pass is carried out is for the passing car to carry more speed into the corner and brake later than the car being passed. To do this, the passing driver either has to have a faster car with better brakes, or have more confidence in the car and his or her ability to get it through the corner safely, or both.

However, as we learned earlier when discussing the fastest line through the corner, we noted that if you turn in too early, you won't be able to get on the accelerator as hard

SCCA and BMW CCA are attracting more and more MINIs every season. It's an inexpensive way to go racing, and with a little work before and after race weekends, you could still drive the car on the street. Think how much fun it would be to take this car to the office or out on sales calls. *Picture by Fred Voit ActionPhotos*

coming out of the corner, if you want to stay on the track. Thus it may seem strange that a passing car can take the slower line through the corner and still come out ahead of the car being passed.

In fact, one way to respond to being passed is to drop back slightly, and make sure you're on the fast line. You can then let the other driver pass you, but still have a chance to accelerate past them as you come out of the corner, since they may not be able to get on the accelerator as quickly.

Keeping Your Passes Safe

If you are passing another car and do decide to do it by taking the passing line and thus blocking them from getting to the apex, don't forget that it is your responsibility to make sure the pass is made safely. Here are a few tips.

First, make sure that the other driver knows you are behind them. You can't always count on them to be checking their mirrors to see that you are coming up and trying to pass. One of the most typical ways in which accidents happen in corners is for the driver ahead to not be aware he or she is being passed, and come over to the apex just at the time that the passing car is going for the same point.

So it is a very good idea to come up next to the other car at one or two corners before you actually try to pass. That way, you can make sure they've seen you before you actually go for the pass.

Finding a good corner to make your pass is another good idea. If you're behind another car and the cars' speeds seem to be pretty evenly matched, you'll have to pass them on the basis of skill. Typically, all drivers, depending on their own skills and the capabilities of their cars, are better at some types of corners than others.

Be patient and follow the other car through several corners, maybe even for a few laps, while you scope out their skill, their ability to drive through specific corners, and their techniques. If it is going to be possible to pass them, you should be able to find a corner that you drive better than they do, or one that your car can handle better than theirs, and then make your pass at that corner.

Track Etiquette and Common Sense

One major difference between professional racing and amateur racing is that, in amateur racing, your car is your own. If something happens to your car, it will be your checkbook that will suffer. There won't be a sponsor or team owner to pay for the damage. As a result, you're going to want to try to protect your car from accidental damage, and you're going to be hoping that everyone else on the track feels the same way about their car.

Fortunately, amateur racing has taken a leaf from the vintage racing rule book and adopted a common code of track etiquette that helps everyone keep the shine in their paint jobs. The first rule is that contact is wrong. Period. No matter what else is going on, no matter how close the racing is, there is never any excuse for cars to get close enough to swap paint.

Most amateur racing organizations have adopted some form of the "13/13 rule" used in vintage organizations. Simply put, drivers involved in any incident that results in

The most important distinguishing feature of racing is that you are sharing the track with other drivers with different attitudes and experience, driving cars with very diverse capabilities. Driving safely and looking out for the other driver should be everyone's number one priority. *Photo by Walt & Louiseann Pietrowicz.*

damage to a car will be placed on probation for 13 months. During that period of time, if they are involved in a second incident where a car is damaged, they will be expelled from the organization for 13 months.

The reasoning behind this rule is that if you're involved in an incident where a car is damaged, whether it's yours or another car, you probably could have helped prevent the incident. Either you're either taking chances beyond your own driving ability, or you're not being cautious enough or paying enough attention to keep out of trouble. Either way, if your car is damaged once, under the 13/13 rule you'll be warned to change your driving.

If your car is damaged twice, even if a reasonable observer might agree that neither accident was actually your fault, it was you who put your car in harm's way by overdriving your abilities, or by not paying attention. Either way, you can be considered to be a risk to yourself as well as others on the track and shouldn't be out there.

You and Other Drivers

What safety on the track boils down to is that you need to be know where the other cars around you are at all times, and you need to leave them enough room to maneuver so that there's never any need for two cars to try to occupy the same space at the same time.

When you're first starting to race, there are some specific guidelines that will both help you stay out of trouble and allow others to race safely while you're on the track. Perhaps the most important practice for you to work on as a novice driver is to check your mirrors frequently. You need to be aware not only of who is ahead of you, but perhaps even more important, who is coming up behind you.

When you do see a driver coming up behind you because they are going faster than you are, or you are shown the blue and yellow flag, both politeness and common sense point to allowing the faster driver to get around with a minimum of fuss. You only need to do two things: be predictable and be polite.

To be predictable, you should stay on the standard track line. The worst thing you can do is to move off the line in order to let them go by. If you move off the line, you might do that just at the time that the driver behind you decides to go off the line in order to pass. All of a sudden, you'll both be trying to be in the same place at the same time.

Instead, simply keep on the line. Then all they need to do is use their relative speed and skill to go around you on the passing line.

To be polite, it is a good thing to signal which side of the car you will be expecting them to pass. All you need to do is use one hand to point the following car by. This accomplishes two things: It lets the overtaking driver know that you know he or she is there, and it tells them where you expect them to pass you.

In the event that you should find yourself overtaking another car, either because they may also be a novice and be more timid than you are, or because they are in a slower car, which can be the case with a multi-marque grid, then keep in mind the rules we talked about above.

As we said, passing safely is the responsibility of the overtaking driver. If that's you, then you're responsible for making sure the car ahead knows you're there, and you're responsible for making a clean, safe pass. If you have any doubts, then back out and wait for a nice wide, straight place on the track where you'll have lots of room to pass. And before you do, check to make sure that you don't have an even faster car on your tail about to pass you.

Keeping Cool in Chaos

Keeping calm and staying focused are probably the two most important aspects of safe racing. When problems do develop, more often than not, the driver who caused the incident will say, at least to him or herself, that they just experienced a momentary instance of "brain fade" or "red mist."

Brain fade occurs when you let your mind wander away from the moment at hand. Red mist is a racer's term for the condition when your desire to beat the other driver, or worse, get even with them, overwhelms your common sense and leads you to do something stupid.

Either way, anything less than 100 percent calm, common-sense driving is likely to get you, and probably someone else, in trouble. So the trick is to keep your cool at all times.

Move up to SCCA racing, as Brad Davis here has done, and the track will be crowded with all sorts of different cars. There are few other sports that can provide so much challenge and excitement. *Photo by Henry Kowalski.*

Keeping calm starts by remembering that your primary reason for being on the track is to have fun. You're not earning your living by racing, and there is no money at stake. At most, there might be the passing glory of being listed as having come in first, or recording a time better than a specific competitor. In most cases, with most clubs there isn't even a first prize to vie for, and if there is, you can buy a better one for a few bucks at the nearest trophy store.

Nothing that you could possible win is worth risking a major dent in your bank account to repair a major dent in your car, much less risking a lengthy and expensive stay in the hospital, or having someone else's injury on your conscience.

But even if you do know that you're just out to have fun, and you don't intend to take any risks, you still need to keep focused. Seasoned race drivers will tell you that the best way to do that is to always keep thinking about the next corner, the next lap, and the next race. If you screw up a corner, or just as bad, if you really nail one and gain a place or two, immediately put it out of your mind. There simply isn't enough room in your head to be regretting or gloating about the last corner while staying on line and hitting your braking point for the next corner.

If you think there's something to be learned from your mistakes or your triumphs— and, quite definitely, there is—then invest a few hundred dollars in a digital video camera that you can attach to your roll bar. Film each race, and then think about it afterward, in the comfort of your own living room. Just don't waste any time thinking about what's passed while there is still racing to be done.

Automobile racing is one of the most exciting ways we can imagine to challenge your skill, intellect, patience, self-discipline and nerve. It isn't for everyone, and many people every year participate in only one or two races before deciding that they don't like the experience.

But if you do discover you like racing, then you will have joined a very small fraternity of men and women who challenge the limits of themselves and their cars for the pure satisfaction of the challenge. And no words you can find will ever be able to explain to the uninitiated the excitement, pleasure and satisfaction you get from racing.

Now that's motoring.

Don Racine exercises the MiniMania SuperCooper S in a BMW CCA event. *Photo by Walt & Louiseann Pietrowicz.*

Regional MINI Clubs

New Hampshire
Monadnock Area Mini Association
www.sirannon.com/mini/

Western New York
MINI Club of Western New York
www.minicooperclubofwny.com/

New Jersey
Mini Owners of New Jersey
clubs.hemmings.com/frameset.cfm?club=
miniownersofnj

Pittsburgh, PA
PittStop MINI Club
www.PittStoptMINI.org

Washington, DC
DC Metro MINIs
www.dcmetrominis.org

North and South Carolina
Mini Motoring Club of the Carolinas
M2c2.org

Atlanta, GA
Atlanta MINIs
www.atlantaminis.net

Northern Florida
Florida MINI Enthusiasts
www.flamemini.com

Central Florida
MINIs of Orlando
www.minisoforlando.org

**Southeast Florida (Broward, Miami
Dade, Palm Beach counties)**
Broward MINI Club
www.browardminiclub.com

Miami, FL
MINIs of Miami
www.minisofmiami.com

Southern Michigan
Michigan Mini
www.michiganmini.com

Northeast Ohio
MINI of Northeastern Ohio
www.minineo.org

Indiana
MINI Car Club of Indiana
www.minicci.org

Kentucky and Southern Indiana
Kentucky and Southern Indiana Mini
Cooper Club
autos.groups.yahoo.com/group/
KentuckyMini/

Tennesee
Smoky Mountain MINIs
www.smokymountainmini.org

Madison, WI
Madison MINI group
Revorg.org/mini.html

Chicago Area
Chicago MINI Motoring Club
www.chicagominiclub.com

Northern Illinois
Minis in Northern Illinois (M.I.N.I.)
Minisinil.com

St. Louis, MO
St. Louis Mini Club
www.stlmini.com

Kansas City, MO
Kansas City Mini Enthusiasts
www.kcminiacs.org

Oklahoma
Oklahoma Mini Motoring Community
okmini.com

Texas
Mini Owners of Texas
www.miniownersoftexas.com

Dallas/Fort Worth, TX
Metroplex MINIs
www.metroplexmini.org

Houston, TX
Houston MINI Motoring Society
www.hmms.cc

South Texas
South Texas Mini Club
autos.groups.yahoo.com/group/
minimotoring/

Rocky Mountain Region
MINI5280 Motoring Society
www.mini5280.org

New Mexico
New Mexico MINI Motoring
www.nmmini.org

Utah
MINI Motoring Club of Utah
www.miniutah.com

Arizona
Arizona Mini Owners
clubs.hemmings.com/clubsites/amo

Las Vegas, NV
Sin City MINI Club
www.sincityminiclub.com

Oregon
PDX MINI Cooper Club
www.pdxmini.org

Northern California
Redwood Empire MINI Enthusiasts
www.redwoodempiremini.com

Northern California/Bay Area
NorCal MINIs
www.norcalminis.com

San Francisco Bay Area
Mini Owners of America – San Francisco
www.moasf.com

Sacramento Valley and Sierra Nevada area
Gold Country Minis
www.goldcountry.com

Southern California
SoCal MINI Maniacs
www.scmm.org

Los Angeles Area
Mini Owners of America Los Angeles
www.moala.org

Los Angeles
C3 Club – MINI Club for Charity
www.C3Club.org

Hawaii
Hawaii MINI Motoring Club
www.hawaiiMINIclub.org

Southern Ontario, Canada
Southern Ontario MINI Club
www.somc.on.ca

Vancouver, BC, Canada
Vancouver Cooper Club
www.vancouverminicooperclub.com/

Network of regional MINI clubs
worldwide
Minicooper.meetup.com

Note: All websites were operational as of February, 2005. Other clubs may have been established and some may have ceased operations since that time.

Useful Links for MINI Information

Where It All Starts

The MINI USA website

This is where you begin to learn about Minis at the website maintained by BMW's MINI USA division. The site includes a neat system to design and price your own Mini before you even visit the dealer.
www.miniusa.com

MINI Parts and Installation

MiniMania

Foremost aftermarket supplier and developer of MINI parts and accessories in North America
www.minimania.com

Online MINI Communities

www.motoringfile.com
www.northamericanmotoring.com

These two websites are terrific time-fillers as well as great sources for MINI news, parts vendors, and best of all, the thoughts, opinions, and experience of other MINI owners through the forums.

www.autocross.com

An excellent basic web resource for anyone interested in autocrossing. The site provides links to information on getting started in autocross, organizations, events, car set-ups and various other useful links.

Track Instruction and Racing Events

BMW Car Club of America

Organizes track club racing events and advanced driving schools for BMW owners. MINI Spec Racing series is a BMW CCA racing series.
www.bmwcca.com/club/

Sports Car Club of America

Organizes racing events and race driving schools, including MINI classes
www.scca.com

National Auto Sport Association

Organizes racing events and High-Performance Driving Events (track days with instruction) at tracks in California, Arizona, and Nevada.
www.nasaproracing.com

NASA Time Trails Program

New time trials program for open track competition against the clock.
www.nasa-tt.com

Driving Schools

Phil Wicks Driving Academy

Presents basic driving schools, especially for younger drivers, with emphasis on MINIs, at various tracks around the United States.
www.minidriving.com

Car Guys On-Track Driver Education

Two- and three-day courses taught in students' own cars at tracks in Virgina, New York, North Carolina, and West Virginia.
www.carguysinc.com

High Performance Driving School

Taught at Thunderhill Park in Northern California in students' own cars, this course is typical of schools available at many tracks around the country.
www.thunderhill.com/school.html

Hooked on Driving

Organizes open track days at Thunderhill Park and other race tracks in northern California/Nevada.
www.hookedondriving.com

Evolution Performance Driving School

Offers multiple-day courses in autocross techniques at venues all over North America, teaching basic and advanced techniques using specialized equipment.
www.autocross.com/evolution

Driving School Directory

Lists a variety of driving schools in all regions of North America that advertise in Autoweek.
www.autoweek.com

Bibliography for Additional Reading

The following books were used extensively in writing this book and we recommend them for any MINI owner who wants additional information about the MINI, about general automotive information, or competitive driving techniques.

Going Faster—Mastering the Art of Race Driving by the Skip Barber Racing School, Foreward by Danny Sullivan, Bentley, 2001. www.BentleyPublishers.com

Perhaps the most comprehensive and easiest to understand of the many books written over the years on race driving techniques.

Secrets of Solo Racing—Expert Techniques for Autocross & Time Trials by Henry A. Watts, Loki Publishing Company, 1989.

This book focuses specifically on the techniques of autocross driving, and to our knowledge is the only textbook that has been written on the topic. It is out of print, but copies can be found through sources such as www.amazon.com

Drive to Win—The Essential Guide to Race Driving by Carroll Smith, Carroll Smith Consulting, 1996. www.motorbooks.com

This book is considered a classic among books on racing techniques and covers all aspects of racing, including driving lines, car prep and race tuning, and driver tips.

MINI Cooper Service Manual 2002, 2003, 2004 Factory publication, Bentley Publishers, 2004. www.minimania.com

Before putting a wrench or screwdriver to the new MINI, every owner should have a copy of this book on the workbench for reference.

Hooked on Driving—Track Day Essentials, David Ray. DVD. www.hookedondriving.com

Excellent video presentation for the first-time track day participant, covering paddock protocol, safety, car preparation, and basic track driving skills.

The New MINI by Graham Robson, Haynes Publishing, 2002. www.haynes.co.uk www.minimania.com

Written by Graham Robson, a noted English automotive historian, with the cooperation of BMW, this book provides an in-depth look at the history and background of development of the new MINI

MINI by Patrick C. Paternie, Motorbooks, 2002. www.minimania.com

Written for Motorbooks with the cooperation of MINI USA, this book by auto journalist Pat Paternie provides a good overview of the car's development from a U.S. perspective.

Essential Mini Cooper—The Cars and Their Story 1961-1971 & 1990-1997 by Anders Ditlev Clausager, Motorbooks, 1997. www.motorbooks.com

Still in print, this illustrated history of the classic Minis was written by the British Motor Heritage historian and is an excellent overview of Mini development with great period and contemporary photographs.

Road & Track Illustrated Automotive Dictionary by John Dinkel. Bentley Publishers, 1999. www.bentleypublishers.com

The R&T automotive dictionary was used extensively in checking and clarifying definitions of terms used in this book.

Index

Disclaimers

The information presented in this book is, to the best of the knowledge of the authors, accurate and represents the best information available to them at the time of writing. However, the authors emphasize that automobile driving, whether on the road or the track, is inherently dangerous, and therefore neither the authors nor the publishers assume any liabilities and make no warranties, express or implied, regarding the application of any of the information presented in this book, whether it relates to automobile mechanics, modification, or operation.

Readers should not rely solely on the information presented in this book for guidance on automobile operation or modification, and should make their own efforts to verify and expand on the information presented here, taking the advice of experts in motorsports and relying on specialists to carry out the modifications described in this book. The authors and publishers also disclaim all liability for direct, indirect, incidental or consequential damage that may result from use of or reliance on any of the examples, instructions, products and brands, or other information presented in this book.

The authors and publishers recognize that some words, model names, and brand names used in this book are the property of other individuals or companies. The authors' and publisher's use of these trade and service marks and brand names is for the purpose of identification only, and is not meant to indicate or imply any endorsement by, or connection, legal or otherwise, with the authors or publishers of this book.

In particular, there is no connection between the authors and publishers of this book and the BMW Group, BMW USA or MINI USA.

Driving is Dangerous

The authors emphasize that driving any automobile, especially in a high-performance manner that approaches the limits of the automobile or driver, is dangerous to the driver, passengers, and pedestrians. No book can teach all aspects of performance driving or racing. Driving should be done in a conservative and responsible manner, whether on public roads or private tracks or courses. Do not race or practice race driving except on a designated and properly supervised race track. When on public roads, obey all laws and regulations, and drive with full respect for the safety of yourself and others, and the limits of your automobile.